Global Cities

Global Cities

Mark Abrahamson

University of Connecticut

New York   Oxford

OXFORD UNIVERSITY PRESS

2004

Oxford University Press

Oxford   New York
Auckland Bangkok Buenos Aires Cape Town Chennai
Dar es Salaam Delhi Hong Kong Istanbul Karachi Kolkata
Kuala Lumpur Madrid Melbourne Mexico City Mumbai Nairobi
São Paulo Shanghai Taipei Tokyo Toronto

Published by Oxford University Press, Inc.
198 Madison Avenue, New York, New York 10016
www.oup.com

Library of Congress Cataloging-in-Publication Data
Abrahamson, Mark.
    Global cities / Mark Abrahamson.
        p. cm.
    Includes bibliographical references and index.
    ISBN 978-0-19-514204-4
    1. Metropolitan areas. 2. Globalization. 3. City dwellers—Social conditions. 4. City
dwellers—Economic conditions. 5. City and town life. 6. Culture. 7. Sociology, Urban.
I. Title.

HT330.A27 2004
                                                                    2003047110

Printed in the United States of America
on acid-free paper

Dedicated,
With love and hope for the future

Rachel

Evan   Leah

Jason

Contents

Preface

For the past twenty-five years, or so, it has been apparent to most observers that some dramatic changes were underway within major cities, and in their relationships to each other. Increasing globalization was obviously at the core of the transformation, but there was little agreement about the most important aspects of globalization for contemporary cities. Approaching the issue from varied perspectives, social scientists offered different explanations for what was occurring. Many analysts were particularly taken by the economic modifications associated with globalizaton, specifically involving alterations in the occupational and organizational configurations within cities and in the inter-urban connections that sustain the global economy.

Other analysts attributed much more significance to two sets of interrelated cultural phenomena. On one hand was the emergence of postmodern culture, which was most visible in the major global cities, where new lifestyles and values seemed to be evolving at a breathtaking pace. On the other hand were the increasingly international and rapidly growing cultural industries located in the global cities, from which many of the new ideas and ways of life were emanating.

Those writers who emphasized economic changes typically paid little attention to the cultural analysts, and vice versa. The result was two separate literatures. One of my principal objectives in writing this book was to try to connect these economic and cultural dimensions. I wanted to see, for example, how economically generated changes in the labor force and new cultural emphases combined to produce large groups of people with distinctive lifestyles. From there, I wanted to identify the particular kinds of places within global cities that such large groups chose for their residential areas.

My other major objective was to try to produce a more detailed and multifaceted picture of the global cities than I was able to find in the literature. There is a substantial degree of consensus that there are four leading global cities—London, New York, Paris, and Tokyo—and that they appear to have been the leading cities for several decades. However, there is almost no agreement concerning which cities, if any, follow the leading four on some kind of ranking. Pertinent findings have differed greatly according to the specific indicator investigators employed, and each study typically relied on only one indicator. Further, almost all of the studies were based solely on such economic measures as concentrations of banking or other financial institutions. I was interested in seeing what the global system—beyond the four leading cities—looked like; and I wanted to glimpse it from an economic angle, a cultural angle, and from a perspective in which both angles were combined.

My intent has been to produce a book that is highly accessible to students and others who are interested in the topic. I strove to minimize the use of jargon so that the material would be useful and understandable to people with limited social science backgrounds. I also utilized numerous examples and detailed case studies to illustrate and explain major topics.

I am grateful to a very large number of graduate and undergraduate students who listened as I talked through the ideas presented in this book, and who offered many helpful suggestions. I regret that I cannot thank them all by name. I am also indebted to a number of reviewers who read, and reread, drafts of the manuscript before it reached this point. Special thanks are due to my editor, Peter M. Labella, who never lost faith in this project, even when there were bumps in the road. As always, I want to express my gratitude to my wife, Marlene, who I know sometimes must have felt as though she was dining alone even when her preoccupied husband sat across the table.

—Mark Abrahamson

Global Cities

ONE

Introduction, Background, and Preview

Major cities have historically been focal points within their nations. Structures in these cities, such as the Statue of Liberty or the Eiffel Tower, often became the icons that represented the entire nation. The major cities became focal points because they contained the activities that tied together diverse parts of their nations. For example, in the 1500s, London was already the crossroads of England. Craftspeople and farmers from miles away traveled unpaved roads to bring their wares to London's markets. The City of London was an important government unit in its own right, but the city also housed the most significant seats of national government. Aspiring actors and writers from all over England, such as Shakespeare, made their way to London's stages. Even going back 2,000 years, when London was merely a Roman army camp, the major city (i.e., Rome) was the focal point because it was the center of commerce, government, theater, and so on. The expression "all roads lead to Rome" was true, literally and figuratively; and it remained an accurate summary of the relationship of most principal cities to their nations for thousands of years.

In addition to housing many of the activities most important to the internal life of a nation, major cities have historically provided their nations with the most significant points of connection to other nations. The English farmers and craftspeople who brought their goods to London markets in the 1500s sold a lot of it to Dutch, German, and French merchants who came to London to export such goods back to their home countries. Furthermore, most of the cargo from around the world, ultimately intended for any place in England, initially entered the country at London's Custom House.[1]

Until sometime in the late middle of the twentieth century, there was a great deal of movement of goods and services and people among cities within the same nations, and relatively little movement among cities that crossed national boundaries. The balance shifted when firms in many cities of the world dramatically increased the amount of business they conducted in other nations:

transnational investment increased, international tourism rose, and there were more exports of movies, music, styles, and fashions. And the people, products, and new ideas all moved with unsurpassed speed among the major cities of the world.

The linkages among cities cutting across nations became a global network. It is important to note here that the key nodes in the international system are (global) cities, not nations. Correspondingly, it is interesting to note that on a space flight, an astronaut looked back at Earth and was surprised not to see any national boundaries. The United States simply "flowed" into Canada, Egypt into Libya, and so on. In daylight, the only human artifact visible from space was a portion of the Great Wall of China. At night, though, the astronaut could see the world's major urban areas appearing as "pin-pricks of electric light on a black canvas."[2] Thus, from space, it was the world's urban settlements that were most apparent. Of course, the massive flows of information among these urban areas, and the numerous linkages and connections between them, were missing from the astronaut's view.

Once the linkages among cities became a global network, nations became dependent upon their major cities for connections to the rest of the world. Paris played this role for France, Tokyo for Japan, Warsaw for Poland, Lima for Peru, and so on. Thus, the role and status of cities *within* their nations became, to a large degree, a function of the international connections of the cities. However, this is not meant to imply that the role of these cities relative to each other is all the same. Links to the global network are more intense in some cities. What occurs in Paris, for example, will ordinarily have more consequences everywhere else than what happens in Lima. Later, we will examine ways the influence of the activities emanating from within these cities might be categorized and ranked. For now, it is important only to emphasize how during the last decades of the twentieth century there was a dramatic increase in interdependence—in styles and fashions and movies and music and, of course, in economic exchanges—among all the cities (and nations) of the world.

To illustrate how interdependent the economies of the world have become, consider the relationship between state employees in Illinois and an upscale mall in Moscow with forty international retailers. The mall, called GUM, was transformed in the early 1990s from a drab department store to a highly profitable shopping center. For example, Samsonite reported that its luggage store in the Moscow mall was outselling any of its other outlets in the world. Dresner Bank in Germany was eager to lend GUM $10 million for expansion, and the mall's liquid assets soared to over $30 million in 1997 as investment funds around the world bought GUM stock.

It was, paradoxically, as GUM's economic fortunes reached their apex in 1997 that its unraveling also began, in Thailand, though the connection was not yet recognized. Unemployment, inflation, and business failures were increasing in Thailand, and businesspeople and investors became nervous about holding local currency. They rushed to convert to U.S. dollars, at almost any rate of exchange, and the value of Thai currency continued to decline. Throughout much of Asia people became anxious that their nation's problems could be the same as Thailand's, triggering fiscal problems in Indonesia, South Korea, Malaysia, and so on. In late October 1997, the panic reached the Hong Kong stock market, which lost 23 percent of its value in just four days. Based on the Hong Kong exchange's size and important international connections, investors around the world reacted in alarm and began to sell their stock holdings. What followed were the largest one-day losses in the pre-1998 history of the stock markets in New York, Mexico, Brazil, and elsewhere. Fortunes that had been quickly made were just as quickly lost. For example, Peregrine Investments, a Hong Kong investment bank with British ownership, simply disappeared. It had been established in 1988 and in its ten-year existence rapidly accumulated $25 billion before it vanished under a tidal wave of debt.

The worldwide economic slowdown reduced demand for Russia's chief exports: oil and gas. Russia's currency fell in value, which had the effect of raising the cost of the merchandise that GUM imported from the United States, England, Germany, and other countries. To make matters worse, with unemployment and business failures increasing, fewer Russians could afford the now inflated prices of GUM merchandise. Sales fell and the final blow was the fact that all of GUM's liquid assets—which once surpassed $30 million—had been invested in stock and bond markets that collapsed. Unable to make payments on loans, including the large loan from Dresner Bank, the desperate management of GUM could only hope that a European company would buy the mall and save them, but given the problems in the Russian economy, no buyers were interested.[3]

In the United States, many banks and large private investors lost large sums of money due to the worldwide recession. Many ordinary working people were adversely affected as well, notably, state employees in Illinois. The state pension fund had invested in Peregrine Investments, the Hong Kong bank that collapsed, and in Dresner Bank, the German bank that lent GUM $10 million it could not repay. While the Illinois state pension fund remained solvent, it lost millions of dollars in retirement funds, reducing the amount that would later be available to retired state workers. Thus, in the global economy, state employees in Chicago or Peoria (Illinois) are closely linked to investors in Hong Kong, to bankers in Dresden (Germany), and to people in Moscow who work for GUM. In sum: What happens in any one part of the world will eventually have some effects everywhere else. What happens in the leading global cities will have more immediate and profound repercussions for us all.

IDENTIFYING GLOBAL CITIES

During the first half of the twentieth century, most major cities in economically advanced nations had an industrial base. They were not only industrial cities, but manufacturing was an integral component of their labor force and economic organization. The decline in manufacturing in cities in these nations during the last half of the twentieth century created severe social and economic problems. To recover, many cities tried to move in a new direction that may be described briefly as "the globalization response": recruit transnational corporations and the specialized firms (offering legal, accounting, and other services) that follow these corporations, and provide cultural attractions for international tourists.

The formerly major industrial cities that were most able quickly and thoroughly to transform themselves into the new postindustrial mode became the leading global cities—the centers of the new global system. Cities that lagged in this transformation process have typically experienced high unemployment, out-migration, neighborhood deterioration, and related problems. Eventually, leaders in most cities concluded that globalization is the strategy most likely to be successful. They have correspondingly tried to strengthen their links to the global urban network and, in effect, become more like the cities that are its hubs. This strategy was apparent in the 1995 report of the Manchester (England) City Council. After twenty-five years of economic deterioration associated with the closing of manufacturing plants, the Council's report stated that the only viable alternative would require that Manchester be "plugged in to the network of world cities . . . developing as centres of decision-making . . . financial institutions . . . the media, culture and sport."[4] (Later in this chapter we describe the specific plans the Manchester City Council pursued and explore how successful they were.)

The pervasiveness of the globalization response means that almost all cities are likely to have some features that make them global. For example, in 1980, Garden City, a small town in Southwest Kansas, was able to induce IBP, Inc., to relocate to the town. (IBP sells meat products around the world.) Over the next decade, the company recruited 3,000 employees who, with their families, raised Garden City's population to over 20,000. As a result of the IBP relocation, Garden City could be placed somewhere along a global cities continuum. However, that city's connections to the global system are not highly consequential from either an economic or cultural perspective. If the concept of global cities is to be meaningful, places like Garden City have to be placed below the cutoff point.

At the opposite end of the global cities continuum is a set of four cities that are at the apex, no matter what criterion is emphasized. These four cities— London, New York, Paris, and Tokyo—are the central hubs of the global network regardless of how it is defined. The consequences of activities contained within them are unequaled. One could therefore write about global cities focusing solely upon this set, or a subset of it, and numerous writers have done just that. However, by so limiting the number of cities to be considered global, one risks seriously underestimating how widely the global city construct might be generalized. And given the pervasiveness of the globalization response, it would not be surprising if a substantial number of other cities were also more-or-less qualified candidates for inclusion.

Between places like Garden City and the four cities at the apex of the hierarchy, there is no agreed-upon point on the continuum above which cities could be labeled global, below which they could be regarded as nonglobal. Right behind the leading centers is a group of between ten and thirty cities that can be considered second-tier global cities. The exact number of such cities and their ranking vis-à-vis each other vary according to the criterion employed. Second-tier cities tend to follow closely behind the four top cities on some, but not all, dimensions. For example, Chicago and Frankfurt are usually considered rather significant global cities when a concentration of economic activities is stressed, but not when the focus is on cultural industries. The reverse is true of Los Angeles and Sydney. In addition, a few other cities are frequently placed in the second tier of global cities, including Hong Kong, Osaka, Toronto, and Zurich. Behind this category is a similarly sized grouping of third-tier cities. Such cities typically fall behind the second-tier cities on every criterion, but they nevertheless remain globally significant given the broad consequences of the organizations and activities they house. The third tier frequently includes such cities as Miami, Milan, San Francisco, São Paulo, and Singapore.

This book begins with the assumption that it will be most fruitful to conceptualize global cities along a continuum, with cities at the upper echelons of the continuum accorded more weight in describing the key features of the construct and the four cities at the apex regarded as the exemplars of the construct. The upper echelon will generally be regarded as including the four cities at the apex, plus the cities located in tiers two and three. This results in a group of between about thirty and fifty leading global cities, depending on the criterion emphasized and the cutoff employed. This broadly—and for now, loosely—defined group of cities will be in the forefront in descriptions of spatial arrangements and lifestyles in global cities. However, at times it will be helpful to examine selected cities, such as Manchester, that are lower in the hierarchy. Through efforts to emulate cities that are more centrally positioned with respect to the global system, such cutoff cities often exaggerate certain tendencies, thereby making features and trends of the global cities more apparent.

Thus far, we have described a transition from industrial social organization in which the primary integrative role of cities was intranational to a postindustrial order in which cities played a more important international role. One key factor in this transition was the decline in manufacturing. However, that decline was only a piece of a picture that included a number of economic and occupational changes. In addition, running parallel to the economic and occupational transformations were a number of changes in people's perceptions, values, and lifestyles that collectively have been described as constituting postmodern or postindustrial culture. Global cities were one of the many new forms to emerge out of this complex set of economic and cultural changes.

To some theorists, postmodern culture is derived from the new postindustrial economic organization, and therefore warrants less independent importance. As you will see later in this chapter, this view was followed in some of the most influential early descriptions of global cities, leading to a stress on the primacy of economics. At the opposite extreme, some theorists have emphasized the shaping power of postmodern culture, believing it has a vital influence on the economy and government.[5] We will generally follow a middle ground that attempts to link cultural and economic changes, noting their inter-relationships without attributing precedence or priority. That approach puts this book with a growing number of others that stress convergence with a "focus on the mutual effects of economics . . . and culture in restructuring processes."[6]

The next section, includes descriptions of some of the more important economic and cultural changes that provided the backdrop for the evolution of industrial cities into global cities. Following each discussion, we review the most influential research on global cities, noting the place that investigators have accorded to economic and cultural dimensions in conceptualizing a global cities continuum.

INDUSTRIAL TO POSTINDUSTRIAL ECONOMIES

Employment and the local economy, for roughly the first half of the twentieth century, rose and fell with manufacturing. Then, in the second half of the century, manufacturing jobs in many cities markedly diminished as a result of several processes, the single most important of which was relocation. The corporate boards of many large corporations moved their manufacturing facilities from cities in the United States, England, Germany, Japan, and other countries to less established industrial nations, such as Mexico, Brazil, and Korea. Companies moved production facilities (but not home offices) to formerly nonindustrial countries because labor costs were a lot less—often due to the absence of unions—and the minerals, crops, and other raw materials used in production were locally more readily available, cheaper, or both.[7]

Manufacturing employment also declined in established industrial countries because of automation, the use of sophisticated machines to replace manual labor. Instead of depending solely on people, during the final decades of the century companies relied more on computers to inspect inventories and design production processes and utilized robots to adjust machines, monitor assembly lines, paint automobiles, and so on. Furthermore, many of the production facilities that remained in these societies were reduced in size because responsibility for many of the functions that were previously handled in-house were subcontracted to specialized, external firms. Many firms found it cheaper to pay outside companies for maintenance, accounting, parts supply, and other tasks than to have their own employees perform such functions.

The loss of manufacturing jobs created long-term social and economic problems from which many cities have still not fully recovered. Successful adjustment to the new conditions has generally required cities that formerly relied heavily on manufacturing to devise strategies for linking to the global economy in new ways. As noted, the city of Manchester, in Northwest England, presents an especially interesting case. Jerome Hodos, who studied Manchester for several years, believes that the city's revival was due in large part to a small association formed by corporate chief executives whose primary purpose was to link leaders of the business community and government officials, without having to go through electoral politics or legislative review.[8] By limiting the association's size to no more than thirty members, the group was able to present a more unified business view than larger and more diverse groups. Many association members were executives of multinational corporations that were headquartered in other nations. One member, for example, was head of a subsidiary of Kellogg's, the American cereal company. These executives designed a strategy of recruiting transnational firms to Manchester and parlaying cultural and athletic activities into economic development initiatives with international marketing.

One direction Manchester followed was to become a world center of puppet animation films. Adding to the animation studio it had housed for years, Manchester attracted other animation and film studios, puppet makers, and set designers. The city became a leading international center for "stop-frame" animation in which puppets are moved slowly and filmed frame by frame. The most popular show created and filmed in Manchester was *Bob the Builder*, which became a hit with preschoolers throughout Britain, Germany, Japan, and the United States.[9]

Sports provided a second arena for Manchester, and, although the city's bid to host the 1996 Olympics did not succeed, the effort galvanized public and private support. Funds were raised to build an impressive ($115 million) football stadium, university dormitories, and hotels, mass transit systems, and so on. The cumulative effect was at least the partial rejuvenation of the formerly deteriorated and moribund downtown, and it positioned Manchester to be selected as the site of the seventy-two nation 2002 Commonwealth Games. This competition provided another important event for the city to use in marketing itself internationally, and the expected influx of visitors spurred the building of two large, innovative museums near the center of the city, plus an extensive addition to Manchester's former Art Gallery.[10]

In sum, Manchester—like numerous other cities formerly dominated by industrial production—had to reinvent itself after many of its factories closed. By focusing on linking to the global economy and the international business community located in Manchester, the city developed such cultural forms as museums, television production, and sports facilities. That route attracts coverage in the world's leading newspapers and may help to lure footloose corporations looking for new locations, although not all segments within a city will necessarily reap much benefit from such developments.

Who Benefits?

At the same time that Manchester's successes are noted it is also important to recognize that global linkages and cultural institutions do not have uniform effects within a city or metropolitan area. When foreign capital flows into a city, it commonly targets the commercial and financial center. Downtown real estate interests tend to benefit from the increase in commercial property values that typically follows. Sectors connected to international trade, finance, or tourism are also likely to benefit directly from more transnational connections. However, other groups (such as the blue-collar workers in Manchester who were still seeking jobs in factories, and their trade unions) are more apt to be adversely affected.[11]

When potential rental properties are converted (often via foreign investment) to commercial uses, the price of the rental properties that remain is usually increased. While this may be good for landlords, it is not good for working-class renters. The city of San Francisco is illustrative: a "dot-com boom" helped fuel a population increase of 7 percent between 1990 and 2000, but the net number of residents who identified themselves as black declined by almost 20,000. This shift did not occur because more African Americans were moving to even more expensive Bay Area suburbs, but because the growing number of start-up companies increased property prices to the point that people of limited means, which included a disproportionate number of blacks, were simply pushed out of the entire metropolitan area.[12]

Recent construction in the heart of old Shanghai has had similar consequences, which is somewhat ironic in light of the fact that the Communist Party's building is near the center of the large, internationally financed development project that is displacing former workers. Specifically, 129 acres in the center of the city were being redeveloped from a crowded, working-class residential neighborhood into a landscaped corporate park. Many residents who received eviction notices liked the location and wanted to remain, but their buildings were torn down. The government offered compensation to the evicted residents, but it was not enough money to enable them to afford a place in the same area after the construction was completed. As one man, who described himself as a true communist, complained with a wry smile, "They want to buy from me at planned-economy prices but sell to me at market-economy prices."[13]

Saskia Sassen, who has written extensively on globalization, views the influence of foreign firms and their executives on urban development as raising a question of moral claims; that is, whose city is it? The international business community, Sassen notes, has been accorded a great deal of legitimacy in making its claims upon cities, and it has consistently tried to transform them into high-tech, international business centers with world-class entertainment. In marked contrast are the low-income "others"—who Sassen identifies as minorities, immigrants, and women—who find their claims overlooked by the new decision makers.[14] (This issue is further addressed in the next chapter.)

The Knowledge/Information Base

The new global order, as seen by sociologist and urban planner Manuel Castells, is based on the ability to store and process information and generate knowledge. Information was always in demand, of course, helpful both to economic accumulation and political power. However, it may have become the most critical capacity. The production of goods, the offering of services, and decision making at every level depend increasingly on information. All other processes are now subordinate to it. And in modern nations, Castells adds, it is the information-processing component that underlies the dramatic recent growth in the services, and producer-services, sector.[15]

One historically unique feature of the new arrangement is the reliance of wealth on knowledge in a global economy. Throughout most of the past several hundred years, economist Lester C. Thurow notes, the richest people in the world owned natural resources, such as land, gold and oil, or factories and equipment. Now consider Bill Gates: What does he own? The answer, according to Thurow, is none of the things that conventionally made people rich. Gates's wealth is based on control of a knowledge process, the most valuable "commodity" in a modern economy.[16] Access to this new base is essential for creating wealth, and differential access within societies is magnifying preexisting income inequalities. Thus, Castells, Thurow, and most other analysts expect that levels of inequality will continue to reach new heights. *New York Times* columnist Thomas L. Friedman illustrated how these disparities in wealth and understanding are growing by recounting his experience in Egypt on a train between Cairo and Alexandria. Friedman sat in a car full of upper-class, urban Egyptians whose cell phones never stopped ringing. As the train passed the Nile, he saw barefoot villagers tilling their fields with water buffalo, much like their ancestors had in pharaoh's day. Inside the train, Friedman concluded, it was A.D. 2000, but outside the train, it was 2000 B.C.[17]

Thurow also observes that the very changes that led to an emphasis on knowledge have, ironically, made it difficult to protect intellectual property rights. The protection of most property rights, in an industrial age, involved patents, copyrights, and trademarks. Such safeguards do not work well today because technologies have created new forms of intellectual property rights that are difficult to patent or copyright. For example, when scientists discover the function of a specific gene, what ownership rights can be patented? And the ease with which software can be illegally duplicated often makes copyrights meaningless.

ECONOMIC MEASURES OF GLOBAL CITIES

During the late 1970s extensive writings began to appear describing the formation of a global division of labor among cities. The way any new topic (such as global cities) is initially examined is typically a function of the theoretical assumptions that predominate in a discipline or its most relevant substantive area. During the late 1970s, a paradigm shift was occurring in urban studies across the social sciences. Specifically, during the earlier decades of the twentieth century there was an emphasis on human ecology. According to this school of thought, changes within cities occurred spontaneously as a result of the same natural laws that operated in plant and animal communities. By contrast, the deliberate actions of groups of people or of governments were considered of little importance in altering city growth and development.

The ecological perspective was quickly being replaced in the late 1970s by a political-economy model that emphasized the importance of wealth and power and people's ability, via planning and concerted actions, to direct change. According to the new perspective, cities and their components were "commodities," subject to marketplace considerations.[18] People with wealth and power (and the two usually go together) were viewed as making investment decisions that determined which neighborhoods would grow, how quickly suburbanization would occur, where various types of businesses would concentrate, and so on. While the role of government was largely ignored in the earlier ecological analyses, the later paradigm stressed the link between economic interests and political actions.

Many global analysts assumed that the principles that governed activities and development within cities were similar to those that affected relations among and between cities. Thus, analysts focused on the cities in which fiscal-economic activity was concentrated in such forms as the largest stock exchanges, banks, and related financial institutions. The decisions that were reached in the cities that contained these economic concentrations, analysts assumed, were almost certainly highly consequential for other cities in the world because they all depended on investments emanating from these centers. Thus, the concentration of capital and economic decision-making influence was assumed to identify the leading global cities.

In addition, World System Theory (WST), which also followed a political-economy model, was pervasive during the 1970s and provided an initial umbrella under which to view the world urban system. According to WST—as formulated during the 1970s—for several hundred years the world had been divided into a core and periphery.[19] These two sectors corresponded with differences in nations' wealth and influence, and relations between the nations in the core and periphery were self-sustaining because of the way those in the core exploited the periphery. The imagery of WST also borrowed heavily on the insights of Karl Marx, but where Marx had primarily focused on capitalism's effects within nations, WST focused on capitalism's international effects. The nations in the core (for example, England and France) initially maintained dominance over the periphery (nations in Africa, Latin America, and elsewhere) via colonization, and later through exploitive arrangements in which firms located in the core paid very little for the raw materials they extracted from the periphery or for the labor they employed in the periphery. As a result, core firms' profits were excesssive, maintaining the wealth and advantage of the core nations at the expense of those in the periphery.

The cities that most analysts agreed belonged at the apex of the global city hierarchy tended to be the major cities within the core nations (again, for example, London and Paris), suggesting that the theoretical underpinnings of WST—its economic emphasis in particular—could be fruitfully applied to the analysis of global cities. This direction, as noted earlier, was congruent with the paradigm shift occurring in urban studies (as well as across many other social science specialty areas).

The impact of both WST and a political-economy model on the study of global cities was clearly evident in an influential early paper by urban analyst John Friedmann. In 1986 he tried to summarize the findings of current studies of world cities and propose the directions he thought future studies should pursue. Friedmann began by noting that the nature of a city's connection to the world economy was the key issue, and that similarly connected cities would necessarily be alike despite differences in history, national policies, and cultural influences. These leading cities were conceptualized as the *global command centers* because they were the "basing points" between world production and world markets. Among the significant features leading cities would always be expected to have, Friedmann emphasized similar divisions of labor (for example, large numbers of professionals in specialized control functions, such as lawyers, computer programmers, and accountants). In addition, he expected all these cities to serve as the major sites for the concentration and accumulation of world capital.[20] Friedmann's proposed hierarchy was based on a number of criteria, but it emphasized fiscal-economic and business services concentrations, and by his definition no primary world city could be located in a country that was considered peripheral.

In an important study of three major global cities (London, New York, and Tokyo), Sassen provided a detailed analysis of the parallel economic developments that were transforming the cities into concentrated financial centers. In a 1991 book, Sassen argued that the global cities had significant consequences both for the nations in which they were located and the global economy, but her analysis was not presented in a WST framework. Instead, Sassen insisted that it was the leading global cities, rather than core nations, that were the key structures in the world economy.[21] This separation of cities and nations was very influential. Even Friedmann, when he looked back at the decade of research after the publication of his early paper, dropped the WST perspective from his framework and simply identified cities in a hierarchy according to his view of the economic power they commanded.[22]

We will explore these issues in greater detail in Chapter 4, which examines fiscal-economic concentrations, specifically focusing on the cities that are headquarters to major stock exchanges, banks and financial institutions, multinational corporations, and financial services corporations. For each of these specific variables, we will describe the leading global cities as well as the secondary and tertiary centers. Chapter 5 focuses on patterns of growing income inequality within and across nations and cities, global cities in particular, and analyzes the relationship between inequality and the global economy.

MODERN TO POSTMODERN CULTURE

Running parallel to the changes associated with postindustrial economies are a number of fundamental cultural changes involving new ways of perceiving and experiencing the social world. All of these changes "distort" cultural features of industrial societies, though they do so in different ways. Some changes drastically exaggerate trends begun in industrial societies. Two of the most important examples are hyperrationality (discussed next) and hyperconsumption, which involves constantly growing desires for more commodities (introduced in Chapter 2). On the other hand are cultural changes (such as dedifferentiation, which is discussed on p. 14–15) that appear to reverse trends that formerly characterized industrial societies.

Hyperrationality

Max Weber, among the most influential theorists in economics, political science, and sociology, observed that a basic trend characterizing Western societies was a "demystification" of the world. Writing early in the twentieth century, Weber contended that magical beliefs, superstitions, and rituals were playing an ever-diminishing role in most people's everyday lives. In their place was an increasing rationality, epitomized by modern science and technology. By rationality Weber meant that decision making within the society, and especially its economy, involved a deliberate assessment of the likelihood that various means (i.e., alternatives) would lead to desired goals. One example is a company's calculation that it would be more efficient to supplement its workforce with temporary workers than to hire permanent employees. Whether permanent workers would be more loyal, and whether such loyalty would make any difference, seems too far afield to be relevant to decision makers who focus solely on an efficient connection between means and ends. This was how Weber anticipated people would make choices. He concluded that in modern societies people would find it so difficult even to conceive of alternative ways of reaching decisions that he likened rationality to "an iron cage."[23]

Writing nearly a hundred years ago, Weber envisioned the kind of rationality that became associated with manufacturing processes. Consider an automobile assembly line as the prototype: each worker contributed a door handle, a seat bolt, or some other small standardized part to the manufacture of an automobile. Highly rational control over the entire production process was apparent. Then rational production was combined with rational distribution and mass marketing to ensure maximum profitability for the firm. Because Henry Ford was the first to utilize assembly lines on a large scale, this entire system of production is often termed "Fordism."[24]

Rationality was not limited to manufacturing, of course. In fact, with the decline in manufacturing, the most important applications of rationality exist elsewhere in the economy and may be best illustrated by fast food franchises such as McDonald's.[25] Such franchises became dominant purveyors of food because they epitomized the rational approach. Buying raw materials in large quantities and selling products to a mass market provided franchises with large-scale efficiencies that small "mom and pop" restaurants could not match. The parent corporations made each decision rationally. How many square feet should be assigned to the eating area? Does a drive-through window maximize the use of space and personnel? Should whole potatoes or precut potatoes be distributed to franchises? In each case, decisions were based on efficiency and opportunities for rational control. For example, the decision to ship potatoes that had been precut in one location was made because it offered more control to the corporation and promised a standardized product that could be nationally priced. Those factors were weighed in the decision about the type of potatoes to distribute to franchises; other considerations, such as which type of potatoes the cooks might prefer to work with, were not.

Every fast food chain promised quick service and the same predictable food, no matter where its products were purchased. In promoting corporate identities, each chain also tended to emphasize the quantitative, rather than qualitative, features of its operation (e.g., how many burgers it had sold, how many seconds it took to fill an order, and so on). Persuading consumers that it was rational to purchase food at the corporation's franchises also led the chains to stress the quantitative characteristics of their products (that is, product size and weight), because consumers can most readily compare such quantitative features across competitors. As a result, franchises market such items as the Quarter Pounder, the Big Gulp, and the Whopper, and all of the fast food purveyors tend to deemphasize qualitative aspects, such as taste, aroma, or texture.

In postindustrial (post-Fordism) societies, the emphasis on rationality may have become excessive, resulting in hyperrationality. This shift is certainly not confined to fast food restaurants: ATMs, weight loss or diet centers, packaged vacation tours, and so on, similarly ensnare people by offering what appears to be highly efficient means to various ends. As rationality has been exaggerated into hyperrationality, however, it may have resulted in practices that only appear to be efficient. Are long lines at ATMs efficient for customers? Is it rational to take a packaged tour that does not permit the traveler to deviate from the beaten path to pursue a personal interest? With respect to fast food restaurants, Ritzer questions whether a better meal could not be prepared at home, for the same money, and be more satisfying than one eaten in a car. Furthermore, he asks, is it rational to eat in a restaurant that looks and feels exactly the same as every other, whose arrangements encourage people to eat as quickly as possible, and then to gather and dispose of their own garbage?[26]

Hyperrationality has become a pervasive feature of everyday life in postindustrial, global cities. Some people object, and try to resist the encroachment by franchises (and their attendant rationality) into every aspect of modern life, but resistance is difficult, and sometimes the alternatives are only superficially different. Tired of McDonald's? An alternative is American-style pizza, readily available everywhere in the world through such chains as Pizza Hut and Domino's. Pizza franchises became popular on a global scale because the type of pizza they sell is also highly uncomplicated to produce, easily standardized, fast, and portable.[27] However, for the same reasons, it may be no more rational a choice for consumers than fast food hamburgers.

Dedifferentiation

It was the view of an other influential classical theorist, Emile Durkheim, that the growing size and density of industrial societies were leading to greater and greater specialization. He particularly emphasized the movement toward more differentiation and stratification among occupational groups. The butchers, bakers, and candlestick makers—and engineers, lawyers, and scientists—were each associated with a specific product or service that in industrial societies was clearly demarcated from the others. Each had its place, and social solidarity in Durkheim's view depended on each group knowing that place. Associated with this rigid division of labor in industrial societies were strict separations among symbols, places, categories, and so on. Everything had to be kept in its proper place. To illustrate, mealtime was a distinct activity with its own set of norms, carried out in settings that were specifically designed for eating.

As the differentiation process continued and then accelerated at the end of the twentieth century, it may have reached a point where the boundaries of numerous symbols and social categories simply collapsed. Previously differentiated entities "imploded" into each other, and all types of distinctions became obscure.[28] Mealtime, as a special ritualized activity, to carry out our example, has become virtually meaningless because people eat while they watch television, walk down the street, drive their cars, or work at their desks.[29]

The increase in the products and services that can be put into a car to turn it into a mobile office is also eroding the distinction between leisure and entertainment, on the one hand, and work on the other. Among the equipment recently designed for automobiles are printers put into folding-down rear seats, special antenna for wireless Internet connection, hands-free telephones, palm-sized computers that transmit information to a dashboard display, and so on. The net result has been to transform automobiles into go-anywhere office cubicles that can be used by people in many occupations other than the sales representatives and insurance claims adjusters who had used mobile offices for years. A business consultant who had been living in an apartment recently bought a 37-foot recreational vehicle and fully equipped it to serve as a mobile office. Now he can visit Death Valley one day and write business reports that night in the same R.V. in which he will go to sleep. The next day he may tour a national park then drive to Phoenix and give a presentation before heading to Montana to view the fall foliage. The business consultant insists that even if he looks like a recreational vagabond, he really is working most of the time. "It's not like I'm sitting outside drinking margaritas all day," he said.[30]

When the partitions that once separated symbols and categories become unclear, the previously distinct dimensions of social life penetrate each other. As a result, social theorist Jonathan Turner notes, any new group can "usurp the symbols . . . of other persons . . . especially in an economy that makes everything available."[31] Consider as an illustration wealthy suburban teenagers who wear beltless jeans slung low on their hips. This was once considered a jailhouse look because prisoners were not permitted to have belts so their pants often slipped down. What do low-slung jeans now signify with respect to the status of the wearer?

The status distinctions between high-brow and low-brow forms of consumption have also diminished. Symphony orchestras whose repertoire was once largely confined to the works of classical composers and whose audiences tended to be well versed in the composer's work now play more "pops" concerts for heterogeneous audiences. The art and artifacts of museums were once arranged for patrons who knew the context and were looking for content. Now there is more emphasis on how to present collections to a mass market in a way that will provide people with a cinematic and interactive experience. One prominent exhibit designer explained that this trend is "an inevitable outcome of a theme-park and movie culture."[32]

CULTURAL MEASURES OF GLOBAL CITIES

The most overt aspects of any culture are most readily observed in people's language, technology, and artifacts. With respect to these more visible expressions of culture, it is clear that societies everywhere became increasingly alike during the last decades of the twentieth century. All around the world the same advertising slogans made their way into everyday speech, the same songs and movies were most popular, children everywhere wore Yankees or Dodgers caps and used the same kind of remote control to change television stations. Telecommunications advances, along with the more efficient worldwide distribution of commodities, were responsible for this visible cultural homogenization. However, the songs, baseball caps, and the like were only the manifest components of more fundamental cultural changes. A transformation of perceptual and value orientations accompanied the changes in overt cultural trappings. Thus, people in many nations ascribed more legitimacy to capitalistic markets and put more emphasis on consumption, leisure, and touring; and everyone's lives were affected by modifications of dominant cultural tendencies, such as dedifferentiation and hyperrationality.

Although what we may term global culture diffuses throughout the world, the cultural industries that transmit it are concentrated in a few cities: New York and Los Angeles (hence, the pervasiveness of Yankees and Dodgers caps), London, Paris, and Tokyo. The cultural industries located in these cities are the major conveyers of ideas and values, influencing the way people everywhere act, think, and feel.

For some theorists, particularly those following a political-economy model, cultural hegemony is real but ephemeral; that is, while an urban hierarchy involving cultural influence might be deduced, some expect that it would reflect nothing more than patterns of economic dominance. In still other words, the cultural dimension was thought only to reinforce, rather than shape, the political-economic nexus, and it was that latter nexus that was regarded as central. Other theorists, however, place the cultural and economic realms on a more even plane, often emphasizing how difficult it can be empirically to distinguish between them. All types of commodities—from movies to athletic shoes—have both cultural and economic aspects, and it can be very problematic to say where one begins and the other ends.[33] Furthermore, for the products of one country to be marketed in another, mass media and advertising have to penetrate people's lifestyles. Thus, sociologist Leslie Sklair contends that finance and economics may be the "building blocks" of the transnational system, but culture and ideology are the nuts, bolts, and glue that hold everything together. Without them, Sklair concludes, the economic building blocks would "drift off into space."[34]

Looking within global cities from a spatial perspective discloses a pronounced overlap between the cultural and economic entities. It is precisely in the central financial districts of global cities, where international economic activity is most highly concentrated, that one also finds the headquarters of the most significant media conglomerates and clusters of museums, galleries, Disney stores, and other representations of the cultural industries. They are all interspersed among the high-rise centers of finance.[35]

From an empirical perspective we may also note that the cities that are the hubs of the cultural industries resemble those that dominate the economic hierarchy, but with some notable variations. The least overlap occurs between the secondary and tertiary economic centers (including Frankfurt and Osaka) and the secondary and tertiary cultural centers (including Luxembourg and Sydney). In this book, we will treat the cultural and the economic realms as conceptually distinguishable, even while recognizing their marked overlap. In Chapter 6 the interpenetration of the cultural and economic realms is further explored, followed by an overview of recent changes in the cultural industries, with emphasis on how mergers and acquisitions produced enormous media conglomerates that control large shares of the world markets. In Chapter 7, a hierarchy of cities is presented based on headquarters of three of the most important global cultural industries: recorded music, movies, and television.

CITIES AND REGIONS

Throughout this introductory chapter we have referred to cities, especially global cities, without clarifying exactly what comprises a city. When specific cities are discussed there are usually appropriate qualifiers; for example, different territorial units are obviously implied by Inner London and Greater London, or New York City and the New York Standard Consolidated Area. However, when discussing cities in general, the term can refer solely to a municipality or politically incorporated area, or the municipality and the built-up area immediately surrounding it, or an extended metropolitan area, including the municipality and its inner and outer suburbs.

As we use the term city in this book, it usually encompasses both the municipality and the extended suburban area. Any other geographical unit is too small to adequately correspond with the way globalization has affected extended metropolitan areas. For example, streams of immigrants have settled in both the center and extended suburbs of global cities. Thus, the major nodes in the world economy are these global "city-regions."[36]

Within these city-regions, however, there are variations in the degree to which global connections are centralized or dispersed. These different patterns are illustrated by the locations of multinational corporations in U.S. cities. As conventionally defined, multinational (or transnational) corporations engage in economic activities in nations other than the one in which their headquarters are located. The larger corporations are involved in production or sales across much of the world, and the vast resources they control make them an enormous asset to the city (and the nation) in which they are housed.

Within the United States, the headquarters ranking of cities and metropolitan areas varies somewhat according to the criteria employed in selecting multinational firms. However, New York is always at the apex, and Chicago, Los Angeles, and San Francisco are almost invariably near the top. One fairly typical result, presented in Table 1.1, displays the location of the 500 largest publicly held U.S. corporations in 1998. Virtually all of these firms engage in a great deal of business across national lines. The table also indicates the number of headquarters that are located in the city (which would ordinarily be in the central business district) and in the suburban area surrounding the city.[37]

From Table 1.1 we can see that the four metropolitan areas with the largest headquarters concentrations actually contain about a third (165) of the 500 largest corporations. The top ten sites (among cities included in Table 1.1) contain over half (258) of the largest corporations. When the next ten sites (not shown in the table) are also included, the top twenty metropolitan areas are found to house nearly two thirds (328) of the nation's 500 largest corporations.

TABLE 1.1   Headquarters Location of 500 Largest Publicly Held Corporations in the United States

Metropolitan Area	Number of Corporations	Number in City/ Surrounding Area
New York	76	29/47
Chicago	35	17/18
San Francisco	29	4/25
Los Angeles	25	5/20
Boston	19	2/17
Dallas	19	13/6
Houston	18	18/0
Minneapolis	14	11/3
Washington, D.C.	12	4/8
Philadelphia	11	3/8

Table 1.1 also discloses an interesting pattern of city and suburban locations. It is only in those cities that grew most recently—the noncoastal cities, including Dallas, Houston, and Minneapolis—that central city headquarters are more prevalent than suburban headquarters. Much of the reason has to do with the availability of space in these cities relative to their suburban areas. The non-coastal central cities are relatively large because their basic shape was set after automobile use was widespread. Cities that developed before the automobile tend to be more compact due to transportation limitations during their formative years. (This would include most of the leading global cities in Europe and Asia as well.) Because the suburban areas of preautomobile cites developed later, they tend to encompass a relatively larger area than the cities they surround, enabling them to house a larger proportion of multinational corporations.

The next two chapters examine locations, activities, and lifestyles within global cities. Specifically, Chapter 2 begins at the center of global cities in the financial services district and works outward until it reaches "edge cities," the concentrations of corporate headquarters, retail agglomerations, entertainment facilities, and dense housing located at the periphery of metropolitan areas. Chapter 3 presents a discussion of immigrants and exiles, examining the enclaves they formed in global cities, and the way immigration has challenged conventional aspects of citizenship.

Figure 1.1   In global cities, both the downtown and the extended urban area house important activities. (Pictured here is Zurich, 2001.)

APPENDIX

The Virtual Workplace

One of the more dramatic changes in postindustrial economic organizations involves the physical separation of many employees from their primary work sites. Telecommunication developments involving the use of digital transmission, fiber optics, and lasers greatly improved the ability of people working at different locations to communicate with each other. They also led to the growth of the virtual workplace in which the work sites of lawyers, accountants, purchasing agents, and others are electronically, but not physically, connected to their co-workers, clients, and customers. To illustrate, the home office of BOC Gases, an international distributor of industrial gases used to manufacture semiconductors, is located just outside of New York, in Murray Hill, New Jersey. BOC maintains an online catalogue of gases on a restricted-access Web site that is available only to select suppliers and customers. Million-dollar orders are placed on BOC's Web site without any phone calls, faxes, or invoices. Managers employed by the Murray Hill facility only have to turn on their home computers to be able to oversee these sales transactions.[38]

What makes the separation of workers and work sites especially interesting is the way it illuminates the congruence between economic and cultural changes. To be more specific, the technological innovations that support the economic-occupational transformation are associated with a blurring (i.e., de-differentiation) in such previously distinct realms as home and office. According to some analysts, the change promotes rationality. Thus, for many people an electronic rather than physical attachment to their work site is an ideal arrangement. Their home office enables them to work the hours they prefer, sit in front of a computer in their underwear, remain close to young children, or the like.

However, other analysts regard the arrangement as blurring the lines between work and nonwork, between private and public space, because one's work site is never further away than the "spare bedroom," converted to a study. There is nothing like a plant whistle at 4:30 to mark the end of a work day. In addition, home work sites separate workers from work groups, which in industrial organizations often provided working people with an important sense of identity and connectedness.

Feelings of isolation among home-office workers are apparently one of the most important reasons for the success of "rent-an-office" complexes in major cities. A number of franchises provide offices for the estimated 40 million people in the United States who now work out of their homes. They can rent everything from compact, modestly furnished offices to executive suites. These furnished spaces are available by the hour, day, or month, and typically offer access to fax machines, color copiers, even shared secretaries. Some home-office workers rent the facilities for short periods in order to have more suitable places to meet clients. Others want to escape from the sound of crying babies or the sight of overflowing laundry baskets at home. For many of the office renters, however, a major objective is to be in a place where there are other working people to talk to during the day. After interviewing people in these rented offices, a *Time* magazine writer concluded, "A key part of [their] success . . . is replicating the sense of community that employees used to find hanging around the water cooler."[39] Thus, in these leased complexes, workers employed by different companies who happen only to share an address, hold Friday afternoon pizza parties, Christmas celebrations, and the like.

John Freie cynically notes that it was when more people were physically separated from their co-workers that American corporations introduced "participatory management" and a variety of other collegial approaches. They promised to increase the sense of connectedness among employees by providing the things people longed for but were no longer getting: recognition and approval. However, according to Freie, contemporary corporate versions of participation provide only "counterfeit communities" that cannot replace the authentic communities that were once based on neighborhoods and families. As the significance of the latter has declined, people have been left feeling isolated. The managerial fads, Freie concludes, "manipulate and exploit" people's longing to belong, but they cannot provide workers with any enduring personal identity or sense of genuine connectedness.[40]

NOTES

1. For further discussion of a number of major cities between roughly 1400 and 1800, see Alan K. Smith, *Creating a World Economy* (Boulder, Colo.: Westview, 1991).
2. Jonathan V. Beaverstock, Richard G. Smith, and Peter J. Taylor, "World-City Network," *Annals of the Association of American Geographers* 90(2000):123.
3. Nicholas D. Kristof, with Sheryl WuDunn, "Of World Markets, None an Island," *New York Times*, 17 February, 1999, p. 1.
4. Jerome Hodos, "Second Cities: Globalist Development Strategies and Local Political Culture," Department of Sociology, University of Pennsylvania, 2001.
5. See the discussion in Frederic Jameson, *Postmodernism, or, the Cultural Logic of Late Capitalism* (Durham, N.C.: Duke University Press, 1991).
6. Sharon Zukin, *Landscapes of Power* (Berkeley: University of California Press, 1993), 21.
7. For further discussion of these processes and their effects, see York Bradshaw and Michael Wallace, *Global Inequalities* (Thousand Oaks, Calif.: Pine Forge Press, 1998).
8. See Hodos, *op. cit.* By the same author, see also, "Globalization, Regionalism and Urban Restructuring." *Urban Affairs Review,* 37(2002):358–379.
9. Chieko Tsuneoka, "A Little Puppet Gets the Job Done, No Strings Attached," *New York Times*, 7 August 2001, p. E2.
10. Alan Riding, "An Industrial City Has an Architectural Rebirth," *New York Times*, 18 July 2002, p. E1.
11. For further discussion of the ways that globalization affects local areas and different segments of local areas, see Robert A. Beauregard, "Theorizing the Global-Local Connection," *World Cities in a World-System*, ed. Paul L. Knox and Peter J. Taylor (Cambridge: Cambridge University Press, 1995), 232–48.

12. Evelyn Nieves, "Blacks Hit by Housing Costs Leave San Francisco Behind," *New York Times*, 2 August 2001, p. A12.
13. Craig S. Smith, "High-Priced High-Rises Displace the Proletariat," *New York Times*, 16 July 2001, p. A4.
14. See especially Sassen's "Introduction," in Saskia Sassen and Kwame Anthony Appiah, *Globalization and Its Discontents* (New York: New Press, 1999).
15. Manuel Castells, *The Rise of the Network Society*, 3 vols. (Malden, Mass.: Blackwell, 1998).
16. Lester C. Thurow, "Globalization: The Product of a Knowledge-Based Economy," *The Annals of the American Academy of Political and Social Science*, 570(July 2000):19–31.
17. Thomas L. Friedman, "One Country, Two Worlds," *New York Times*, 28 January 2000, p. A23.
18. For further discussion of the paradigm shift, see Mark Gottdiener and Joe R. Feagin, "The Paradigm Shift in Urban Sociology," *Urban Affairs Quarterly*, 24(1988):163–87. The paradigm shift is discussed, and applied to several issues, in John R. Logan and Harvey L. Molotch, *Urban Fortunes* (Berkeley: University of California Press, 1987).
19. Immanuel Wallerstein, *The Modern World System*, vol. 1 (New York: Academic Press, 1974).
20. John Friedmann, "The World City Hypothesis," *Development and Change*, 17(1986): 69–84.
21. Saskia Sassen, *The Global City* (Princeton, N.J.: Princeton University Press, 1991).
22. John Friedmann, "Where We Stand: A Decade of World City Research," *World Cities in a World-System*, ed. Paul L. Knox and Peter J. Taylor (Cambridge: Cambridge University Press, 1995), 21–47.
23. See Hans Gerth and C. Wright Mills, eds., *From Max Weber: Essays in Sociology* (New York: Oxford University Press, 1958).
24. For a discussion of Fordism and the ways it has and has not changed in postindustrial societies, see Jerald Hage and Charles H. Powers, *Post-Industrial Lives* (Newbury Park, Calif.: Sage, 1992).
25. Much of the following discussion is based on George Ritzer, *The McDonaldization of Society*: New Century Edition (Thousand Oaks, Calif.: Pine Forge, 2000).
26. Ritzer, *op. cit.*
27. Barbara Crossette, "Burgers Are the Globe's Fast Food? Not so Fast," *New York Times*, 26 November 2000, p. WK2.
28. Ritzer describes the process by which previously differentiated entities collapse onto each other as implosion. See George Ritzer, *Enchanting a Disenchanted World* (Thousand Oaks, Calif.: Pine Forge Press, 1999).
29. For additional examples of the blurring of snack times and places, see Dirk Johnson, "Snacking Today: Any Time and Anywhere," *New York Times*, 30 July 1999, p. 1.
30. Todd Lappin, "When the Cubicle Has a Crankshaft," *New York Times*, 13 April 2001, p. F7.
31. Jonathan Turner, *The Institutional Order* (New York: Longman, 1997), 40.
32. Peter Hall, "Now Showing: Something Dazzling," *New York Times*, 2 May 2001, p. 17 (special section on museums).
33. Roland Robertson, "Globalization Theory 2000+," in *Handbook of Social Theory*, ed. George Ritzer and Barry Smart (London: Sage, 2001), 458–71.
34. Leslie Sklair, *Sociology of the Global System* (Baltimore: Johns Hopkins University Press, 1995), 63.
35. Sharon Zukin, *The Culture of Cities* (Oxford: Blackwell, 1995).

36. For further discussion, see the essays in Allen J. Scott, ed., *Global City-Regions* (Oxford: Oxford University Press, 2001).

37. The listing of corporations from which Table 1.1 was prepared is *Ward's Business Directory*, vol. 4 (Detroit: Gale, 1999). Figures pertain to 1998.

38. Bob Tedeschi, "The Net's Real Business Happens .Com to .Com," *New York Times*, 19 April 1999, p. D1. For a discussion of how jobs come to be located outside of an employer's place of business, see Alison Davis-Blake and Brian Uzzi, "Determinants of Employment Externalization," *Administrative Science Quarterly*, 38(1993):195–223.

39. Daniel Eisenberg, "Offices by the Hour," *Time*, 1 February 1999, p. 41.

40. See especially Chapter 5 in John F. Freie, *Counterfeit Community* (Lanham, Md.: Rowman and Littlefield, 1998).

TWO

People, Places, and Lifestyles

In this chapter we examine the spatial arrangements and lifestyles that are most characteristic of the leading global cities and their metropolitan areas. These attributes do not make them totally unique because many less global cities, especially large ones, partially share some of these features. The differences are typically more a matter of degree than kind. However, the leading global cities are set apart by their tendency to be uniformly high on all of the distinguishing spatial and lifestyle characteristics to be described here.

Our analysis will begin in the center of the city, in the downtown area that is dominated by high-rise office buildings catering to professional and financial services corporations from throughout the world. We will analyze the reasons for the financial agglomeration and the characteristics of the people who work in the district. Remaining near the city center, we will then turn to a distinctive type of neighborhood that frequently surrounds the financial center, namely a gentrified area. We will describe the physical characteristics of such neighborhoods and examine the lifestyles of the mobile young professionals who are its primary residents.

This chapter will also discuss the ways in which tourism and the heightened emphasis on consumption associated with postmodern culture are defining and shaping global cities, from financial services districts to urban neighborhoods to shopping venues. Our analysis will finally move out to the periphery of metropolitan areas of global cities to examine "edge cities," with their enormous concentrations of office complexes, housing, retail shopping, and entertainment.

When people encounter the built environment of cities and suburbs it is often difficult for them to imagine how that environment could be any different from the current setup. Frequently, however, a city's seeming "naturalness" obscures the fact that there is usually a struggle between competing groups to define space. Gender, race, and economic interests, for example, are typically associated with the attribution of different meanings to the same space. Is an acre of grass and trees in the center of a city to be considered a "green space" for the visual enjoyment of office workers or a park to be used by the children of nearby residents? The prevailing definition of the space will influence whether ball fields are built or "keep off the grass" signs are installed. Whose definition of the place wins out ordinarily depends on resources and access to decision makers. It is only after a usage competition has been resolved that it becomes difficult to imagine how space could be put to any other use. The constructed landscape then, has "the capacity to legitimize the powerful, by affirming the ideologies that created them in the first place."[1]

THE FINANCIAL SERVICES SECTOR

The concentration of high-rise office buildings that has become a hallmark of the center of global cities tends to contain large numbers of banks, insurance companies, law firms, stock brokers, and companies that buy, sell, and manage real estate. These activities correspond with the role of global cities as centers of the international flow of money, information, and commodities.[2] Affiliates or branches of the same companies are consistently found in the financial services sectors of global cities because these giant firms want access to all the urban centers with similar agglomerations.

Within these high-rise office buildings, employment is predominantly in highly skilled, knowledge-intensive producer services involving accountants, site analysts, lawyers, computer programmers, financial analysts, and so on. These professionals earn large salaries and their clients are more likely to be firms than individuals. Within this same sector is a second type of service work, involving such low-skill, low-wage positions as security guards, mail sorters, people who prepare and fill orders in fast food restaurants, and so on. Many service workers are employed in the lobbies of high-rise buildings, where they stand guard at entrances, shine shoes, or take orders at the counter of a Starbuck's or a McDonald's that serves the building. In contrast to the highly skilled people in the upstairs offices whose clients tend to be firms, people in this second type of work typically provide services directly to individuals.[3]

The large number of people working in low-wage service occupations in financial services sectors was vividly illustrated by unemployment figures following the September 11, 2001, terrorist attack on the World Trade Center in New York. In the month following the destruction of the Twin Towers, business activity in the vicinity largely halted and an estimated 80,000 people lost their jobs. Some who lost jobs were stock brokers, bankers, other managers, and executives. The occupations most affected in terms of unemployment, however, were waitstaff, food preparation workers, and others in restaurant and fast food services.[4] Unemployment among lower-end service workers was only part of the story. Even though thousands of people kept their jobs, they saw their incomes plummet. To be specific, limousine and cab drivers received fewer calls to transport bankers and lawyers, nannies found their schedules cut, and bellhops lost tips due to fewer guests at hotels in the financial district. New York, like other global cities, has a lower class that provides luxury services for upper-class professionals and their families. One New York historian observed that "when that upper class catches a cold," as in the aftermath of the World Trade Center destruction, "those who rely upon them catch pneumonia."[5]

Concentration and Agglomeration

For the past several decades, the headquarters locations of multinational corporations and specialized service firms have followed two trends: concentration (i.e., each firm has brought diverse functions to its primary location) and agglomeration (i.e., different firms have sought the same locations resulting in clustering of similar types of enterprises).

The explanation for the concentration of financial services in global cities, according to sociologist David Meyer, lies with flows of information. The global economy is, of course, dependent on modern telecommunications. The growth in international financial transactions and in imports and exports could not have occurred without satellite transmission, fiber optics, and other telecommunication innovations. Connecting to this global flow of information has never been easier; some information is accessible to anyone with Internet access. Yet, firms have tended toward large size and concentration despite the fact that, at first glance, technology might seem to support small size and decentralization. Why the seemingly contrary trend? According to Meyer, it is due to differences in the *kinds* of information available. Anyone can obtain stock and bond prices, for example, but specialized firms that have sophisticated software and other information processing technology with which to analyze trends in prices are more likely to have unique insights. The infrastructure that gives this advantage to firms is expensive, though, and concentration helps justify the high fixed costs.[6]

Sassen agrees that the concentration of financial service firms over the past few decades can, at first glance, seem counterintuitive, but she offers several additional reasons why these firms did not disperse. One important reason is that the branches and affiliates of firms headquartered in the major cities are carrying out activities throughout the world, which places a premium on centralized control and argues against dispersion. Sassen also points out that the scale of modern business, with huge mergers and mega-acquisitions, requires enormous resources, which also favors consolidation. Finally, she notes, the growth of the global economy has diminished the significance of national boundaries. As a result, externally moving investment flows are less likely to arouse nationalistic concerns, so companies do not have to locate major components everywhere they are doing business.[7]

In addition to all Meyer's and Sassen's reasons for the growth and concentration of financial services, large size is also indirectly encouraged by problems of trust, which are at least partially resolved by government "certification." To understand this government role, Meyer notes that it is helpful to remember that these firms are not routinely buying and selling (or advising ɔuy and sell) actual physical assets. While transactions can involve ɪdities as automobiles, gold, or timber, they more often consist of ;" that are symbols of these assets or else are derived from them. ɪo illustrate, real estate portfolios may repeatedly change hands without anyone taking physical control of the property involved or altering that property in any way. Similarly, outstanding loans may be "bundled" and sold from firm to firm with virtually no impact on the debtors whose loans are the objects of the transactions.

With symbolic exchanges, trust is essential because no one is handing over a visible truckload of automobiles or a ton of wheat. On the other side of the transaction, buyers are not bringing stacks of currency to the table. Buyers must assume that sellers own the items they are offering, and sellers must assume that buyers have the funds (or access to the funds) to cover the cost of the transaction. Furthermore, these transactions are occurring between people who ordinarily do not know much about each other's backgrounds, and whose relationships are confined to this one set of work roles. Lacking personal familiarity with each other, buyers and sellers must rely on trust precisely when its potential is receding.[8]

A premium is also placed on trust because the speed and volume of exchanges in stocks, bonds, currencies, and the like typically precludes the detection of malfeasance until it is too late. If each aspect of a potential exchange required scrutiny and confirmation, the pace of exchange would be slowed to a crawl. Therefore, Meyer points out, elaborate methods have been devised by which nations certify the trustworthiness of firms and provide means by which an aggrieved party could seek redress. This commercial legal code is crucial to the successful operation of any nation's international financial center. However, by limiting the number of firms that are certified, a nation also places an entrance barrier to the market, and this limitation on the number of firms that can compete also favors the growth in size of the designated firms.[9]

POWER AND OPPOSITION

While recognizing the role played by national governments in supporting financial services agglomerations, it is important not to overlook the strategic part played by host cities and their metropolitan areas. Host cities create an environment conducive to agglomeration by cooperating in building and maintaining infrastructure conditions, such as global telecommunication and air transport facilities, and providing tax incentives. City leaders tend to emphasize the anticipated rewards for making such investments: more jobs, an improved tax base in the long run, image enhancement, and so on. The costs that will likely accrue, such as airport noise or congested highways, tend to receive scant attention.[10] Furthermore, almost any type of development is likely to benefit some segment of the city at the expense of others. Few changes will actually turn out to be neutral in their consequences, regardless of how ideally they may be presented as serving the interests of everyone. To illustrate, in the late

1980s, the metropolitan Los Angeles transportation authority (MTA) proposed a long-range plan for the metropolitan area. Its centerpiece was a light rail system linking downtown Los Angeles with several suburban areas. By enticing commuters to leave their automobiles at home, the planners believed the new system would cut pollution and sprawl. What group could object to these goals?

Opposition arose later when, to offset high construction costs of the subway system, the MTA slowly reduced bus route expenses by putting fewer new buses into service, raising fares, and eliminating monthly bus passes. In response, a Bus Riders Union formed to advocate against these reductions. The union pointed out that buses were heavily used by people from working-class neighborhoods, minorities in particular, many of whom had no alternative means of commuting to work. The suburban rail line, by contrast, primarily served more affluent (and fewer minority) suburbanites. Eventually, lawyers from the NAACP Legal Defense Fund took an interest and argued that by degrading bus service in favor of rail transit the agency was engaging in de facto racial discrimination. The Bus Riders Union won a few small court cases, including one resulting in a judge requiring the MTA to order some new buses. In the larger scheme of things, however, the bus riders and their association have not been able to do more than slow the process. Where Los Angeles' transportation policies have been concerned, the interests of the working class, minorities, and their communities have taken a back seat to the interests of affluent suburbanites. As rail construction proceeded at the expense of support for bus service, ridership on metropolitan Los Angeles buses declined by a third between 1985 and 2000.[11]

When corporations have designs on economically depressed areas, there is a power mismatch. Because these communities tend to have limited political clout, any conflict that occurs between local and corporate interests is usually of short duration. Gerald Suttles, a sociologist who studied poor areas of cities for many years, described the process as resembling a con game because poor areas rarely get what they are initially promised. A corporate representative (someone like a modern Professor Harold Hill in *The Music Man*) comes to town and makes a dramatic announcement about what the community really needs: renewal. The presentation is scheduled in a place that is too important for the media to ignore; for example, the mayor's office. The representative promises that, as a side benefit of community renewal, neighborhoods will be improved by the corporation's benevolent donation of well-equipped parks or plazas, and lots of jobs will be created. The representative neglects to mention that the only jobs likely to be filled by local residents are in the low-wage service sector.

As part of the presentation, the media are given access to scale models or architect's drawings that give the plan a solid, real feeling. However, the schedule requires that the project be approved at once, the corporate representative insists. Preparations must begin: old housing has to be razed immediately, even if it is still occupied; expressways or subway stops must be rerouted through neighborhoods, even if it creates barriers to everyday activites. The benefits?

They come later—honest! On the other hand, if there are delays, the representative threatens, there will be cost overruns that could jeopardize the entire project: no free parks or plazas, no jobs. Those residents who still object are typically steamrolled.[12]

It is also important to recognize that initial construction decisions do not put an end to the struggle over how space will be utilized because most spaces are compatible with a variety of uses. To illustrate, in central Hong Kong's financial district, corporations have tried to restrict the use of public spaces, such as squares and the areas around fountains. Development practices in Hong Kong give corporations broad powers to limit use and access. The regulations typically state that people can be excluded if they create a nuisance or use the space for unintended purposes. One might then ask, a nuisance to whom, or unintended by whom? The answer to both questions is the corporations who wield the power to make their definitions of the space stick. In effect, during the week, given corporate power in Hong Kong, the general public can use these "public" spaces only to pass over.

On Sundays, when the corporate offices are closed, control over the use of public space in central Hong Kong is relaxed, but not removed. For example, police still place barriers around a central fountain in order to keep people from sitting on its ledges. With control lessened, thousands of Filipino women, most on whom work in Hong Kong as domestic workers, crowd the public spaces on Sundays. They sit on straw mats and gossip, talk about their children's schooling, and reminisce about life in the Philippines. It becomes a place for women to "reimagine" their homeland and try to make sense out of life in Hong Kong. It also becomes a potentially political site in which women can make public the conditions under which Filipino domestics work.[13]

CASE STUDY: LONDON'S FINANCIAL SERVICES DISTRICTS

Like many European cities, London was a former Roman army encampment, initially selected because the Thames River was ideal for transporting troops and supplies. Flat meadows and plains on London's other borders made it easy to monitor the settlement against surprise attacks. To further enhance security, the Romans enclosed the city in a semicircular wall. Over the next 1,600 years this enclosed area of approximately 1 square mile contained most of the city's craftspeople and merchants. With England's industrialization in the eighteenth century, there was expansion, but the core area north of the Thames remained the center of commerce. In 1803 it was described as a "shopping centre" dominated by two sets of east–west streets lined with the shops of clockmakers, tailors, pastry cooks, book and music sellers, and small manufacturers of tobacco, mattresses, and other goods.[14] Some of these streets at one time contained concentrated numbers of particular types of merchants from which they derived such names as Garlic Court, Poultry Street, and Threadneedle Street.

The most dramatic changes in this square mile began in the 1970s, when banks, brokers, insurance companies, and capital management and investment firms from everywhere in the world sought space in the center of London. The specialized legal, accounting, and other firms that serviced them also wanted a nearby London address. Within a decade, this square mile north of the Thames River (called the City of London or the City) contained one of the largest concentrations of banks and financial service institutions in the world. It is a dense clustering of buildings, though it lacks the skyscraper skyline of some cities, like New York, because of historic restrictions imposed on the height of buildings in certain parts of London. To form a mental picture of this area in 2001, take a "virtual walk" down a couple of blocks of historic Threadneedle Street. You will pass large buildings containing the Bank of Scotland, several international capital management firms, Lloyds (the world's largest reinsurer), the London International Financial Futures Exchange, the Bank of England, and the London Stock Exchange. When Threadneedle meets Poultry, turn left and walk over to Lombard Street. In the next two blocks you will pass a large German bank, several asset management and professional services firms, a large Japanese bank, and so on.

To build this financial district, large office complexes were built as quickly as smaller, older buildings could be knocked down. However, the demand for space, especially large amounts of space in the compact center of London, could not be met. The supply–demand mismatch was exacerbated by the city's prohibition against building any high-rise edifice that would block the public's views of historic landmarks, such as St. Paul's Cathedral, the Tower of London, and the Palace of Westminster. Large international firms often require hundreds of thousands of square feet of office space, and any building that could accommodate them would occupy an enormous amount of scarce land unless it was built vertically.

The backlog of unmet demand led to new commercial development east and west of the main financial district. The West End became headquarters for some international manufacturing and service industries, but it had been a prime residential location for a couple of hundred years, which limited commercial development. To the east of London were the docklands: an old, rundown area containing warehouses and boarded-up factories. One 71-acre site in docklands, near the Thames, located east and south of the "square mile," was Canary Wharf. Development of this area began in 1982, when a British television network built a studio in what had been a rum and banana warehouse. The studio became the home of a popular business news show (*The Business Programme*) that brought bankers and industrialists to the docklands as guests of the show. One banker, impressed with the area's potential, put up £1.4 billion (about U.S. $2 billion) to turn the rundown area near the Thames into "Wall Street on water."[15]

Canary Wharf attracted firms, mostly in financial services, and by the 1990s established itself as London's second financial center. The larger it became, the more the agglomeration of firms made it attractive to others as a business site. By 2001 a total of about 41,000 people were working at Canary Wharf, but there were ten high-rise buildings still under construction, accounting for 50 percent of all of the commercial development in greater London at the time. The completion of these buildings was expected to more than double the number of people employed in the area, raising the total to about 90,000. Still further expansion and development of Canary Wharf is planned, however, and total employment of as many as 130,000 people is envisioned by 2010.[16]

The initial growth of Canary Wharf—"overflow" from London's square mile—represented little threat to the Corporation of London, the group that oversees the main financial district, and to the main figures in London's city government. However, when large banks and investment firms such as Lehman Brothers (with 2,800 employees in its investment banking operation) and even the London Stock Exchange expressed an interest in moving to Canary Wharf, the City and the Corporation of London responded. In 2001, the mayor of London and other influential politicians in the city insisted that height restrictions on buildings in the older financial center had to be modified. Unless taller buildings were constructed, they argued, the largest financial services firms would all wind up outside of the city, in Canary Wharf. Given those consequences, the mayor stated, spoiled views do not mean very much to most Londoners.[17] Heritage and environmental groups were opposed to the proposed changes, and skeptics warned against London engaging in "vulgar international height competitions" like Chicago but competition with Canary Wharf was considered likely to lead to at least some future relaxation of London's building code.[18]

As Canary Wharf's skyscrapers have continued to attract more large firms, the difficulty of moving the workforce in and out of the area has multiplied. To illustrate, Citigroup relocated employees that had been scattered among a half-dozen buildings in London to a forty-two story high-rise in Canary Wharf. Many of the transferred employees wanted to remain in the same London housing, even though their commute had been increased. As a way of alleviating the traffic jams produced by the employees of numerous relocated firms, in late summer 2001, Canary Wharf began a campaign to alter a previously proposed rail route through some of London's poorest boroughs in order to build an east–west rail link between it and London. The poorer neighborhoods from which the rail would be diverted, if Canary Wharf has its way, have limited public transportation, and the ability of residents to find and hold jobs might be substantially improved by a rail line. The issue is far from resolved as this is written, but we can note that when such conflicts have arisen in London in the past—or Los Angeles or Shanghai or other global cities—it has been the interests of corporate and financial service centers, such as Canary Wharf, that have generally been given precedence.

YUPPIES AND DINKS IN GENTRIFIED AREAS

As financial services districts emerged during the 1980s, at their outskirts tended to be older, deteriorated areas of the central city. The residents were generally poor, often minorities, and lived in small, old homes (aged brownstones,

Victorians, or row houses). In many cases the residents shared their neighborhood with warehouses and small factories that located there because of the low cost of land. Despite age and deterioration, however, these areas retained an important asset, namely, their proximity to the financial services district—and this proximity typically led to changes.

In some cases, old buildings were demolished and replaced by high-rise office buildings to expand the central financial district. In the late 1980s in central Tokyo, for example, a growing number of international firms wanted to locate close to the city's other corporate headquarters and providers of business services. The demand led to wild land speculation that fueled dramatic increases in land prices, beginning in the central business district and diffusing to adjacent areas. As the value of property increased, taxes associated with property assessments went up, and the residents of the small, older housing units were forced to move because they could not afford the higher taxes. Facilities associated with the former neighborhood were also affected. Elementary schools were closed due to falling enrollment and once successful retail stores were pushed out due to a diminished customer base. Office buildings replaced these structures, and were quickly occupied by firms that found ways to reduce or circumvent taxes that pushed out the former residents.[19]

Despite the changes that occurred in various sections of central Tokyo, the neighborhoods as they once existed have remained within the collective memory and are still topics of discussion. In recent years foreign travelers have visited the places described by natives, looking for the traditional shops and neighborhoods that once existed. Such trips are in vain, of course, because the communities are now only places of retrospection and nostalgia.[20]

In other global cities, the deteriorated areas adjacent to the financial services districts underwent a gentrification process. With respect to housing, gentrification sometimes involves replacing older buildings with new, high-rise apartment buildings or condominiums. There also tends to be a great deal of renovation of existing structures. Many major cities had a stock of office buildings erected prior to 1930 that forty to fifty years later, when financial districts were expanding, were no longer attractive to potential business clients. Retrofitting these buildings for modern office use is prohibitively expensive because it involves new wiring, the construction of parking garages, and so on. Converting to residential use is cheaper. In addition, the oddly shaped "funky" spaces in older offices buildings are much better suited to remodeling as luxury apartments.[21]

Two types of new residents predominate in these gentrified areas: young, urban professionals (yuppies) and dual-income, no kids (dinks) households. A large proportion of yuppies and dinks are in professional occupations (lawyers, accountants, information technology specialists, etc.). Many are employed by multinational corporations and are frequently relocated from one international city to another, typically working in the financial services district. They have low rates of automobile ownership and want to minimize commuting time, which is why they choose to live in these nearby gentrified neighborhoods.

Years after the expansion of Tokyo's financial district engulfed older residential areas, a number of large corporations committed billions of dollars to build residential complexes offering high-rise rental apartments and condominiums in central Tokyo. They made these commitments in 2002, based on two major considerations:

1. the fastest growing segment of Tokyo's population were dinks,
2. many of the young professionals had worked overseas and learned to appreciate living close to work to cut commuting times.[22]

Thus, in central Tokyo, the growth of the financial services district first pushed out older, horizontally congested housing and replaced traditional neighborhoods with high-rise office buildings. However, this growth later provided the incentive for the construction of newer, vertical housing for yuppies and dinks, likely leading to gentrified areas like those in other global cities.

Displacement and Isolation

Once gentrification begins, the lifestyle of the young professionals attracts retail enterprises, such as eat-in and carry-out restaurants, cleaners, specialty food and liquor stores, designer clothes boutiques, and so on. The commercial expansion then makes the area more attractive to other yuppies and dinks, which, in turn, promotes more commercial development, stimulating more residential development, and the cycle continues. Residential and commercial interests then compete for the unconverted land. This competition causes land values to increase further, and many of the neighborhood's long-term residents find it impossible to pay the escalating rent or taxes.

The consumption patterns of the high-end professional service workers generate employment for lower end service workers (in the fast food industry, cleaning and maintenance work, as governesses, beauticians and barbers, and so on). However, the former residents of the neighborhood, who could fill these types of service positions, especially if they were able to live nearby and hence minimize commuting costs, are priced out of the area. Some former residents move to other neighborhoods, but others become the homeless "casualties" of gentrification.[23]

Geographer Neil Smith notes how an area in the process of gentrification is frequently described, by newspapers and realtors, as a "new frontier," complete with latent images of the wild, wild West. The young professionals who are among the first to renovate old brownstones are seen as courageous homesteaders or perhaps like the first *StarTrek* crews, traveling where no one had gone before. Some of the appropriation of frontier language might seem playfully innocent, Smith comments, except that it happens also to convey a negative image of the ("untamed") pregentrified community and its (barbaric) former inhabitants, who become modern counterparts to a mythical tribe of savages, thereby justifying extreme measures by the brave, outnumbered settlers.[24]

The precise boundaries of these gentrified areas typically do not correspond with municipal or town borders, and there often are no landmarks, such as parks or major thoroughfares, to demarcate the edges. Residents, therefore, are often uncertain exactly what space their neighborhood includes. There may be more consensus about which places are categorically excluded. To illustrate, in the high-density, upper-middle-class neighborhood of Tai Koo Shing, on Hong Kong island, one young investment banker was asked to define the neighborhood. She was only sure about what it did not include, namely an adjacent area with housing that she described as "old, deteriorated and the prices are much cheaper."[25]

The final step in solidifying a gentrified neighborhood is to assure that potential interlopers (who are poor or members of minority groups) are kept outside. The new residents typically believe that their personal security and the safety of their property depend on their ability to maintain the new homogeneity of their upscale community, resulting in a "fortress-like" mentality. Empirical data to support such excessive fear of crime are usually lacking, but the perception sticks and it is sufficient to motivate new residents to erect physical and symbolic barriers.[26] In downtown Los Angeles, social critic Mike Davis describes how big American and Japanese investors built billion dollar megastructures, such as CitiCorp Plaza and Crocker Center, and then used public funds via the Community Redevelopment Agency to remove almost all of the pedestrian links to older, minority communities. To maintain the stylish shops and gourmet strips, Davis concludes, requires the "social imprisonment' of the minorities who provide the wage labor.[27] Except for their work shifts, minorities have to be kept out of the area.

To prevent these "undesirable" outsiders from even temporary nonwork intrusions, Davis points out that many communities have been eliminating virtually all public spaces, like parks, playgrounds, and beaches. The contempt currently attached to the term "street person," he contends, indicates the way public spaces have been devalued. Further, public spaces that cannot be eliminated—such as in underground subway stations—tend to be tightly monitored, restricting the access of street musicians, beggars, the homeless, and others. (The fortress-like structure of heavily patrolled suburban malls similarly controls public spaces, banning any activity owners consider detrimental to shopping.[28])

Social Life of Young Professionals

Young professionals employed in the financial services district typically work long hours. In their limited free time, yuppies and dinks tends to emphasize convenience over cost in making lifestyle decisions. A Chicago bank vice president in her early thirties explained that the time factor determines most of her dining decisions. To cook at home requires planning: one must first go to the store and shop, and when she gets home at eight o'clock it is too late to start. "So we pick up the telephone, call a bunch of local restaurants and ask about the waiting times."[29]

Many residents of gentrified areas can afford to emphasize convenience over cost because they have a lot of disposable income. As professionals, they earn high salaries and have few dependents because they tend to be either single or, if married, childless. The result is a conspicuously high-consumption lifestyle. Social critic David Brooks calls them "bobos," an abbreviation of bourgeois bohemians, due to their proclivity for combining conventional and unconventional tastes.[30] (Perhaps they merely reflect the way this distinction has also become blurred?) In decorating their homes, for example, bobos in America prefer furniture that is new and expensive, but has a distressed look to mask its newness. They also believe it is okay to display religious items on tables or walls if the objects are associated with distant or remote religions (for example, a shaman's mask is acceptable but a crucifix is not).

Dating patterns among young professionals are also shaped by the time constraints of work, plus new norms that emerged during the 1980s regarding how single people ought to meet. These new norms were associated with the societal transformation from industrial/production to postindustrial/consumption. Through the transformation, identity and sense of self became less work based, instead deriving more from leisure styles and consumption patterns. As a result, people's identities are more fluid (less locked into class and occupation, which are more enduring), created and displayed through consumption choices that reflect cultural preferences.[31] In this consumer-dominated context, in which the media and advertising are of heightened importance, self-advertising became a socially acceptable means of making contact. An increasing number of people turned to personal sections in newspapers, magazines, and other periodicals to design and present an image of themselves for the social marketplace: "attractive and witty . . . enjoys music and food and shopping. . . . "[32]

Like their eating habits, dating and mating among young professionals emphasize a commitment to convenience, and are shaped by technology. The same e-mail that enables them to order lunch without leaving their computer screen has become a preferred means of finding others with whom to connect. One twenty-nine-year-old business executive in Boston, who worked in e-commerce and spent much of his day on the Internet, explained that meeting someone online "seemed more natural."[33] E-mail has also become an important means of managing relationships. For example, after meeting in a bar, yuppies may be more likely to exchange e-mail addresses than phone numbers. E-mail also provides a convenient and tasteful way to follow up on a first date. A thirty-one-year-old publishing executive in Manhattan talked about how e-mail resolved the "next day" problem. Having just seen her date the night before, the executive thought it would be awkward to telephone (she feared seeming pushy or too anxious), so sending her date an e-mail was a handy solution. And it certainly provides the ideal way to end a relationship because neither party has to see or hear the other party when that message is conveyed.[34]

The telephone continues to be an important part of everyone's lives, though for young professionals in particular cell phones have become omnipresent. Whether in a bar or restaurant, waiting for an elevator or walking down the street, young professionals rely on their cell phones to make dates, keep in touch, or simply impress others. The use of cell phones is a part of their generation's lifestyle that is generally frowned on by people over about age thirty-five or forty. To these older people, who did not grow up with cell phones, public use of them is often seen as "appropriating others' space and forcing them to eavesdrop."[35] To younger people, by contrast, the cell phone is a symbol of social importance and is something to be flaunted, leading some users to engage in "stage-phoning": using public space to make unimportant calls solely to impress others.

The status aspects of cell phones appear to be especially important for men, according to two researchers in Liverpool, England. They spent several months observing young professionals in one of Liverpool's upscale singles bars and found that male patrons conspicuously displayed or used their cell phones about two and a half times more often than female patrons. The men in the bar fiddled with their phones, turned them over and stared at them, checked the battery, and so on. The investigators concluded that it was a "courtship display" intended not only to reflect the male's status, but his social importance as someone who had to be reachable at all times. Thus, for these young professional men who were trying to attract females' attention, the researchers concluded that exhibiting a cell phone was akin to other male animals' preening or strutting to distinguish themselves from the rest of the pack.[36]

INTERNATIONAL TOURISTS AND TOURISM

Tourists have become an integral part of daily life in the heart of the leading global cities. International tourist favor many of these cities over anywhere else. Specifically, the leading destination for international tourism during the 1990s was Paris, followed—at a distance—by New York, Madrid, Rome, and London.[37] Within these cities, tourists got off at the same subway stops as corporate personnel, window-shopped at the same stores, ate in the same restaurants, and so on. This influx of international tourists is partly responsible for the spatial intertwining of finance and cultural diversions in global cities. Galleries, Disney and Warner Brothers Studio stores, museums, nightclubs, bars, and sports arenas all tend to be concentrated among the high-rise office buildings of the global cities' financial centers.[38]

People have always traveled, Fainstein and Judd observe, but tourism—which involves traveling in conjunction with the tourist industries—is a much more recent phenomenon. A complex of industries is involved, including hotels and convention centers, agencies (such as visitors bureaus) that promote officially recognized sites and attractions, the production and marketing of souvenirs, and so on. These industries that attract and cater to visitors transformed mere travel into modern tourism by making it a more socially distinct and recognizable activity.[39]

Which cities international tourists visit seems to be related to two characteristics: more travelers are attracted to cities that have a financial-commercial concentration (e.g., Wall Street) and that have buildings or specific places that have become "enshrined" as attractions (e.g., the Eiffel Tower). These two variables tend to operate congruently because the cities that have large financial centers usually have significant cultural, political, and military traditions as well, and have thereby generated potential historical artifacts (e.g., places where treaties were signed, artworks were created, and the like). Paris, New York, and London are ready examples of global cities with both enticements. These cities, according to Fainstein and Judd, are so established as "must see" places that people who consider themselves to be world travelers feel obligated to visit them. Cities that are perceived to be outside of this circuit, but nevertheless aspire to tourist revenue, must somehow transform themselves. This typically requires that the cities emphasize and promote a specific quality that can set them apart, such as gambling, climate, entertainment, or a combination of special qualities.[40]

Some cities and regions lacking in historical importance have been successful in marketing themselves as tourist cities. Examples include Atlantic City in the United States, the Sunshine Coast in Australia, and Cancun in Mexico. These cities have developed into tourist meccas that are global in that they attract large numbers of international visitors, but they differ from the major global cities in several important ways: the population size of tourist cities is usually much smaller; their labor forces are dominated by service positions in the entertainment industry; they house few corporations with international affiliations; and although many have large groups of segregated minorities, they do not have diverse racial and ethnic enclaves.[41]

Selling Places

International tourism involves a great deal of money. In 1998, 625 million people spent at least one night outside of their home country, and on average each traveler spent over $1,000 (U.S.).[42] Cities and private promoters throughout the world all want a share of the billions of dollars that travelers spend annually. Toward this end, government and private interests collaborate to "sell" an image of a city, or a distinct place within it, that will make it attractive to potential tourists. (At the same time, they are usually trying to make the city look appealing to firms considering relocation.)

The recent selling of cities, according to London geographer Mark Goodwin, is part of the "commodification" of the everyday world. Life in major cities is now marketed via myths—in movies, novels, and the brochures of property developers—to the point where the difference between reality and its representation is moot. Los Angeles, for example, has gone through several cycles of revision, first emphasizing its film industry, then its entertainment complexes, and finally its visual and museum arts. Each time promoters symbolically redefined the city in the way that they believed would best attract tourists and investments.[43]

Miriam Greenberg calls the marketing of a distinct vision of a city "branding," a term she derived from the recent growth in the importance of brand value, as something that has worth apart from the tangible assets of a firm. (For example, when the value of the tangible components of a firm are added together to arrive at a selling price, an additional figure is often added for intangibles, such as name worth or the value of the brands it owns.) Brand value grew in importance during the last quarter of the twentieth century as popular marketing increasingly stressed the link between consumer lifestyle and brand name items. Once an automobile, running shoe, perfume, or lipstick found a lifestyle niche, its brand value increased. A new occupation simultaneously emerged, the brand manager: a specialist in overseeing a product's image. Given international competition for tourists, it was a logical progression for cities to try to increase their own brand value and to do so by employing brand managers (though they are called public relations experts, convention and tourism managers, and so on).

Periodicals that portrayed the lifestyle a city wanted to project became important instruments to brand managers. New York, Paris, London, and other major cities promoted magazines with their names in the title. Each of these monthly publications was designed to present a picture of the city that would make it exotic and attractive to potential visitors. To illustrate, the magazine, *New York* regularly included columns on unusual restaurants ("underground gourmet") and out-of-the-way stores ("undercover shopping"). The apparent objective was to entice upper-middle-class tourists to shop and eat in various ethnic enclaves by branding them in the magazine as exciting and special places to visit.[44]

To be successful, the marketing effort must ordinarily convince people that the place has something "authentic" that they should find appealing. In this context, *authentic* means that the tradition, object, or event being promoted is intrinsically rooted in the place. A museum devoted to industrial history, for example, would be difficult to market in an area that is regarded as having only an agrarian past. Therefore, to promote such a museum as a tourist attraction, it would probably be necessary simultaneously to promote the city's industrial traditions. This may, of course, require some manipulation or reinvention of culture and history that will leave some locals feeling left out of the public representation of the place. Farmers, unemployed laborers, and others may feel that the selling of an industrial museum in their city presents an inauthentic cultural representation, or at least one that seriously departs from the meaning of the place that they share.[45] For example, the working-class residents of London's docklands, who lived there before the area became a financial district, were unable to prevent the marketing of Canary Wharf as a professional service center with housing for yuppies and dinks, with little in the way of job retraining projects or child care services.

TOURISM AND HYPERCONSUMPTION

The connection between tourism and consumption is not new. Tourists have for a long time spent money to view attractions and buy trinkets and souvenirs as part of their traveling experience. However, sociologist George Ritzer has written that the boundaries between tourism and consumption have eroded. Consumption, which was once incidental to tourism, has become one of its major objectives. To support his argument, Ritzer notes the degree to which giant malls have become dominant tourist attractions. In Canada, the Edmonton Mall draws more visitors than Niagra Falls; Potomac Mills in suburban Washington, D.C., has more visitors than Arlington National Cemetery.[46]

As consumption has become more salient—that is, hyperconsumption—entrepreneurs across the world have built what Ritzer terms "cathedrals of consumption." He uses religious imagery because of the reverence with which people describe trips to mega-shopping malls and other retail concentrations. Visiting them has become almost like making a pilgrimage to a holy site. People also tend to treat the commodities they purchase on these trips as though they were out-of-the ordinary items requiring special treatment. For example, souvenirs acquired in the course of these shopping pilgrimages may be assigned to exclusive locations on bookshelves, over fireplaces, or in display cases—spaces not shared with items purchased locally. Such special treatment was precisely the quality that, in his classic theory, Emile Durkheim associated with religious (sacred) rather than everyday (profane) objects.[47]

In addition, James Twitchell notes, upper-status shopping emporiums and elaborate churches also resemble each other in appearance. To see what he

Figure 2.1 Tourism and shopping have become increasingly important to the economies and images of global cities. (Pictured here is Wangfujing Street, Beijing's premier shopping district, in 2000.)

means, Twitchell suggests walking down Fifth Avenue in New York and comparing the fine jewelry stores (BVLGARI, Cartier, Fortunoff) to the imposing St. Patrick's Cathedral. Twitchell emphasizes their numerous overt similarities, including marble facades, tall ceilings, and highly ornate but empty expanses around displays.[48]

The exemplar of the mall as a cathedral of consumption, at least in the United States, is probably the Mall of America, in suburban Minneapolis. In four levels, the mall houses 550 stores, plus a theme park, aquarium, petting zoo, miniature golf course, and a wedding chapel right next to Bloomingdale's. The mall boasts of being the largest, "fully enclosed retail and family entertainment complex" in the United States. Within its enveloped space, the connection between tourism and consumption is unmistakable. The mall operates its own tourism department, offering numerous vacation packages in which visits to the mall are the centerpiece. From Japan alone, there are an average of nearly ten tour groups visiting the mall each week of the year. Travel themes also predominate in the decor of the mall and its stores. To illustrate: Timbuktu Station displays women's clothing around antique suitcases; the Rainforest Cafe is designed to make eating a hamburger feel like going on a safari; the entire West Market district of the mall is filled with street furniture and vendors evoking the feel of a European marketplace, and its European Gift Shop even sells souvenirs of Europe!

After spending ten days observing and interviewing people at Mall of America, Jon Goss wrote that he was struck by how retailers and shoppers both acted as though inauthentic objects (like European souvenirs made in Pakistan and sold in Minnesota) were genuine. By socially defining them as real, however, the objects take on an authentic feel. The mall functions like a modern temple, Goss concludes, offering an antidote to a capitalist world that has become meaningless because of its overemphasis on commodities.[49] As Twitchell puts it, people could rationally make decisions about which products to buy following *Consumer Reports*, but given the cultural emphasis upon materialism, people want products that tell everyone, themselves included, who they are. To achieve this, people need brand names: products with stories behind them created by advertisers.[50]

The cathedrals of consumption are often designed to re-create communities of the past; that is, to provide replacements for the neighborhoods they helped to destroy or that never really existed except in people's imaginations. Thus, within Mall of America employees talk about being parts of neighborhoods where people know each other and keep up on the gossip. A nurse practitioner at the mall's women's clinic explained, "We've bonded on this arm of the mall."[51] Apart from malls, consumer-oriented venues have often tried explicitly to re-create communities. Outside of Los Angeles, for example, Disney's California Adventure and Universal Studios' City Walk are both examples of theme parks as urban spaces. They have been successful as shopping meccas, but their private, gated properties with security cameras and closing hours do not really simulate urban neighborhoods. They "fake a village."[52] However, consumption-

Figure 2.2   BVLGARI is one of many "cathedrals of consumption" on New York's Fifth Avenue. (Pictured in 2003.)

oriented spectators, temporary pseudo citizens of these communities, do not seem upset by the discrepancies.

As capitalistic South Korea and communist North Korea made steps toward reunifying at the beginning of this century, the different place of cathedrals of consumption in their cultures was dramatically expressed by their reactions to South Korea's megamall, Lotte World. Its 29 acres in Seoul, South Korea, include not only three shopping centers, but a large hotel, amusement park, indoor golf course, and museum. In late summer 2000, South Korean officials hosted groups of visitors from the north. Not having had any opportunity to travel to South Korea for many years, the visitors were hoping to see family, old friends, and familiar sites. However, the South Koreans apparently thought the most important place for their visitors to see was Lotte World because there was nothing like it in North Korea. The hosts walked their guests past franchised restaurants, clothing and shoe stores, then to an upper level of the mall that was filled with exhibits of Korean history and local areas. The visitors tried to be polite, but they were not impressed with the mall's representations of Korean places. "I saw the real thing on a school trip a long time ago," one older visitor explained.[53]

EDGE CITIES

When the first modern suburbs formed in the middle of the twentieth century, they primarily involved residential concentrations and young families predominated. These suburban areas, during the industrial era, became synonymous with middle-class lifestyles and commuting into the city to work. The suburban ring soon expanded into exurbia, but the basic lifestyle remained unchanged. Geographical expansion was made possible by improvements in expressways and mass transit systems that increased average trip speed. However, rather than result in shorter commuting times, faster speeds only increased the distance of the daily commute in large international cities. Suburbanites in global cities—such as London, New York, Paris, Sydney, and Toronto—continued to spend an hour, on average, in each one-way commute to work, but instead of going 11–12 miles, they went 13–14 miles in the hour they traveled.[54]

During the latter decades of the twentieth century, however, as the industrial nature of many urban areas declined, they became parts of the global informational network. Corresponding with this change in functions, the spatial structure of entire urban areas was also transformed.[55] For many tracts that continue to be classified as suburban (given their location near the outskirts of metropolitan areas), the recent changes have involved far greater diversity in land use and in occupants than in traditional suburbs. One of the first observers to chronicle the change in some of these suburbs was Robert Fishman, a historian specializing in twentieth-century cities. He called the suburbs "technoburbs" because they could function at a great distance from the heart of central cities through advanced communications technology (even though a majority of employment in the area was not in high-tech industries).[56] Fishman described technoburbs as self-contained areas that spread out along highway growth corridors, encompassing: shopping malls, industrial parks, office complexes, and a full range of housing types.

The term that is now most commonly used to describe these self-contained suburban areas is "edge cities," following journalist Joel Garreau. He offered a more precise definition than Fishman, specifying 5 million square feet of office space (about equal to the downtown of a midsized U.S. city) and 600,000 square feet of retail space (a good-sized mall) as minimum requisites. In addition, Garreau added to the definition the presence of entertainment (bars, nightclubs, theaters, and so on) and the view of local residents that the components of the edge city were bound together by their common locale. To people in the metropolitan area, its name connotes a single destination for jobs, shopping, and entertainment.[57]

Garreau and Fishman wrote almost exclusively about American cities, noting as examples some of the suburban areas outside of major cities such as New York, Washington, D.C., Chicago, and Los Angeles. However, the same transformations were occurring in suburban areas of global cities everywhere, producing edge cities in La Defense, in Paris' suburban periphery; Eschborn, on the outskirts of Frankfurt, Germany; Odaiba, near the bay area outside of Tokyo. Regardless of where they formed, however, there were a few qualities that consistently characterized edge cities. To begin, almost all edge cities were built in places that at the time would have seemed unlikely candidates for such development: orchards, pastures, deserted factories, and the like. Thus, edge cities did not typically grow out of small commercial-residential-retail complexes.

Once clearing and building began it usually proceeded rapidly, in a series of distinct phases. The basic features of an edge city are typically in place in less than a decade. In the Merry Hill Centre, located near Dudley in the West Midlands outside of Birmingham, England, the first phase, begun in the early 1980s, was a modest industrial park. It was followed by retail warehousing and fast food restaurants. Developers next built a conventional two-story retail mall, then a fashion mall containing specialty shops and department stores. A finance court was created in the next phase, with major banks, insurance agencies, and stockbrokers. The final development in this section of the West Midlands was a waterfront leisure complex with hotels, an ice rink, sporting facilities, and so on. Then, between 1987 and 1992, the Dudley Council invested nearly $40 million to promote Merry Hill as an international tourist destination.[58]

Another feature common to most edge cities is the active role played by local, regional, and national governments in promoting or subsidizing them. Edge cities do not just develop "naturally" as a result of location or other ecological considerations. For example, the catalyst to the development of Tyson's Corner, in the Virginia suburbs of Washington, D.C., was federal funding for a Beltway to bypass the city and the simultaneous expansion of two local roads. The transformation of the apple orchards formerly owned by William Tyson began where the newly widened roads met the Beltway. The assistance of the county government was also required to rezone the land for commercial and retail use, despite large and well-organized opposition.[59] Similarly, Merry Hill Centre probably would not have been built if developers had not received exemptions from local planning authorities, long-term tax relief, and large government grants (because it was built within a formerly depressed Enterprise Zone).

Perhaps because of the important part played by government support in the creation of edge cities, critics have frequently held government to a high standard in evaluating the consequences for the public good. Some specific criticisms mirror those now leveled at many other kinds of urban areas. For example, edge cities, like gentrified inner-city areas, have been accused of providing relatively little unrestricted open space. Fairfax County, Virginia, in which Tyson's Corner is located, is among the wealthiest communities in the world, but it has little public space, such as parks. The reason: fear of encroachment by outsiders. Planners in Fairfax do not want parks, Garreau notes, because they "know from Washington, D.C., that parks get filled with bums."[60] Similarly, Merry Hill Centre's advertisements promote it as providing "safe, secure family shopping," and its large, private security force tightly controls space in and around the mall.

The Problem of Sprawl

Social critics have indicted edge cities for their unique contributions to postindustrial "sprawl." Precisely what is meant by sprawl varies. Defined narrowly, it refers to the (usually rapid and unplanned) expansion of a metropolitan area, leading to the loss of farmlands and wetlands. However, because such expansion is ordinarily dependent on private automobile use, sprawl is often more broadly associated with traffic congestion, drive-through retail facilities, and air pollution, as well as the loss of farmlands and wetlands.[61] In Tyson's Corner, this sprawl has even extended to paving over front lawns. Because more of the suburb's residents own more cars, they have not been able to find enough off-street places to park the automobiles when they get home from work at night. To solve the problem, many homeowners took to paving over their front lawns, to create additional parking spaces. That may have been the last straw because in 2002 the county council passed a law prohibiting "pave overs" to preserve what little green space remained.[62]

Suburban gridlock was once confined to suburban-to-city commuting in morning and afternoon rush hours, but in and around edge cities, heavy traffic can be a serious problem at almost any time of the day or night. In part, these problems arose because the growth of edge cities continuously outstripped the expansion of the expressways and highways that served them. In addition, improved connections between edge cities and downtown financial districts—via expressways or mass transit—does not alleviate the gridlock *within* edge cities that involves people traveling among residence, employment, entertainment, and shopping.

Sprawl has also become a defining feature of edge cities due to the absence of centralized planning and control. Because edge cities typically transcend the boundaries of any suburban town or borough, no one government unit can effectively exert control. The ability of public and private groups and suburban governments to cooperate with each other, especially across town lines, has historically been limited. Further, responding to changes in the global economy, local activities can be reconfigured quickly, much more rapidly than government institutions have been able to respond to the changes.[63]

It is also important to ask to what degree edge cities are a cause of sprawl at the periphery of metropolitan areas, as critics contend, or are a consequence of that sprawl. After all, metropolitan areas were highly dependent on automobiles and were already expanding outward before the formation of edge cities. Data that could clarify the direction of the relationship between expansion and edge cities are limited, but some suggestive findings have been reported in a study of the Cleveland metropolitan area. Two researchers obtained yearly data on employment and household moves between 1989 and 1996 for the entire metropolitan area. During this period suburban Cleveland contained three edge cities and the investigators proceeded to compare changes in household moves around the edge cities to changes in suburban areas lacking edge cities. They found that, indeed, edge cities did tend to lead to further expansion of the metropolitan fringe.[64] In other words, the researchers concluded that people followed jobs; so, as more employment was offered in edge cities, concentrated numbers of people moved further out toward the periphery of the suburban area, thereby contributing to the spread of sprawl.

In an optimistic vein we can note that there appears to be greater awareness of the problems associated with sprawl. Environmental groups have been monitoring cities in the United States and hoping to alert citizens in those areas most threatened by sprawl. European cities, many of which have experienced sprawl, are examining tax and transportation policies to avoid following in the footsteps of many sprawl-threatened U.S. cities.[65] And there are recent case studies to suggest that faster and more effective private-public and intertown government cooperation may be possible in the future.[67]

NOTES

1. Lily Kong and Lisa Law, "Introduction," *Urban Studies*, 39(2002):1505. For an overview of the role of meanings in the struggle to define space, see Donald Mitchell, *Cultural Geography* (Walden, Mass.: Blackwell, 1999). For a focus on how gender can generally influence the contest over places, see Doreen Massey, *Space, Place and Gender* (Minneapolis: University of Minnesota Press, 1994).
2. This was the view of world cities presented by Jonathan Friedmann, "The World City Hypothesis," *Development and Change*, 4(1986):69–84.
3. For further discussion of the two types of service workers, see Saskia Sassen, *Cities in a World Economy* (Thousand Oaks, Calif.: Pine Forge Press, 2000).
4. Leslie Eaton and Edward Wyatt, "Attacks Hit Low-Pay Jobs the Hardest," *New York Times*, 6 November 2001, p. B1.
5. Quoted in Steven Greenhouse, "As the Rich Do Without Extras, Service Workers Do Without," *New York Times*, 29 November 2001, p. D4.
6. David R. Meyer, "World Cities as Financial Centres," in *Globalization and the World of Large Cities* ed. Fu-chen Lo and Yue-man Yeung (Tokyo: United Nations University Press, 1998), 410–32.
7. Sassen, *Cities in a World Economy*; see especially pp. 107–12.
8. For an interesting theoretical discussion of how changes in people and roles have made trust problematic, see Adam B. Seligman, *The Problem of Trust* (Princeton, N.J.: Princeton University Press, 1997).
9. Meyer, "World Cities."
10. For further discussion of the local costs of global involvement, see Joe R. Feagin, *The New Urban Paradigm* (Lanham, Md.: Rowman & Littlefield, 1998).
11. James Sterngold, "A Los Angeles Commuter Group Sees Discrimination in Transit Policies," *New York Times*, 16 September 2001, p. A25.
12. Gerald D. Suttles, *The Man-Made City* (Chicago: University of Chicago Press, 1990).
13. Lisa Law, "Defying Disappearance," *Urban Studies*, 39(2002):1625–45.
14. David Barnett, *London, Hub of the Industrial Revolution* (London: Tauris Academic Studies, 1998).
15. The television executive who began the docklands boom was Jeremy Wallington, who died in 2001. The early history of Canary Wharf was recounted in his obituary in *London Times*, 15 August 2001.
16. Angela Jameson, "Canary Wharf Set for Capital Return," *London Times*, 10 March 2001.
17. See the editorial on "Plans for London," *London Times*, 8 May 2001.
18. "The Caneletto Effect," *The Economist*, 17 April 2001, p. 61.
19. Masahiko Honjo, "The Growth of Tokyo as a World City," in *Globalization and the*

World of Large Cities, ed. Fu-chen Lo and Yue-man Yeung (Tokyo: United Nations University Press, 1998), 109–31.

20. Paul Waley, "Moving the Margins of Tokyo," *Urban Studies,* 39(2002):1533–50.
21. Ellen Perlman, "Downtown: The Live-in Solution," in *Annual Editions: Urban Sociology,* ed. Fred Siegel and Jan Rosenberg (Guilford, Conn.: McGraw-Hill/Dushkin, 2001), 219–21.
22. James Brooke, "A Builder Sees Tokyo Rising Ever Upward," *New York Times,* 4 January 2002, p. C1.
23. See Saskia Sassen, *The Global City* (Princeton, N.J.: Princeton University Press, 1991).
24. Neil Smith, "New City, New Frontier," in *Variations on a Theme Park,* ed. Michael Sorkin (New York: Hill and Wang, 1992).
25. Ray Forrest, Adrienne La Grange, and Yip Ngai-Ming, "Neighborhood in a High Rise, High Density City," *The Sociological Review,* 50(2002):225.
26. On the nonrational basis of fear of crime, see Barry Glassner, *The Culture of Fear* (New York: Basic Books, 1999).
27. See Mike Davis, *City of Quartz* (London: Verso, 1990); and Mike Davis, *The Ecology of Fear* (New York: Metropolitan Books, 1998).
28. For further discussion on security and control in urban and suburban shopping malls, see Margaret Crawford, "The World in a Shopping Mall," in *Variations on a Theme Park,* ed. Michael Sorkin, 3–30.
29. Susan Stephenson, "DINKs Dine Out," *Restaurants & Institutions,* 107(1 April 1997):78.
30. David Brooks, *Bobos in Paradise* (New York: Simon and Schuster, 2000).
31. See Anthony Giddens, *Modernity and Self-Identity* (Cambridge: Polity Press, 1991).
32. Perhaps surprisingly, Jagger reports that these self-advertisements continue gender stereotyping, with women emphasizing physical attractiveness and nurturing qualities and men describing themselves as sexy in a self-confident way. For further discussion of self-advertising, see Elizabeth Jagger, "Marketing Molly and Melville: Dating in a Postmodern, Consumer Society," *Sociology,* 35(2001):39–57.
33. Reena Jana, "Arranged Marriages, Minus the Parents," *New York Times,* 17 August 2000, p. G1.
34. Ed Boland, "In Modern E-Mail Romances 'Trash' Is Just a Click Away," *New York Times,* 19 October 2000, p. G8.
35. Eric A. Taub, "Cell Yell: Thanks for (Not) Sharing," *New York Times,* 22 November 2001, p. G1.
36. John E. Lycett and Robin M. Dunbar, "Mobile Phones as Lekking Devices Among Human Males," *Human Nature,* 12, no. 2(2001), 29–42.
37. For recent tourism figures, see the World Tourism Organization's Web page: www.world-tourism.org
38. The selling of commercial areas within cities, targeted at outside firms that may be planning to relocate, tends to make heavy use of the ready availability of culture and entertainment. For example, the Corporation of London (which oversees the City) and the Docklands Development Corporation (which oversees Canary Wharf) were among the co-sponsors of a project to call attention to London's abundant theaters, museums, galleries, sports arenas, and so on. Both of these commercial-financial sites thought it was in their interest to market London as a world city based on its cultural amenities.
39. An elaboration of this transformation is provided in Susan S. Fainstein and Dennis R. Judd, "Cities as Places to Play," in *The Tourist City,* Dennis R. Judd and Susan S. Fainstein ed. (New Haven, Conn.: Yale University Press, 1999), 261–72.

40. Susan Fainstein and Dennis R. Judd, "Global Forces, Local Strategies and Urban Tourism," in *The Tourist City,* ed. Judd and Fainstein, 1–17.
41. Gladstone further divides tourist cities into two types: leisure cities and tourist metropolises. See David L. Gladstone, "Tourism Urbanization in the United States," *Urban Affairs Review,* 34(1998):3–27.
42. See Table 9 in UNESCO, *Study of International Flow of Cultural Goods Between 1980 and 1998* (New York: United Nations, 2000).
43. Mark Goodwin, "The City as Commodity," in *Selling Places,* ed. Gerry Kearns and Chris Philo (Oxford: Pergamon, 1993), 145–62.
44. For further discussion of the place of urban lifestyle magazines in several American cities, see Miriam Greenberg, "Branding Cities," *Urban Affairs Review,* 36(2000): 228–63.
45. Chris Philo and Gerry Kearns, "Culture, History, Capital," in *Selling Places,* ed. Kearns and Philo, 1–32.
46. George Ritzer, *Enchanting a Disenchanted World* (Thousand Oaks, Calif.: Pine Forge Press, 1999).
47. The sacred-profane distinction is analyzed in Emile Durkheim, *The Elementary Forms of Religious Life* (New York: Free Press, 1965).
48. One could make similar observations in other global cities, for example, Bond Street in London. For further discussion of the religious undertones of shopping emporiums, see James B. Twitchell, *Lead Us into Temptation* (New York: Columbia University Press, 1999).
49. For further description of the Mall of America, and Goss's interpretations of its symbolic meanings, see Jon Goss, "Once-Upon-a-Time in the Commodity World," *Annals of the Association of American Geographers,* 89(1999):45–75.
50. Twitchell, *Lead Us into Temptation.*
51. Maria Puente, "Mall of Them All Turns 10," *USA Today,* 9 August 2002, p. 6D.
52. Wade Graham, "It Fakes a Village," *Los Angeles,* September 2001, p. 80.
53. Samuel Len, "Like It or Not, North Koreans Tour a Mall in Seoul," *New York Times,* 17 August 2000, p. A3.
54. These studies are reviewed in Roberto Camagni, "The Economic Role and Spatial Contradictions of Global City-Regions," in *Global City-Regions,* ed. Allen J. Scott (Oxford: Oxford University Press, 2001), 96–118. Interestingly, it was more than fifty years ago that one hour was proposed as the maximum commuting time. See Amos Hawley, *Human Ecology* (New York: Ronald Press, 1950).
55. For a theoretical discussion of this transformation, see Manuel Castells, *The Rise of the Network Society,* 3 vols. (Walden, Mass.: Blackwell, 1998).
56. Robert Fishman, *Bourgeois Utopias* (New York: Basic Books, 1987).
57. Joel Garreau, *Edge City* (New York: Doubleday, 1991).
58. This discussion of Merry Hill Centre is based on Michelle Lowe, "Local Hero! An Examination of the Role of the Regional Entrepreneur in the Regeneration of Britain's Regions," in *Selling Places,* ed. Kearns and Philo, 211–30.
59. Garreau, *Edge City.*
60. Quoted in Michael Leccesse, "Edge City," *Landscape Architecture,* 82(June 1992):63.
61. For further discussion of the dimensions of sprawl, see George Galster, Royce Hanson, Hal Wolman, Stephen Coleman, and Jason Freihage, *Wresting Sprawl to the Ground* (Washington, D.C.: Fannie Mae Foundation, 2000).
62. David Plotz, "A Suburb All Grown Up and Paved Over," *New York Times,* 19 June 2002, p. A23.

63. For further discussion of the political problem see Jon C. Teaford and Jon T. Teaford, *Post-Suburbia: Government and Politics in the Edge Cities* (Baltimore: Johns Hopkins University Press, 1997).

64. Chengri Ding and Richard D. Bingham, "Beyond Edge Cities," *Urban Affairs Review*, 35(2000):837–55.

65. See Pietro S. Novola, "Are Europe's Cities Better?" *The Public Interest* (Fall 1999): 73–84.

66. Douglas Henton, "Lessons from Silicon Valley," in *Global City-Regions*, Allen J. Scott ed. (Oxford: Oxford University Press, 2001), 391–400.

THREE

Immigration

In addition to a worldwide flow of capital and of ideas, globalization involves the movement of people, temporarily as tourists and students, and more permanently as immigrants. By the late 1990s, about 125 million people were living in a nation other than the one in which they were born. That figure constituted about 2 percent of the world's population, and immigration numbers have been growing by between 2 and 4 million people each year. The favored destinations selected by immigrants have been the world's wealthiest nations: Canada, France, Germany, Italy, Japan, the United Kingdom, and United States. These seven nations received about a third of the world's total immigration.[1]

It is not coincidental that these seven nations also contain all of the leading global cities (and a high proportion of the second-rung global cities) because getting to these cities, in particular, has been at the top of the the list of immigrant objectives. The influx of newcomers during the last two decades of the twentieth century raised the percentage of the population that was foreign born to as high as about 40 percent in some of the leading global cities (e.g., New York and Toronto) and to about 20 percent or more in several others (e.g., London and Paris).

One of the defining features of most global cities is that they are the destinations of large numbers of highly diverse groups of immigrants. The major exceptions are in Asia, notably Tokyo and Singapore. It is true that many cities, not all important global cities, have grown from a stream of immigrants from one or two nations, but what sets global cities apart is the heterogeneity of the immigrant flow in addition to the group's size. To illustrate, during 1995 and 1996, 230,000 immigrants settled in New York City. Just during this two-year period, over 5,000 immigrants came from each of the following nations: Bangladesh, China, the Dominican Republic, Ecuador, Guyana, Haiti, Jamaica, the Philippines, Poland, the former Soviet Union, Trinidad, and Tobago.[2]

Large and diverse streams of immigrants also moved to London, Paris, and most of the other principal cities of Europe, as well as to Los Angeles, Toronto, and other large North American cities. They came from more varied international origins during the 1980s and 1990s, and immigrants' destinations also became increasingly targeted, as they tended to cluster in a small number of major cities. In order to appreciate the concentration of contemporary immigrants, it is instructive to compare the pattern to an earlier period when immigrants seemed concentrated, but were actually dispersed by contemporary standards. For example, in the United States in 1910, an apex in early immigration, the five largest U.S. cities contained a fifth of all of the nation's foreign-born inhabitants. By contrast, in the mid-1990s, well over half of the foreign-born population in the United States resided in the five largest U.S. cities.[3]

Before proceeding further there is an important distinction to make between two types of immigrants. First is the traditional immigrant: typically lacking much formal education or specialized skills, immigrants of this type usually move in anticipation of finding better work opportunities than they left behind. Traditional immigrants typically qualify only for unskilled jobs, so how well they do after moving depends on the abundance of such positions. When the manufacturing sector of the economy in the United States, United Kingdom, and elsewhere was very large, for example, traditional immigrants rather quickly found work in steel mills, paint factories, and automobile assembly lines. Those positions are now scarce. People with similar backgrounds who relocate today are more likely to find employment in the low status end of the service sector in jobs that entail such activities as cleaning, delivering, and serving.

The second type of immigrant is well educated, with resources and marketable skills, and often with capital. This type of mover is more common now than in the past, especially among those whose destination is a global city. To differentiate this latter group of modern sojourners, they are often described as exiles rather than immigrants. Their major motivations to move are institutional, that is, they want more freedom in the economic, political, or religious realms.[4] Representative of contemporary exiles are thousands of young Iranian college graduates who have recently gone, in large numbers, to Berlin, Toronto, Sydney, and cities in several other nations where they found greater personal freedom as well as better jobs. When they remain in Iran, even most of those with advanced technical degrees wind up driving a taxicab and living under strict repression. So, the educated young people make the rounds of embassies in Tehran hoping for work visas, and one in four Iranians with a college degree is now an exile, working outside of the country.[5]

HOSTILITY AND DEPENDENCE

In some of the early publications that first defined global cities, diverse immigrant flows were an important feature.[6] As previously noted, Tokyo is the most significant exception to the pattern that characterized immigrant flows of most other global cities. In Japan, the percentage foreign-born continues to be less

than 1 percent of the population, and laws of the nation provide part of the reason. Japan's constitution, written in English by American officials during the
post–World War II occupation, specifies that all people are equal under the law,
but in the Japanese version of that constitution, people are translated to mean,
in effect, *only* Japanese people.[7] Given the Japanese tendency toward xenopho-
bia (dislike of foreigners), there are multiple forms of discrimination against
which immigrants have no legal redress. Combined with difficulties in entering
Japan, discrimination against outsiders has kept down the size of that nation's
foreign-born population. However, as Japan's native population ages, combined with its low birth rate, the nation may soon face a host of problems unless its immigration policy changes. An agency of the United Nation estimates
that by 2010 Japan will need to import 600,000 workers per year to fill vacant
positions in the labor force and to keep pension systems from collapsing (because it is younger workers whose contributions support retired workers).[8]

Many other nations, though less extreme in their sentiments and less restrictive in their policies, resemble Japan in terms of being hostile to immigrants despite the important contributions they typically make to a city and a
society. Although immigrants are often viewed negatively because they are
culturally different, the reality is that they routinely fill niches left vacant by
natives. For example, thousands of immigrant laborers from sub-Saharan
Africa are employed in leather tanneries in central Italy and steel mills in
northern Italy. These industries, of vital importance to Italy's economy, rely
on an immigrant workforce to fill almost all of the particularly unpleasant
jobs because these positions are shunned by natives. In recent years in Brook-
lyn, to illustrate further, Millman notes neighborhoods in which housing
stock deteriorated and commercial activities vanished until there was an influx of immigrants from Haiti, Jamaica, and Guyana. The immigrants reno-
vated blighted housing, opened small businesses, drove cabs at night. They
went where natives did not want to go and did work that natives did not
want to do, and their children, striving for success, helped to invigorate city
schools. It was not a coincidence, Millman states, that when the United States
had its most restrictive immigration policies (1945 to 1965) its major cities seriously deteriorated.[9]

Nevertheless, public hostility to immigrants tends to be an overriding
theme. Italy's prime minister was echoing popular sentiments when early in
this century he ignored the role played by his nation's immigrant laborers and
promised that Italy would restrict future immigration. The nation was drown-
ing, he warned, in "a wave of immigrants."[10] Paradoxically, it was Italian immigrants who were treated with hostility, considered inferior, and held up to
public ridicule in the United States a hundred years earlier. The popular press
in the United States complained in 1900 that a "swelling tide of immigrants"
from central and southern Europe (Italy, Poland, Russia, and so on) had become
"a startling national menace."[11]

The tension between immigrants and other groups in any society often
seems to revolve around competition—real or imagined—over employment.

Resentment aroused by immigrants taking jobs, even jobs that nobody else wants, transcends differences in places, people, and times. The dramatic increase in globalization between about 1950 and 2000 made it easy to move capital, but friction remains when it comes to moving labor. Thus, it may be that more resistance is generated when Mexican American workers seek jobs in Detroit's automobile industry than when plants in Detroit close and move to Mexico.[12]

THE IMMIGRANTS

Many of the people who immigrate to global cities are desperate. Their ability to support themselves or their families is so limited in their native country that they may perceive emigration as the only solution. To emigrate, they are often prepared to take enormous risks, such as sailing across perilous seas in small boats. One Liberian who swam to Sicily after his boat sank and was brought to

Figure 3.1 Temporary housing for newcomers and "informal" businesses crowd many streets in the center of Beijing. (Pictured is a street near Longfusi, in 2000.)

an Italian refugee center said, "If they send me back, they send me back. . . . I don't care. I've already lost everything."[13] Although constrained by circumstances, these would-be immigrants' movement is voluntary, especially in contrast to people who are coerced, tricked, or kidnapped across national boundaries. (Involuntary immigrants are discussed in a later section.) The traditional immigrant, as previously noted, typically has little formal education or specialized skills. To survive, many are pushed into an "underground economy" in which goods and services are exchanged for cash (and sometimes bartered), but the economic activity is neither regulated nor recorded by the government.[14] Because the underground jobs and the revenue generated do not "officially" exist, laws and codes pertaining to wages, workplace safety, and health are not applied.

Many illegal activities, such as prostitution, sale of illicit drugs, and loan sharking are parts of the underground economy, as are numerous activities that are not intrinsically illegal, such as children operating a neighborhood lemonade stand or people driving a commercial van—but without a license or registration and not reporting income. In New York City, there are hundreds of unlicensed vans that drive down major thoroughfares at morning and afternoon rush hours, picking up and discharging passengers as they go. Both drivers and passengers tend to be immigrants from the Caribbean. Riders usually pay $1 as they board, less than the cost of subways or taxis. The vans are frequently noisy and in poor condition, and the qualifications of the drivers are unexamined because they typically lack commercial licenses or insurance. The operators of the vans, whose work is not officially recognized by any governmental unit, are not covered by worker's compensation and they have no retirement plans, health insurance, or other benefits. For drivers, who have limited work alternatives, it is a job. For the riders, a reduced fare to work is the incentive. And for both riders and drivers the unlicensed vans are a "comfortable" arrangement because they re-create the transportation system that operates in their island cities.[15]

Ties and Identities

Many immigrants continue to feel a strong attachment to the country they left behind. In some instances they remain heavily involved with institutions in their homelands. To illustrate, many Pakistani immigrants in Bradford, England, rely on networks in Pakistan to arrange marriages for their British-born children with native Pakistanis. Then the married couple returns to live and work in Bradford. According to one British observer, "the immigrants live with one foot in Pakistan."[16] Mexican immigrants concentrated in Chicago, Los Angeles, and New York commonly send a portion of their earnings to parents and siblings who remained behind and to their former towns as well. Typically working as laborers for minimal wages, the Mexican immigrants still manage to remit an average of about $200 monthly. Living close to others from the same hometown, they pool funds to help their towns in Mexico build roads, schools, and sewage systems. Programs of Mexico's federal government match the public works remittances of immigrants, peso for peso. By 2002, these remittances amounted to over $9 billion and had become Mexico's third largest source of revenue.[17]

Given strong attachments to former homelands it is not surprising that a sizable percentage of immigrants aspire eventually to return, and some do, but not usually in large numbers. The size of the immigrant group that returns to their former nations increases when their current country of residence experiences an economic downturn or other adverse event. In the two months following the terrorist attacks that destroyed the World Trade Center on September 11, 2001, an estimated 350,000 Mexicans returned home.[18] For most immigrants who express a desire to return home, most of the time the sentiment is probably a way of showing solidarity with compatriots. It is meaningful symbolically, but may not be indicative of a genuine intent. For example, a common toast in Miami's Little Havana is "next year in Havana." One Cuban-American who insisted he would be on the next plane to Cuba if Castro were out of office was asked if he was really sure of that. "Well," he smiled, "Who can tell?"[19]

The longer the period of time immigrants are out of their native country the more difficult it can become to return because their identities change as a result of living away. Each immigrant from Central or South America, for example, may leave with one specific national identity (Bolivian, Dominican, Venezuelan, and so on). Once they arrive in most global cities, however, the majority population is likely to respond to them as Hispanics and disregard variations in origin. The same process leads to the grouping of other disparate nationalities into such ethnic-racial categories as Arab and Asian. Over time, the immigrant groups may cultivate the broader label themselves when they discover that it facilitates political or economic coalitions. Thus, more inclusive ethnic or racial labels are imposed from without, but also develop from within.

The general process by which panethnic identities form is illustrated by a study of immigrants from the Dominican Republic who moved to New York. The greater their role in American life—as indicated by their length of time in the United States, knowledge of English, or status as U.S. citizens—the more likely they were to identify themselves as Latino/a or Hispano/a. As one immigrant explained, "I am Hispanic, that is how we are called here."[20] Note, however, that more inclusive identities (e.g., Asian, Hispanic, or the like) do not correspond with the place anyone left or with any concrete nation. Thus, panethnic labels provide identities that only make sense in the new context (e.g., New York).

When immigrants do return home it is not uncommon for them to discover that Thomas Wolfe was right: You can't go home again.[21] For example, many Japanese who move to cities like Paris or London feel nostalgic for familiar foods, smells, and places in Japan. They may even miss the crowded subways, but when they return home they are struck by how much everyday life in Japan, even in Tokyo, continues to be closely regulated by traditional norms.

They experience a dramatic loss of freedom. According to surveys, Japanese who have spent time abroad report that they were a lot happier overseas. That is true for men and women, but more so for women, especially those who lived in Western cities.[22] Shortly after they return, many Japanese expatriates make a "U-turn" and go back overseas.

The ties immigrants maintain with others in their former countries and the kinds of identities they develop in conjunction with their experience as immigrants depend on whether or not they are living in a self-contained enclave with others like themselves. In a later section of this chapter we turn to a lengthy discussion of enclaves and how life within them affects immigrant identity.

Immigrant Women

In most societies of the world, women are economically disadvantaged relative to men and are vulnerable to being exploited because they are less powerful. The degree to which women are subordinate to men correlates with the economic development of nations. The greater the overall wealth, the less women's role is confined to raising children, the less they are subjected to patriarchal decision making in the household, and the more they can compete on an equal footing with men for formal education and prestigious occupations.[23] Note that the preceding statements are phrased in terms of more or less: women have not literally attained equality in most societies. Because immigrant women (like men) usually move from economically less developed nations to more prosperous nations, one might assume that immigration enhances their status. However, women usually continue to face numerous barriers after they emigrate. Some obstacles are imposed by their own cultural traditions that justify the subordination of women, others are due to the host society's discrimination against women, immigrants, or both. In any case, as women and as immigrants they are often vulnerable to exploitation.

The exploitation of women immigrants can take many forms. In and around Taipei, Taiwan's principal city, thousands of young women, many of whom are immigrants from a number of Asian nations, support themselves selling betel nuts. The nuts, when mixed with herbs, produce a mild high, and an estimated 2 million mostly male Taiwanese regularly chew them. (They are legal products, but the Taiwanese government discourages the habit because of an apparent link with mouth cancer.) Almost all of the Taipei saleswomen, immigrants plus migrants from other parts of Taiwan and local teenagers, are young, between about seventeen and twenty-five years old. They must also be physically attractive because their standard work outfits consist of lingerie, miniskirts, or skimpy uniforms. When selling the betel nuts, they are on display, perched on stools in garishly lit glass booths. Because selling the nuts is highly competitive and the women only receive commissions, they are pushed to be more revealing in the way they dress and more flirtatious in their interactions with potential buyers. One of the producers of the movie, *Betel Nut*

Beauty, which won a major award at the 2001 Berlin Film Festival, described the movie as telling the story of "how young people get lost in a modern, materialistic society."[24]

It would be a mistake to equate the exploitation of immigrant women with blatant sexual exploitation, such as selling betel nuts (or working as exotic dancers, prostitutes, and so on). An even larger number of immigrant women are probably employed in domestic service work as servants, maids, nannies, home care providers, and the like. Much of the service work is poorly paid through the underground economy, taking advantage of the women's limited alternatives. It would also be erroneous to assume that gender discrimination involving immigrants is only a contemporary phenomenon To illustrate, in Paris around 1850, women who emigrated from other European nations or from the French countryside were at the center of a public controversy over two types of commerce that coexisted in the city:

1. "Bourgeoisie" commerce was conducted in enclosed boutiques, governed by fixed prices, and served a fashionable clientele. It was regarded as a symbol of French civilization.

2. "Popular" commerce was conducted by traveling street merchants, with prices subject to negotiation and a mixed clientele. It was viewed as the dangerous "underside" of the market.[25]

A growing number of women, mostly newcomers to Paris, sought to support themselves, and sometimes their families, by working as merchants. They were a diverse group that included young single women, widows, unwed mothers, and wives of nonworking husbands. Lacking start-up capital, popular commerce was the only alternative open to most of them. However, the crowds that sometimes formed around popular merchants were regarded by journalists and the police as potentially fermenting political unrest or providing cover in which criminals, such as pickpockets or con artists, could operate. Popular misgivings about women as entrepreneurs, and immigrant women in particular, interacted with people's suspicions about popular commerce in general, and gave public officials license to restrict the women's activities. Correspondingly, the condition of the goods that women tended to sell (such as milk and oysters) was scrutinized more carefully than the goods men sold, making women more likely to be arrested for commercial fraud, such as watering down milk. To further control the women's marketplace activities, the police tended to be less tolerant when crowds of customers formed around female than male merchants, claiming they blocked public access and had to be dispersed. When the women merchants persisted, city ordinances finally required that the items typically sold by women had to be dispensed out of permanent locations, as in the bourgeoisie market. The rent this would have required was beyond immigrant women's economic means, so the net effect was to push them out of the marketplace, marginalizing them economically by removing even their limited opportunities to produce and manage wealth.[26]

ILLEGAL ENTRANTS

Officials in the United States and the European Union, the two principal immigration destinations, estimate that their nations are illegally entered by several thousand people every month, but there is, of course, no way to ascertain the precise number of people that enter or the number that remain only a short while before returning home. One limited measure of illegal immigration that can be more reliably measured concerns the number of persons who remain in the United States after they are ordered to leave. Because the U.S. Immigration and Naturalization Service (INS) does not always follow up on deportation orders, a clearly defined group is known to have stayed in the country illegally. The INS refers to them as "alien absconders" and, from an analysis of court records reported in 2002, there were at least 320,000 of them.[27] We know that very few people who enter the United States without papers ever become known to a court, let alone be ordered to return home. So, if there are over 300,000 alien absconders in the United States, how many millions of illegal immigrants must there be? (From Mexico alone the number is estimated to be 3.5 million people.)

From Central America and Mexico, immigrants without documents sneak across the U.S. border, and from Turkey and Africa they clandestinely enter Italy and Spain. Their ultimate destinations, however, as previously noted, tend to be global cities. Thus, many of the Mexicans who enter the United States somewhere in Texas make their way to Los Angeles or Chicago. Many immigrants who initially disembark in Italy or Spain are hoping ultimately to wind up in London or Paris.

When immigrants are not only unskilled, but enter a country illegally, their work options are especially limited. Employment for them is often buried deep within the underground economy. The garment industry in and around Los Angeles is illustrative. It consists primarily of small sewing operations; typically fewer than fifty employees per (sweat) shop. Combined, though, these small shops employ thousands of illegal immigrants, mostly from Mexico, and are estimated to contribute well over $13 billion to the U.S. economy.

The Mexicans in the Los Angeles garment shops typically worked twelve hours per day, seven days each week, but they were fortunate (in 1996) to earn $80 per week. Those who were paid an hourly rate were often not permitted to punch in until after they had worked a few hours. Others, who were paid on a piece rate for finished goods, were routinely told by their supervisors that some of their work was not acceptable or that they had already been paid for it. Not only did their pay fall well below minimum wage, but they worked in shops with unsafe equipment, leaking roofs, filthy toilets, and rats—and there were no officials to whom they dared turn for fear of being deported.[28]

Smuggling

Smuggling people across national boundaries has become a multibillion dollar global enterprise, with the most marked increases beginning in the late 1980s.

By the turn of this century, a United Nations analysis estimated that worldwide profits from human smuggling were about equal to those from the sale of illegal drugs.[29] Within any region of the world, following the analysis by Kyle and Dale, human smuggling—the cargo of the modern pirate—can take either of two distinct forms: immigrant exporting or slave importing, or it can be a mixture of both.[30]

Immigrant exporting schemes provide a package of services for would-be immigrants, including fake papers and expertise in eluding capture as well as basic transportation. One distinguishing feature is that services end on arrival at the immigrant's destination. Like much of the work that falls into the underground economy, immigrant exporting is not an intrinsically illegal activity (unlike the distribution of heroin, for example). People often work as export smugglers temporarily and on a part-time basis. When the demand for passage out of a nation intensifies, boat or plane owners, mountain guides, and others may be enticed into smuggling by the lure of quick money. The immigrants they move out, though not well-off, tend to have some resources or they would not be able to pay the exporter's fee.

Slave importing operations, by contrast, tend to involve specialized criminal organizations, with full-time, permanent staff. For them to persist on a large scale over time smuggling operations have to be allied with corrupt government officials in all of the nations involved, and they are frequently recruiting immigrants for intrinsically illegal activities, such as prostitution. In further contrast to export smugglers, the clientele of slave importers typically comes from the lowest socioeconomic strata of the nations they hope to leave. They tend to be both impoverished and without prospects.

Some of the immigrants who wind up in slave importing operations are kidnapped; others are sold by indebted families. According to Kyle and Dale, however, most often they are tricked. In one ploy, a criminal organization uses a seemingly wealthy woman from the same ethnic group as the potential immigrants to make the initial contacts. She is designed to look like the images the would-be immigrants have seen in the media and to represent the kind of worldly success they hope to achieve. The less the economic resources and power of the targeted victim, the greater the likelihood that the sales pitch of the slave importing organization will be successful. That is part of the reason women are more likely to be tricked into being trafficked than men. In addition, the organizations target women because of their greater potential value as sex workers or domestics.

Men can also become unwitting slaves when they are conned into importing operations searching for physical laborers. To illustrate, in the Amazon frontier of Brazil, thousands of workers are needed to harvest mahogany and other tropical hardwoods. Recruiters, known as "cats," are stationed in Brazilian cities and frontier towns looking for immigrants or migrants. They promise steady jobs at good wages, free housing, food, and other benefits, but that is not what they deliver. As one former victim recounted, "They talk a good game . . . but they change their tune just as soon as they have you in their clutches."[31] At the work camps, armed guards oversee the laborers who work long days and live in wretched conditions. If they try to escape, they are usually captured by local police (who have been paid off by the importing operation) and returned to the work camp.

CASE STUDY: SMUGGLING CHINESE IMMIGRANTS

During the last two decades of the twentieth century, thousands of immigrants from Mainland China were illegally smuggled into the United States each year. Their exodus involved importing, exporting, and mixed-type operations. Many of the immigrants came from Fujian Province, a poor area with the city of Fuzhou in its center. A large percentage of the immigrants eventually wound up in New York, but their routes were typically circuitous, especially after the United States increased border surveillance in the mid-1990s. Many smuggled immigrants traveled by air to Mexico or Central America, then by land to the United States. Others flew to Moscow, waited for a plane to take them to Cuba, then tried to come to the United States by boat. The standard fee paid to smugglers by a would-be immigrant during the 1990s was $18,000—with most of it to be paid, in installments, after they reached the United States. The fee led to the immigrants becoming known in the local Chinese community as "Eighteen Thousand Dollar Men" or as "Snake People," the latter term derived from the Chinese name for the human smugglers, "Snakeheads."[32]

The global structure of the smugglers included safe houses from Moscow to Hong Kong to Bolivia. They surreptitiously moved their human cargo from place to place, but once their clients crossed the U.S. border, control over them passed from the Snakeheads to local Chinese youth gangs. The gangs threatened and tortured the debtors to make sure they kept up with their payments. Living in constant fear, the illegal immigrants would take any job, no matter how poorly it paid: in garment sweatshops, as domestic help, in the kitchens of restaurants. Their wages were kept low by the continuing stream of illegal immigrants, all of whom had to have jobs to make payments on the smuggling fee. The circumstances of the illegal Chinese immigrants resembled that of indentured servants in that as they continued to work their situation did not improve.

Some of the immigrants came to the United States as single adults, others as married couples, and some families came with children. Those who came with children sent them to work at an early age, and their meager earnings helped the families survive. When young couples or single women had babies while they were in the United States it frequently created a totally unmanageable problem, an ironic situation after leaving China—and its rigid one-child policy—and achieving the freedom to have many children. Because of their living conditions, however, smuggled immigrants often cannot afford to raise even one child. There are usually no extended family members around to help and parents are unable to pay for child care. To keep up with payments on their smuggling debts, new parents must soon return to work and some are left with no way to keep their infants in New York. Hoping to be able to bring the child back one day, as many as 20 percent of illegal Chinese immigrants find that the only solution is to send the child to China to be raised by extended family. This practice is common enough to have given rise to a courier business, well advertised in clinics in the Chinese community, that charges a fee of $1,000 to fly an infant to China.[33]

Sex Industries

Many of the immigrant women who are coerced or tricked into immigrating by slave importing operations are recruited for international sex industries. From poor nations of the world, women are brought to rich nations, and global cities in particular, to work as prostitutes, escorts, exotic dancers, and so on. The young women who are recruited are almost invariably betrayed by worthless contracts or phony promises. Prior to leaving home, they expected easy work in pleasant, if not glamorous, settings for a brief period of time, after which they envisioned marriage, exciting careers, or both. When the women discover they have been deceived on all counts it is too late to do anything about it because, once smuggled out of their home countries, they are under the control of organized crime groups that buy and sell people like commodities.[34]

Physical beatings and threats of retaliation against their families back home are obvious external constraints that keep the women in line, despite being forced to work long hours under degrading conditions with no end in sight. The victimized women are also unlikely to see any alternatives open to them. As illegal aliens they have few rights to exercise, and because of their complicity in the smuggling activity the women may consider themselves to be criminals and fear prosecution if they come forward. They also find it difficult, if not impossible, to formulate post-escape plans because they lack both material resources and familiarity with their host country's language and customs.

Due to the fact that the activities they are forced to perform are "underground" in most places, and because the women are smuggled in and out of nations, precise data on the number of international sex workers are not available. However, the International Labour Organization (ILO) of the United Nations has provided figures that suggest the number of people involved probably far exceeds what most people imagine. Each year during the 1990s, ILO estimates that 120,000 Asian, Eastern European, and Latin American women were imported to Japan for sex industry employment, and were either brought in against their will or under deceptive conditions. Most wound up in brothels in Tokyo. An additional 50,000 women, largely from China, Mexico, and Poland, were estimated to be brought as sex workers into the United States, and the nation's major global cities—Los Angeles, Miami, New York, and San Francisco—were their principal destinations. Smaller, but sizeable, numbers of women were also smuggled into London, Paris, and other major world cities. The ILO refers to this international movement of sex workers as the "underside" of globalization.[35]

ENCLAVES

Immigrants have historically tended to congregate in enclaves: places in which members of an ethnic, religious, or racial group, sharing common traditions, support specialized shopping venues, such as ethnic groceries or religious goods stores. Many of these shops are owned by co-ethnics who reside in the same community. Enclaves also tend to be relatively self-contained institutionally; that is, there are usually institutions attached to the enclave that support people's distinctive ways of life, such as schools that teach in their native language or homes for the aged that accommodate cultural dietary preferences. If the community is large enough, it can also have a same-language newspaper, radio, or television station located within the enclave. Because so much of the lives of residents revolves around the enclave, their identities are frequently associated with it as well. Many Cuban Americans living in Miami's Little Havana, for example, think of themselves both as Cuban Americans and as residents of that enclave. Correspondingly, they consider Cuban Americas living anywhere else in the United States as being in diaspora.[36]

Immigrants initially form an enclave partly because they are pushed to it by the discrimination they face in other parts of the city. Landlords may refuse to rent to them, employers may be unwilling to hire them, and their children may feel uneasy in the city's public schools. In Vienna during the 1990s, for example, there was a large influx of Muslim immigrants from Turkey and Egypt. A crucifix, obligatory in every public school classroom in Austria, made the Muslim children feel unwelcome. The other children's antagonistic reactions to the Muslim girls' head scarves and the Muslim boys prostrating themselves in noon prayer made them feel even more out of place. Parents were prodded, as a result, to establish a private Islamic school connected to the Muslim community.[37] In addition, for newcomers with limited economic resources, an inner-city enclave might provide the only housing they can afford.

Some of the people who are pressured into an enclave do not fit well. The outside majority view them according to one master status: their race or religion, for example. Based on this one status they are made to feel unwelcome everywhere but in the enclave. However, other of their statuses, such as their educational level or lifestyle, may differ significantly from others who share their dominant status. Thus, some people are *in* the community, but not *of* it. Purkayastha refers to them as "alien insiders."[38]

Immigrants form an enclave because of pull factors as well, including the desire to be close to others who speak the same language and to stores that sell familiar foodstuffs. Research on several immigrant groups in New York and Los Angeles reported that even when immigrants could afford housing outside of their enclave, many chose the enclave instead.[39] Similarly, a recent survey of housing in cities in England suggested that different ethnic groups were "increasingly segregating themselves from each other and retreating into comfort zones made up of people like themselves."[40] Beyond often making immigrants feel more comfortable, studies indicate that immigrants' careers are enhanced by employment within the enclave economy rather than in the outside metropolitan area. In particular, working with and for co-ethnics has been described as resembling a "school for entrepreneurs" because it provides the knowledge and skills that enable employees eventually to acquire businesses of their own. By contrast, immigrants working in establishments that are not owned by co-ethnics are much less likely to acquire these entrepreneurial skills.[41]

After an enclave has been formed, it typically acts like a magnet to attract later arriving co-ethnics, a phenomenon known as chain migration. Suburban Toronto provides an interesting example. Between 1986 and 2001, the Chinese population living in metropolitan Toronto increased from about 150,000 to nearly a half million. In several of Toronto's suburbs, the Chinese formed classic enclaves that continued to attract later arriving immigrants because of their commercial and institutional offerings. The Pacific Mall, for example, is a shopping center with over 200 stores in suburban Toronto that caters to local Chinese customers. Its travel agency specializes in trips to Hong Kong and Taiwan, its music stores feature CDs by popular Hong Kong singers, home accessory stores are stocked with statues of Buddha and dragons. On the second floor is a popular feng shui consultant who tells fortunes and advises clients how to assure good luck and prosperity. While one middle-aged woman was waiting for a feng shui consultation she was asked what she liked about the mall. She answered, "When I am here, I feel like I am back in Hong Kong."[42]

Immigrant and Enclave Differences

Enclaves vary in physical condition, affluence of residents, location in a metropolitan area, and employment opportunities. The main variable that differentiates enclaves is compositional. Those enclaves that comprise solely, or almost solely, traditional immigrants tend to be in deteriorated condition, located in central cities, have little wealth, and offer limited opportunities.[43] To illustrate, near the stockyards on the south side of Chicago at the turn of the twentieth century, thousands of Lithuanian immigrants worked in slaughterhouses and meat packing plants owned by prominent (non-Lithuanian) Chicago families. The immigrants worked long hours, in unsanitary conditions, under the scrutiny of non-Lithuanian managers. Their jobs were physically demanding and did not lead anywhere. Meat cutters remained meat cutters, carcass haulers remained carcass haulers. There were few wage differences among these laborers, and almost all lived in similar conditions in a Lithuanian enclave adjacent to the stockyards. This area, called the Back of the Yards, was described as crowded, foul smelling, rat infested, and noisy.[44]

A second type of enclave, more common in contemporary global cities than in the past, includes both traditional immigrants and more well-to-do exiles. Little Havana, in southwest Miami, for example, was initially formed by industrialists, professionals, and landowners who fled Cuba after Castro came to power in 1959. They considered themselves political exiles, and when it became apparent that Castro's regime was not going to be short lived, the exiles opened restaurants, cigar stores, clothing shops, and funeral homes, typically the same types of businesses they had operated in Havana. Later groups of Cuban refugees more closely resembled traditional immigrants. They lacked formal education, skills, capital, and so on. Many of them settled in Little Havana and found employment in the businesses established by the exiles that arrived earlier.[45]

Stratification within a mixed enclave is necessarily more extensive than in an enclave comprised almost entirely of traditional immigrants. A group of exiles is usually at the top, living in the most desirable section of the enclave and possessing the greatest ability to influence collective-decisions made in the enclave. Most immigrants are in a middle group, with some variations among them that tend to be related to time of arrival. Illegal immigrants (if there are any) are ordinarily at the bottom of the hierarchy.

The relatively homogeneous enclaves comprised of traditional immigrants tend to be seen by residents as a place to live temporarily, until they can acquire the resources required to be mobile. To move up socially means moving out geographically, and to move out geographically usually means living in an ethnically and racially more diverse community in which co-ethnics do not predominate. Social scientists historically assumed this would result in assimilation, but that concept can be problematic when it implies that a previously distinctive group is simply absorbed by a dominant culture. The concept disregards the way an immigrant group and the larger society mutually influence each other. The food, holidays, music, clothing, and recreational activities once associated with one particular group often become part of the larger society, just as components of the larger society become incorporated into the lifestyles of immigrant groups and their children. In addition, many aspects of an immigrant group's culture need not disappear as its members adopt the practices associated with another society. People may acquire a new language, for example, without discarding their old one and simply become bilingual (likewise, they may learn to celebrate two sets of holidays, and so on).[46]

Within a mixed enclave there may even be strong inducements not to assimilate beyond a minimal degree due to the linkages between the enclave economy and the group's original homeland. In New York City's Chinatown, for example, banks headquartered both in New York and in China connect large corporations and wealthy individuals in the two nations. The global banks help to finance import–export trade between businesses in Chinatown and China, the sale of foreign currencies in each place, and real estate investments in the New York enclave. Local and overseas investors pooled resources to establish large financial investment firms in Chinatown, build multilevel department stores and retail malls, apartment and condominium projects, and so on.[47]

The bulk of the employment in Chinatown's retail stores, financial services, and property management firms has gone to Chinese Americans, most of whom live in Chinatown. Many of these jobs are in the high-status services category, as described earlier. They provide meaningful career opportunities without requiring geographical mobility. As a result, assimilation into the outside society has become less emphasized even as an ideal. In fact, the crossnation

Figure 3.2 Enclaves have become housing and employment centers for their ethnic group. (Pictured is Chinatown, New York, 2003.)

business dealings place a premium on the exiles' retention of many aspects of their traditional culture. Chinese Americans in New York's Chinatown maintain their commercial edge over non-Chinese in dealing with firms from the People's Republic of China by retaining their shared language and customs.

Several studies indicate that it has become commonplace for foreign minorities living in global cities to utilize their connections to their countries of origin as a means of adapting in the countries that received them. In many nations, this involves transnational entrepreneurs whose businesses depend on the desires of co-ethnics to have cultural goods from their countries of origin (newspapers, compact discs, foodstuffs, clothing, and so on). To be successful, the owners must maintain their networks and contacts in their countries of origin. Furthermore, these transnational entrepreneurs tend to experience upward mobility; thus, not assimilating is an effective way for them to adapt to a new economy.[48]

Enclave Tourism

Ethnic enclaves are one of the few areas in the center of global cities that have not been cleared and redeveloped, and that is in part because they can be marketed as important components of a tourist's overall experience in a city. That is how brochures for Paris travel advertise the Arab Quarter, how New York publicizes Chinatown, and so on. Enclave restaurants, nightclubs, and specialty shops can be promoted both as exotic and authentic, hence important for any serious tourist to visit. Enclaves also project an image of multiethnic invest-ment, which is important to the global financial services district.

To be marketed for tourists, however, ethnic enclaves have to be "sani-tized." Tourists will not visit an area unless they feel safe, and that requires con-trol over crime and street commerce (involving peddlers, prostitutes, beggars, and so on). Control usually entails passing city ordinances that prohibit street commerce (by defining it as "loitering," for example) and then directing city police to enforce the ordinances rigorously. However, this control, combined with the marketing efforts of image managers, can lead to ironic contradictions in realities between the "picturesque image of the sanitized ethnic village" that tourists see and the "gritty, littered urban district" with immigrants working in the backs of restaurants and sweatshops.[49] They do not see the latter. The en-clave as witnessed by most tourists is, therefore, only a partial and highly selective representation of the actual place. Similarly, in selecting cultural at-tributes to pass on to future generations, residents of an enclave may be most likely to emphasize aspects that are congruent with the (managed) images that are projected to outsiders. The authenticity of these traditions is then some-times open to question and there is likely to be some discrepancy between a group's history, as it was actually lived, and its history as remembered.[50]

CITIZENSHIP AND THE NATION-STATE

By the twentieth century, the nation-state was regarded not as one form of gov-ernment, but as *the* form of government. People fought over whether to divide a nation-state into smaller and more homogeneous nation-states (as in the for-mer Yugoslavia), or whether to create a nation-state (as in Palestine), but not over whether the nation-state was a desirable model. To illustrate how taken for granted this one form of government has become, John Meyer and his associates at Stanford University's Sovereignty Project present the hypothetical situation of an unknown society on an unknown island suddenly becoming known to the world. It is easy to image how the rest of the world would respond to the "dis-covery" and what would then happen on the island. The Stanford researchers speculate that the islanders would begin to form a nation-state, with the usual agencies: the natives would be given citizenship, with the usual rights and priv-ileges, and they would (with outside assistance) begin to develop modern insti-tutions, such as education and medicine. All of the preceding would occur rapidly and the island's unique traditions would have a limited effect on the structure of government, citizenship, and institutions because the model of the nation-state is now so clear and widely diffused that the rest of the world would convince the islanders that there really was no alternative.[51]

However, during the last third of the twentieth century, extensive immi-gration associated with globalization shook the foundation of the nation-state as a political form, making the possibility of alternatives more viable. Specifically, immigration challenged the cultural underpinnings of nations and the sovereignty of states in relation to their citizens. In order to understand these effects, it is helpful to pull nation and state apart, and separately examine immigration's impact on each.

Nation and Culture

We often use the terms nation and state interchangeably and, although they do overlap, there are important distinctions between them.[52] Nation invokes the cultural and symbolic dimension. It involves "myths" of common ancestry and experience that create a shared sense of community among people. It is a term that joins individuals and the collectivity by its dual referent. Thus, "national" pertains to a shared identity or experience (e.g., baseball is the national pasttime in the United States) and to an individual's citizenship (e.g., she is a French national).[53] Within most nations, tastes and experiences, identities and symbols, were historically widely shared; but with the growth of immigrant populations, consensus and similarities declined. In the public parks of Vienna, for example, Muslims cook lamb while native Austrians cook pork, and each is revolted by the smell of the other's food.

Immigration-induced diversity has been most pronounced in the leading global cities and it has had a limited *direct* effect outside of metropolitan areas. In the United States, for example, only about 5 percent of the foreign-born population was living in a rural community (i.e., outside of a metropolitan area) in 2000.[54] However, the global cities are media centers, both in their nations and globally. What happens in these cities is therefore magnified in importance and can persuade people everywhere that their distinctive way of life is disappearing. When that occurs or people believe that it has, the cultural base of a nation is weakened. As one native Anglo in Birmingham, England, explained: "There is no such thing as England anymore. . . . Welcome to India, brothers! This is the Caribbean!. . . . Nigeria!. . . . There is no England, man."[55]

States, Citizens, and Sovereignty

A state, in contrast to a nation, involves power and has more of an instrumental than affective connotation. It encompasses the activities of officials, such as formulating laws, mobilizing armies, and collecting taxes. While individuals are tied to a nation primarily via subjective emotional and symbolic bonds, their connection to a state is more formal and contractual. It involves citizenship, which confers legal privileges, such as voting, while requiring individuals to subject themselves to the laws of the state. In principle, there is symmetry to the relationship: on one hand, the state is sovereign in exercising control over its citizens, and on the other hand, the state is a product of the self-determination of its citizens.

In most places, residents who were not citizens were in a status, such as student or guest worker, that implied only temporary residence, thereby justifying their nonsymmetrical relationship with the state: bound by its rules, but without a voice in determining those rules. There were also more permanent residents who were excluded from citizenship because they were born elsewhere or were the offspring of noncitizens, but the nonsymmetry in their relationship with the state was not problematic because the number of people involved was usually small enough in relative size to be disregarded.

The historical assumptions became tenuous during the last third of the twentieth century, when large numbers of people more or less permanently emigrated, but were denied citizenship in their new nations.[56] Growing economies in Western Europe, beginning in the 1960s, lured millions of "guest workers" from southern and eastern Europe (Turkey, Italy, and so on) and North Africa (Morocco, Tunisia, and so on). These ethnically and racially diverse immigrants frequently remained in enclaves comprised of people from the same countries, none of whom were granted citizenship because of stringent laws of descent. In Denmark, for example, a child's citizenship is exclusively determined by birth to a mother who is Danish. That means that there are many second- and third-generation residents who are still officially considered foreigners. These more or less permanent noncitizens now comprise a significant proportion of the population in most of the E.U. nations: nearly 10 percent in Germany, between 5 and 6 percent in France, Denmark, and Sweden, and so on.[57] In the United States there are sizeable numbers of people whose citizenship status is ambiguous. During 2000, on the average day there were 20,000 immigrant detainees awaiting a resolution of their status.[58]

International human rights groups, such as Amnesty International, have prodded the nations that host large numbers of permanent residents who are not citizens to recognize that anyone living in a place ought to have some rights, citizen or not.[59] The nations from which large numbers of people have emigrated have also looked after the interests of their citizens living elsewhere. For example, in 2001 there were an estimated 3.5 million Mexicans living illegally in the United States and who therefore lacked all civil rights and were ineligible for government benefits. When in 2001 the president of Mexico visited the White House on a state visit, his public speech emphasized the importance of building "new conditions of fairness" for these undocumented Mexican immigrants.[60]

A number of nations have responded to the inequities facing their immigrants by enacting laws pertaining to foreign nationals, granting them political and civil rights, educational and welfare benefits, and so on. For example, in the United States, many noncitizens are granted some of the same due process rights as citizens in Immigration and Naturalization Service hearings. David Jacobson surveyed these developments, primarily in Western Europe and the United States, and concluded that the criterion being stressed by international advocacy groups is *residency, not citizenship*. Nation-states have been reluctant to embrace this change in emphasis, but they have grudgingly moved to a degree. More progress in this direction seems likely and will—in Jacobson's view—devalue citizenship and compromise the ability of nation-states to define themselves and their citizens.[61]

In looking to the future, it is likely that the wealthier nations, and their global cities in particular, will continue to attract large numbers of immigrants. The pressures this will place on the traditional nation-state, as a political form, will correspondingly continue to grow. It is unclear exactly where it will lead, though. What form could replace the nation-state? One interesting possibility is that the future may look a lot like the distant past, namely in the shape of city-states—or global city-states. Given the importance these urban centers have attained in economic and cultural realms, it might be reasonable to align the political form with them. (A description of how these global city-states may look is presented in Chapter 8.)

NOTES

1. These figures are from United Nations Population Information Network, *Population Today* (various dates, 1996 to 2001), New York: United Nations.
2. Susan Sachs, "As New York City Immigration Thrives, Diversity Broadens," *New York Times*, 8 November 1999, p. B1.
3. See Roger Waldinger, "From Ellis Island to LAX," *International Migration Review*, 30(1996):1078–86.
4. For further discussion of the distinction, see Georges Sabagh and Mehdi Bozorgmehr, "Are the Characteristics of Exiles Different from Immigrants?" *Sociology and Social Research*, 71(1987):45–61.
5. Afshin Molavi, "Sluggish Economy Spurs an Iranian Brain Drain," *Washington Post*, 17 April 2000, p. A12.
6. See, for example, Jonathan Friedmann, "The World City Hypothesis," *Development and Change*, 4(1986):69–84.
7. Howard W. French, " 'Japanese Only' Policy Takes Body Blow in Court," *New York Times*, 15 November 1999, p. A1.
8. Brazilians of Japanese descent are one of the few groups that are being integrated in Japanese cities. See James Brooke, "Sons and Daughters of Japan, Back from Brazil," *New York Times*, 27 November 2001, p. A4.
9. The deterioration continued after immigration "reform" in 1965 because it was another decade until immigrants again moved to U.S. cities in substantial numbers. See Joel Millman, *The Other Americans* (New York: Penguin Books, 1997).
10. Quoted in John Tagliabue, "Italy Says It Can Destroy Illegal-Immigrant Ships," *New York Times*, 29 March 2001, p. A16.
11. This was a popular newspaper and magazine position in 1900; quoted in Rita J. Simon and Susan H. Alexander, *The Ambivalent Welcome* (Westport, Conn.: Praeger, 1993), 93.
12. Bruce G. Carruthers and Sarah L. Babb, *Economy/Society* (Thousand Oaks, Calif.: Pine Forge Press, 2000).
13. Over a third of the one hundred Liberians crowded onto the boat drowned. See Frank Bruni, "Off Sicily, Tide of Bodies Roils the Debate Over Immigrants," *New York Times*, 23 September 2002, p. A10.
14. A number of studies examining the scope of the underground economy in Canada, the United States, and elsewhere are included in Owen Lippert and Michael Walker, eds., *The Underground Economy* (Vancouver, B.C.: The Fraser Institute, 1997).

15. Garry Pierre-Pierre, "Livery Vans Are Feeling Pinch of the Metrocard," *New York Times,* 14 January 1999, p. B1.

16. Sarah Lyall, "The Immigrant Journey Gets No Easier in Britain," *New York Times*, 31 July 2001, p. A3.

17. Ginger Thompson, "Big Mexican Breadwinner: The Migrant Worker," *New York Times*, 25 March 2002, p. A3.

18. Tatasha Robertson, "Many Immigrants Giving Up on the American Dream," *Boston Globe*, 10 February 2002, p. A19.

19. David Rieff, *The Exile* (New York: Simon and Schuster, 1993), 45.

20. Their growing panethnic identity did not necessarily occur at the expense of their Dominican identity; it was not an either-or situation. See Jose Itzigsohn and Carol Dore-Cabral, "Competing Identities?" *Sociological Forum*, 15, no. 2(2000):238.

21. That is the often quoted title of a book by Thomas Wolfe originally published in 1940 (New York: Harper).

22. Howard W. French, "Japan Unsettles Returnees, Who Yearn to Leave Again," *New York Times*, 3 May 2000, p. A1.

23. The relationship between economic development and women's status is discussed along with feminist aspirations in Nitza Berkovitch, "The Emergence and Transformation of the International Women's Movement," in *Constructing World Culture*, ed. John Boli and George Thomas (Stanford, Conn.: Stanford University Press, 1999), 218–235.

24. Mark Lander, "Taiwan's Betel Nut Habit and Voyeurism Merge," *New York Times*, 16 March 2001, p. A4.

25. Victoria E. Thompson, *The Virtuous Marketplace* (Baltimore: Johns Hopkins University Press, 2000).

26. In addition, it subordinated women to men and emphasized their role as consumers rather than producers. For further discussion, see Thompson, *Virtuous Marketplace*. For additional background, see also Ann-Louise Shapiro, *Housing the Poor of Paris, 1850–1902* (Madison: University of Wisconsin Press, 1985).

27. Susan Sachs, "U.S. Begins Crackdown on Muslims Who Defy Orders to Leave Country," *New York Times*, 2 April 2002, p. A13.

28. This description of illegal Mexican workers in the Los Angeles garment sweatshops is based on case studies presented by Jo-Ann Mort, "Immigrant Dreams: Sweatshop Workers Speak," *Dissent* 43 (Fall 1996):85–87.

29. For more figures and additional discussion, see Debarashmi Mitra, "Globalization, Inequality and Trafficking in Women" (paper presented at the Eastern Sociological Society annual meetings, Boston, March 2002).

30. This discussion of the two forms of smuggling is taken from David Kyle and John Dale, "Smuggling the State Back In." in *Global Human Smuggling*, ed. David Kyle and Rey Koslowski (Baltimore: Johns Hopkins University Press, 2001), 29–57.

31. Larry Rohter, "Brazil's Prize Exports Rely on Slaves and Scorched Land," *New York Times*, 25 March 2002, p. A8.

32. Peter Kwong, *Forbidden Workers* (New York: New Press, 1997). The $18 thousand label has stuck, even though the fee now often exceeds $20 thousand.

33. Somini Sengupta, "Squeezed by Debt and Time, Mothers Ship Babies to China," *New York Times*, 14 September 1999, p. A1.

34. See Mitra, "Globalization, Inequality, and Trafficking." For historical perspective on the international sex industry and organized crime, see Eileen Scully, "Pre-Cold War

Traffic in Sexual Labor and Its Foes," in Kyle and Koslowski, *Global Human Smuggling*, 74–106.

35. International Labour Organization, *The Elimination of All Forms of Compulsory Labor* (New York: United Nations, June, 2001).

36. Similar bonding of identity and enclave occurs for religious groups (Hasidim in Crown Heights, New York), lifestyle groups (gays in Castro District, San Francisco), and so on. For further discussion of diverse types of enclaves, see Mark Abrahamson, *Urban Enclaves* (New York: St. Martin's, 1996).

37. Roger Cohen, "Austrian School Drama: Crucifix Meets Ramadan," *New York Times*, 20 March 2001, p. A4.

38. Bandana Purkayastha, "Contesting Multiple Margins," in *Women's Activism and Globalization*, ed. Nancy A. Naples and Manisha Desai (New York: Routledge, 2002), 99–120.

39. John R. Logan, Richard D. Alba, and Wenquan Zhang, "Immigrant Enclaves and Ethnic Communities in New York and Los Angeles," *American Sociological Review*, 67(2002):299–322.

40. Quoted in Sarah Lyall, "The Immigrant Journey Gets No Easier in Britain."

41. For a general discussion of how an ethnic economy promotes entrepreneurship, see Ivan Light and Steve Gold, *Ethnic Economies* (San Diego: Academic Press, 2000). For a detailed study of how business ownership was enhanced in one community involving Mexican Americans in Chicago, see Rebeca Raijman and Marta Tienda, "Training Functions of Ethnic Economies," *Sociological Perspectives*, 43(2000):439–56.

42. Clifford Krauss, "Green Tea Favors the Land of the Maple Leaf," *New York Times*, 21 March 2002, p. A4.

43. For further analysis of the differences between city and suburban enclaves in the United States, see Richard D. Alba, John R. Logan, Brian J. Stults, Gilbert Marzan, and Wenquan Zhang, "Immigrant Groups in the Suburbs," *American Sociological Review*, 64(1999):446–60.

44. The Back of the Yards is described in Thomas J. Jablonsky, *Pride in the Jungle* (Baltimore: Johns Hopkins University Press, 1993).

45. For further discussion, see Alexjandro Portes and Alex Stepick, *City on the Edge* (Berkeley: University of California Press, 1993).

46. A thorough analysis of the inadequacies of the concept of assimilation is presented by Richard Alba, "Immigration and the American Realities of Assimilation and Multiculturalism," *Sociological Forum*, 14(1999):3–25.

47. Jan Lin, *Reconstructing Chinatown* (Minneapolis: University of Minnesota Press, 1998).

48. A number of these studies are described in Alejandro Portes, William J. Haller, and Luis Eduardo Guarnizo, "Transnational Entrepreneurs," *American Sociological Review*, 67(2002):278–98.

49. For further discussion of Chinatown, see Lin, *Reconstructing Chinatown*.

50. Any group's culture and experience are eclectic enough to allow many different values, meanings, or practices to be emphasized. Which will be considered to be genuine, or authentic, is dependent on a process of social construction. For further discussion of how culture is authenticated in different settings, see Samuel Gilmore, "Doing Culture Work," *Sociological Perspectives*, 43(2000):S21–S41.

51. John W. Meyer, John Boli, George M. Thomas, and Francisco O. Ramirez, "World Society and the Nation-State," *American Journal of Sociology*, 103(1997):144–81.

52. This discussion of the distinction between nation and state is based on Herfried Munkler, "Nation as a Model of Political Order and the Growth of National Identity in Europe," *International Sociology*, 14(1999):283–299.

53. For further discussion of this dual referent, see Jean L. Cohen, "Changing Paradigms of Citizenship and the Exclusiveness of the Demos," *International Sociology*, 14(1999): 245–68.

54. U.S. Census Bureau, *Current Population Survey* (March 2000, Washington, D.C.: Government Printing Office, January 3, 2001).

55. Quoted in Robert Holton, "Globalization's Cultural Consequences," *The Annals*, 570 (July 2000):149.

56. See Cohen, "Changing Paradigms of Citizenship," and Jurgen Habermas, "Citizenship and National Identity," in *Theorizing Citizenship*, ed. R. Beiner (Albany, N.Y.: SUNY Press, 1995), 255–82.

57. See Martin MacEwen, *Tackling Racism in Europe* (London: Berg Publishing, 1995).

58. Chris Hedges, "Policy to Protect Jailed Immigrants Is Adopted by U.S.," *New York Times*, 2 January 2001, p. A1.

59. There is also the obligation of nation-states to noncitizens living elsewhere who may, for example, be affected by that nation's environmental regulations.

60. Ginger Thompson, "Mexico President Urges U.S. to Act Soon on Migrants," *New York Times*, 6 September 2001, p. A10.

61. David Jacobson, *Rights Across Borders* (Baltimore: Johns Hopkins University Press, 1996). In addition to human rights groups and pressures from specific nations, immigration-related issues have also been subjected to courts, whose rulings can potentially further erode the sovereignty of nation-states over people residing within their boundaries. Created by the United Nations and located in The Hague, Netherlands, the oldest is the International Court of Justice, often called The World Court. The content of the cases this court considers often intrudes into areas where nation-states were historically considered to have exclusive jurisdiction. For example, in 1999, Germany sued the United States for executing two German brothers who were convicted of murdering a bank manager during a robbery in Arizona. The court ruled, in 2001, that the United States should have informed the German consular offices of the arrest and allowed those offices to assist the prisoners. The ruling was too late for the German brothers—Arizona had already executed them—but it could affect the twenty German citizens who were still in American jails at the time, four on death row. Marlise Simons, "World Court Finds U.S. Violated Consular Rights of 2 Germans," *New York Times*, 29 June 2001, p. A10.

FOUR

Cities in the Global Economy

Throughout most of the twentieth century, urban rankings and classifications typically focused on the role or place of a city in its nation. At one extreme, a city might be at the literal and figurative center of its nation, ecologically, economically, politically, and so on. At the opposite extreme, a city might be of little significance to its nation. This difference involves degrees of primacy, and those cities that are at the highest end are considered to be primate cities. The most frequently relied on measure of primacy is a demographic ratio that compares the size of the largest city in a nation to the next largest city (or cities) in that nation.[1] To illustrate, Santiago, Chile, is a highly primate city because its population of more than 4.5 million people is over ten times greater than any other Chilean city, none of which has as many as 400,000 people. In contrast, Rome, Italy, is not much of a primate city because its population of 2.7 million is just about twice the size of Milan, the next largest Italian city (and Naples and Turin also have populations of about a million or more).

This straightforward demographic ratio typically reflects the degree to which a city dominates the rest of its nation in terms not only of population, but all types of economic resources, such as jobs and investment funds. In addition, primate cities are likely to be the nation's capital and educational and religious centers. Primacy also provides a summary measure by which cities can be compared (e.g., Santiago is more primate than Rome), though the different configurations of national urban systems often detract from primacy's value in comparing cities.[2]

During the last decades of the twentieth century, the transnational linkages of cities grew in importance. Imports and exports, for example, comprised a steadily growing proportion of the economies of the world. This was part of a long-term trend toward more global trade that has characterized the past 200 years, though it has been periodically interrupted by wars and recessions. Consider the cereal that people eat for breakfast as an illustration. The sugar and wheat it contains have long been international commodities in the sense that, since 1800, the production and distribution of sugar and wheat have been strongly affected by global market forces. Other products, such as many of the fresh fruits people eat in the morning, did not become global commodities until they could be transported more quickly. Thus, the average breakfast, eaten anywhere in the world, became more globalized during the last third of the twentieth century, though portions of it had been globalized for many years.[3]

The closest approximation to the pure form of a global economy is probably provided by the world's financial markets. They consist of networks of banks and other traders that buy and sell currencies, options, and other securities. The traders are in dispersed locations around the world, but electronic information technologies link them together as though they were in a single place. The system would be truly global, or globally inclusive, if exchanges were completely unimpeded by national boundaries. While such a system may be established in the future, at the start of the twenty-first century these markets were still based on "trading bridgeheads" in the financial centers of a few major global cities.[4]

GLOBAL CLASSIFICATIONS

As international economic and financial linkages grew in importance, social scientists turned to the question of how cities could best be ranked and classified in a global framework. Primacy was not particularly useful once analysts began trying to describe the relationships among cities apart from their national contexts. The size of cities could probably best be used only to identify world city "nominees" from specific nations. For example, Janet Abu-Lughod selected the three largest cities in the United States—New York, Los Angeles, and Chicago—when she wanted to describe a small sample of the presumably most global cities in the United States.[5]

It is impossible to state, unambiguously, where contemporary, nondemographic analyses of cities in the global economy began. A good case might be made for Peter Hall's 1966 book, in which he proposed that world cities, such as London and New York, were those in which a large percentage of the world's business was conducted.[6] Few studies immediately followed Hall's lead, then after about 1980 there were a host of publications. Of particular importance, as noted in Chapter 1, were several articles by John Friedman that attempted to synthesize the growing body of literature on world cities and to suggest several directions that future research should follow.

While Friedman acknowledged that it might be premature, in 1986, he nevertheless thought it important to present at least an initial hierarchy of world cities based loosely on the amount of international capital they contained and the number of multinational corporations headquartered within them.[7] Nine years later Friedman presented another hierarchy, again based on what he termed "rough notions."[8] Some of the categories he employed were different, making exact comparisons difficult, but there appeared to be both continuity and change in the rankings. London, New York, and Tokyo were among the top cities at both times, and Friedman referred to them as "the command and control centres of the global economy" (p. 23). On the other hand, there were some marked changes. For example, Rotterdam was in the highest category in the 1986 paper, but was not included in any of the top four categories in 1995.

While we expect some changes in the rankings of cities to occur over time, a decade is probably too short a period for changes of this magnitude actually to occur. Perhaps a portion of the excessive change occurred in error, due to Friedman's use of "rough notions." More likely, much of the excessive variation was due to the fact that different indicators yield different results. For example, the concentration of wealth and capital in a city is an important consideration. It could be measured by the location of leading banks or by financial institutions more broadly defined to include insurance companies, stock and bond brokers, and related firms. Which is the better measure? In the absence of other information it is difficult to say which is better, but which one is used certainly does matter. There are marked differences in the ranking of cities each of these different measures produce. New York is first when wealth and capital are measured more broadly, but fifth in terms of banks only. Paris ranks second on leading banks, but eighth on the more inclusive measure.[9]

It is not surprising then, that when investigators use a single indicator of a city's global rank, there are especially marked divergences in their findings. Kunzmann illustrates this principle by noting that between 1986 and 1996 four different studies each presented a list of Europe's leading world cities and each was based on different economic indicators. The only cities all four studies agreed on were London and Paris. Seven other urban areas appeared in at least one of the studies, but five of the seven were included in only one.[10] Such variations in findings provide a strong argument for relying on multiple indicators, that is, the use of a number of separate indicators combined into a single index. When indicators are combined, the idiosyncracies of specific indicators are reduced and one probably gets closest to the heart of the matter.

In this chapter we examine the global rankings of cities that are produced by several sets of indicators: stock exchanges, banking and finance, multinational corporations and foreign direct investment, and corporate services. The locations of these firms and activities help define the most important centers of the global economy and several also provide a picture of linkages among these urban hubs. Some of these indicators partially overlap, but that is not necessarily a problem.[11] Each reflects a somewhat different aspect of how the international economy is hinged on the most important global cities and, as we shall see, using fewer indicators would result in missed nuances in the urban hierarchy. It is also important to recognize that, although these indicators are being separately discussed, they are often interdependent. For example, the development of Tokyo's stock exchange in the 1960s was an important impetus to attracting large banks, financial institutions, multinational corporations, and financial services firms to the city.[12] The conclusion to this chapter presents a single global economic hierarchy based on the combined index.

LOCATION OF STOCK EXCHANGES

The major stock exchanges are special types of markets in which individuals and firms buy and sell several types of stocks, or shares, in publicly traded corporations. (Most of the largest corporations in the world are publicly traded.) In addition, most exchanges offer bonds, mutual funds, and a variety of specialized financial mediums, such as "options" (contracts to make purchases in the future at a designated price). Some exchanges also operate commodity markets, in which supply and demand fix the price of items such as cattle or cotton. In the larger exchanges, over half of all trading involves foreign entities, such as the stocks of corporations located in countries other than the exchange's.

The major exchanges can be viewed, first, as centers of world capital where the major corporations of the world go to raise equity, or loan capital. Thus, whether or not a business enterprise in Italy can raise the funds required to expand its operations into Poland may depend on the willingness of investors to buy shares of the Italian company when it is offered for sale on the Tokyo stock market. The second way to view exchanges is as marketplaces where the price of everything from soybeans to a government's bonds is continuously set. Thus, the price of oranges grown in Brazil for shipment to London is set by transactions that occur on the New York Stock Exchange. The cities in which these major exchanges are located can therefore be viewed as cornerstones of the world's economy in the sense that they house the activities that set the conditions under which economies and businesses operate across the entire world. It is important also to note that a major exchange acts like a magnet, attracting financial service firms and a variety of investors, advisors, and so on. Thus, the presence of a stock exchange also indicates a likely concentration of financial activity.

The world's oldest stock market is in London, England, but the largest by far, in terms of shares traded or the market value of the listed corporations, is the New York Stock Exchange. NASDAQ, roughly tied for second place with the Tokyo exchange, is also in New York, giving that city a clearly preeminent position in the world. (Until late 2000, NASDAQ was alone in second place, but then it began a long decline because the price of many technology companies it listed moved lower.) The London exchange, in fourth place, is close behind the NASDAQ and Tokyo exchanges in size. Before electronic trading opened much of the world to twenty-four-hour trading, the exchanges in these three cities, given their time zones, made a worldwide, around-the-clock market possible because the exchange in Tokyo opens just when New York's closes, and it closes as the London exchange opens.

An international ranking of stock exchanges, arranged according to the market value of the corporations whose shares are traded on them, is presented in Table 4.1. However, these rankings are subject to change as a result of:

1. mergers and joint ventures among exchanges in process across the entire globe,
2. new Internet companies offering electronic trading across national boundaries.

TABLE 4.1   Location of World's Largest Stock Exchanges

Market Capitalization	Headquarter City
Over $10 Trillion	New York (NYSE)
$1 to $3 Trillion	Frankfurt*, London, New York (NASDAQ), Paris[†], and Tokyo
$½ to $⅔ Trillion	Hong Kong, Milan, Osaka[††], Toronto, and Zurich[§]

* This exchange is also referred to by the name of its parent company, Duetsche Borse. It offers the world's largest market for trading derivatives, financial contracts based on assets such as stocks and bonds.
[†] Amsterdam and Brussels are joined to this exchange, formally known as Euronext.
[††] Also linked to NASDAQ in 2000.
[§] Basle and Geneva are also linked to the Swiss Exchange.

In addition, as individual stocks vary, there are fluctuations in the values of shares traded on an exchange. To iron out these short-term variations, Table 4.1 presents a ranking of cities averaged by total market size in 1998, 1999, and 2000.[13]

Trailing in size behind the world's leading exchanges, as noted in Table 4.1, are a number of secondary exchanges, beginning with Chicago's. That city houses the largest exchange in the United States outside of those in New York, and it also contains its nation's major agricultural commodities and futures markets—for cattle and hogs, corn and wheat, and so on—and these agricultural products still comprise the largest export category of the United States. In addition, a subsidiary of the Chicago Mercantile Exchange sets international prices for silver and the future U.S. rates of exchange for most foreign currencies.[14]

In the same general range as Chicago's are stock exchanges located in Madrid, Stockholm, and Sydney. Finally, there are several other exchanges located in "emerging market" nations. They are still relatively small, with market capitalization in billions rather than trillions, but any or all of these exchanges may be of substantial global consequence in the near future. The largest in this group, in order of market capitalization, are the exchanges in Taipei, Seoul, Mexico City, and São Paulo.

INTERNATIONAL BANKING AND FINANCE

International banking began in the thirteenth century, when commercial establishments in Italy, based in Florence, opened branches and subsidiaries in several European nations. The banks' primary objective was to assure local representation of their interests as they financed the silk and wool cloth trade across Europe. Pursuing similar objectives, over the following centuries banks in other cities followed suit. The first major change in the nature of international banking occurred in the nineteenth century, when the predominant activity became raising loans for foreign governments and investing in foreign nations. (The United States was a major recipient.) At this time, large banks in London were the world's leading arrangers, underwriters, and holders of foreign bonds.

The economic rise of the United States in the early twentieth century was associated with the expansion of U.S. banks. The U.S. dollar replaced the U.K. sterling in international trade, and New York took London's place as the world's financial center. However, international finance remained relatively small compared to domestic finance until the 1970s, when another major change occurred in conjunction with the growth of transnational corporations. The banks followed their corporate customers, and soon realized it would be even more profitable to service the local market in the host country at the same time they handled the transnationals' accounts. Modern telecommunications also played a role, making it increasingly easy to transfer funds, arrange loans, and convert currencies between a parent bank and its distant branches or among bank affiliates thousands of miles apart.[15] Although of major significance, commercial and investment banks are only part of the modern financial services complex. Also included are financial advisors, insurance and stock brokers, and the like.

There have been accelerating mergers and linkages among firms in the financial services complex, cutting across both business sectors and national boundaries. The purchases in the United States by the giant Swiss bank UBS A.G. are illustrative. During 1997 and 1998, the bank acquired three specialized money management and corporate advisory firms in New York and Chicago, and then in 2000 purchased PaineWebber, the fifth largest brokerage house in the United States. The bank could then directly provide and manage a wide array of services to corporations and wealthy individuals in Zurich, New York, Chicago, and so on.[16]

The financial service firms in the major world centers have the advantage of what Sassen terms "global connectivity." Their staff members know how to

Figure 4.1   Banks from all over the world are part of the financial concentrations of global cities. (Pictured is the Arb Bank in Zurich, 2001.)

execute major international deals. With modern telecommunications, firms in cities like Dayton, Ohio, or Palermo, Italy, know the day's closing prices on the New York Stock Exchange the same time as everyone else in the world. They may not fully understand its significance, though. What the staff members of firms in the major financial centers uniquely possess is the expertise to interpret what those closing prices will likely mean for future investments and to guide a client by assessing the risks of specific crossnational ventures.[17]

An excellent example of a firm with this type of specialized knowledge is Goldman Sachs, a leading New York investment bank that has concentrated on global communications. During the 1990s, when government-owned telephone and telecommunications companies in Europe and Asia either became private or offered shares to the public, Goldman Sachs was often their advisor. The firm was the lead banker for billion-dollar public stock offerings in Denmark, Hong Kong, and Japan, and was consultant to giant telecommunications mergers in England, Germany, and the United States. One industry observer described the highly successful Goldman Sachs strategy for its client companies as: "If it was owned by the government, take it private. If it is private, take it public. Then merge it. They are a transaction machine."[18] And each transaction meant a fee for Goldman Sachs.

Many of the most successful of these international firms have contacts to open doors in the capitals of the world. For example, the Carlyle Group is a private equity firm based in Washington, D.C. Its specialty is buying and selling companies, often across national lines. The funds used in Carlyle Group's purchases come from such diverse sources as pension funds in Texas and California and oil money from Saudi Arabia. The advisors and directors of the Carlyle Group include former president George H. Bush and former presidents or prime ministers of Britain, Thailand, South Korea, and elsewhere. Specializing in the purchase of foreign companies regulated by their governments, the Carlyle Group has used its connections to learn when there will be shifts in government spending that could affect the value of companies in the future.[19]

In order to illuminate the general place and role of banking and finance in the global economy, it is instructive to examine the Bank of New York (BNY), a large institution that was especially successful in attracting foreign clients, particularly from Eastern Europe. As Russia, Poland, and other Eastern European nations moved into a capitalistic mode during the last decades of the twentieth century, cooperative arrangements with U.S. banks became especially critical. For example, most of the foreign suppliers to Russian companies wanted payment only in U.S. dollars. This required that the companies' Russian banks establish "dollar settlement accounts" in American banks. In addition, to increase their capitalization, a number of Russian banks wanted to be listed on U.S. stock exchanges and needed the expertise of American financial specialists to arrange it. Large banks in cities with major stock exchanges, like New York, have departments that specialize in stock capitalization.

Many U.S. banks were eager to do business with the Russians, but because of their locational advantage, New York banks, especially BNY, were able to obtain most Russian business. Banks were interested because it meant new clients who, in addition to paying commissions for special services, could be billed for transaction fees on their accounts. Even though each transaction (e.g., a deposit, withdrawal, transfer) involved only a nominal fee (typically about $3), many of these accounts had extremely high volume. For example, in a six-month period between October 1998 and March 1999, one BNY account that linked firms in New York and Moscow had 10,000 transactions. Unfortunately for the bank and several of its chief executives, this account was apparently used to move profits from illegal activities in Moscow to a "front" company's account at BNY. The money then was sent to banks in England, Italy, and Switzerland before being returned—its origins moot, hence "laundered"—to a bank in Russia.

The BNY money laundering scandal was a criminal corruption of the international banking system and a deviant exception to the way the system normally operates. However, it is instructive to examine the BNY fiasco because criminal, or deviant, behavior typically provides insight into the societal (or intersocietal) arrangements in which it occurs. The same Internet technology that makes it possible for distant friends to stay in touch via e-mail messages also improves the access of child molesters to kiddie porn. In the future scientists wishing to study our current technology would learn much by studying the actions of those convicted of transmitting or receiving illegal images of children. To illustrate further, criminal groups—mafias, *La Cosa Nostras*, and so on—have usually organized following the same forms (e.g., familial or bureaucratic) that predominated in legitimate sectors of society. Thus, one could gain insight into a wide range of legitimate business operations by studying how criminal syndicates were organized. In a parallel way, money laundering through BNY helps us understand many conventional aspects of international banking.

The central figure in the story was Natasha Gurfinkel Kagolovsky. Russian born, Princeton educated, Kagolovsky was a senior vice president at the BNY's main office in New York, in charge of the bank's Eastern European Division. Her husband, who lived mostly in Russia, was a banker and oil executive and Russia's former representative to the International Monetary Fund (IMF). He was apparently of great help in steering corporate clients in Russia to BNY. (U.S. investigators later accused him also of diverting $200 million in IMF loans through the bank.) Reporting to Ms. Kagolovsky and working as head of the Eastern European Division in the bank's London office was another Russian-born executive, Ludmila Edwards. Her husband, living mostly in New York, opened the BNY accounts to which the Russian funds flowed. The source of most of the money, according to the FBI, was the Russian mob's profits from drugs, extortion, arms traffic, and prostitution. From New York, Mr. Edwards moved the funds to European banks and eventually the laundered funds returned to Russia. There was apparently enough money for everyone to make out nicely. Ms. Kagolovsky purchased a condominium in Manhattan in 1997 for $796,000 and Ludmila Edwards bought a $500,000 apartment in central London—and both paid cash.[20]

The importance of U.S. dollars to world trade made it likely that Russian money laundering would involve changing local currencies into U.S. dollars. New York's role as the leading financial center in the United States made it likely that a bank located in New York would be involved. The amount of money crossing borders is so great, making the potential for bank profits so large, that normal safeguards are sometimes relaxed. BNY is not alone in this regard. Its problems would be less interesting to us if they were unique. Thus, at the same time that key officials at BNY were being indicted, a congressional committee began to examine Citibank of New York which, during the 1990s, became the preferred banker for elite families in Asia. That probe focused on illegal transfers between Citibank's corporate parent in New York and its Hong Kong branch.[21]

There are at least two indicators that can be employed to focus on the concentration of capital in major financial centers:

1. the location of the largest banks in the world as defined by their total assets,

2. the location of the world's largest financial service institutions, as reflected by market capitalization (i.e., the value of their common stock). Included in the latter category are banks, plus insurance companies, brokerage firms, holding companies, and the like. Both measures reflect the presence of extensive capital in a city, and the likely availability of financial expertise to go with it, though as noted in the introduction to this chapter, each indicator yields a somewhat different ranking of cities. It is important, therefore, to examine both indicators, and the two sets of findings—involving the thirty largest banks and one hundred largest financial institutions—are presented in Table 4.2.[22]

TABLE 4.2 Location of Leading Financial Firms*

City	World's Thirty Largest Banks (%)	Top One Hundred Financial Institutions (%)
Tokyo	27	9
Paris	13	2
London	10	10
Frankfurt	10	6
Bejing	7	1
New York	7	14
Osaka	7	2
Munich	3	4
Zurich	3	4
Chicago	0	4
Total	87	56

* This table includes only the ten cities that house 2 percent or more of either type of firm. For this reason, neither of the columns totals 100 percent.

From Table 4.2, we can see that the location of the largest banks is especially highly concentrated: 60 percent of the total are in the four principal centers: Tokyo, Paris, London, and Frankfurt. Add Bejing, New York, and Osaka, and the seven principal centers contain over 80 percent of the world's total. The location of the leading financial institutions is more dispersed, though still quite concentrated, as the seven leading cities contain over half of the world's total.

Several other cities contain some of the largest banks or financial institutions, but fewer than the leading cities listed in Table 4.2. The most important of these cities to consider are Amsterdam, Dusseldorf, and Geneva.

MULTINATIONAL CORPORATIONS AND FOREIGN INVESTMENT

Perhaps the most significant form of conglomeration in the major global cities involves multinational (or transnational) corporations. Included here is any corporation that engages in economic activity in nations other than the one in which its headquarters is located. The largest of these corporations are involved in production and sales across much of the world. The vast resources controlled by the largest multinationals make them an enormous asset to the city and nation in which they are housed.

Many of the largest multinational corporations are household names, familiar to people everywhere in the world. Others have less public recognition either because their products are not sold to the general public (e.g., industrial chemicals) or because they have brought together a number of product lines that are marketed separately, so many people do not recognize their vast consolidation of ownership in the marketplace. For example, the Diageo Corporation is a consumer goods company whose size is interesting precisely because it is *not* among the top fifty multinationals in yearly income or total assets. It is a London-based corporation that many people have never heard of but almost everyone is familiar with some of their products. Diageo's holdings fall into three categories[23]:

1. spirits and wine, labeled under such names as Johnnie Walker and J&B (the two best-selling brands of scotch in the world), Smirnoff, Baileys, and Guiness beer and ale

2. packaged foods, under the following labels: Pillsbury dough products, Green Giant vegetables, Old El Paso Mexican foods, and Häagen Dazs ice cream

3. fast foods: Burger King

Most of the products sold by the various divisions of Diageo Corporation are virtually identical throughout the world. Among Burger King Whoppers, for example, there is essentially no variation. However, like many multinationals, Diageo subsidiaries also make some concessions to local tastes. In Japan, for example, the second leading Häagen Dazs ice cream flavor, after vanilla, is green tea, and it is only marketed in Asia. (This type of localization is not unique to Diageo. Domino's best-selling pizza in England is topped with sweet corn and tuna.)

Throughout the world, one can find salesrooms for the same automobiles or television sets and franchised restaurants serving the same food, but about 90 percent of the headquarters of multinational corporations tend to be concentrated in a few of the economically most advanced nations. The United States, the United Kingdom, Germany, France, and Japan are the leading nations in this regard. If one looks at all corporations conducting business in more than one nation, then Germany is found to house the most parent corporations and the United States is in fourth place.[24] When the size of firms—and indirectly, therefore, their wealth and importance—is taken into account, the headquarters of firms is even more highly concentrated in a small number of nations and the hegemony of the United States becomes more apparent. To illustrate, Table 4.3 focuses solely on the headquarters of the one hundred largest multinational industrial corporations. (If other types of companies had been utilized, the specific numbers would change, but the overall pattern would remain the same.) Table 4.3 makes it clear that, although the United States has lost some of its large share of the top global firms, mostly to Japan, it nevertheless headquartered the greatest percentage of the largest firms throughout the twentieth century.[25]

The small group of nations (and cities within them) that house the multinational corporations (see Table 1.1 in Chapter 1) are highly advantaged because extremely large amounts of capital flow *to* the headquarters nations, and enormous influence over decisions made throughout the world emanates *out* from the national homes of multinational corporations. The largest transnationals are, in fact, richer (and probably exert more influence in the world) than many moderately well-off nations. To illustrate, in 2000, a typical year, Exxon-Mobil and General Motors Corporation both exceeded entire nations such as Peru, New Zealand, and Hungary in wealth.[26]

As noted earlier, one reason firms establish production facilities outside of their headquarters nation is to find relatively cheap labor and raw materials.

TABLE 4.3 Headquarters of Top Global Industrial Firms

Country	1912 (%)	1995 (%)
United States	52	40
United Kingdom	15	13
Germany	14	7
France	6	5
Japan	0	21
Rest of Europe	6	12
Rest of Non-European World	7	2
Total	100	100

Within the Diageo Corporation, for example, Guiness established a brewery in Tanzania (Africa) and Pillsbury operated a plant in Irapuato (Mexico). Other reasons for transnational investments are access to new markets, especially when trade barriers discourage imports, and for economies of scale. The latter has been especially important in recent years to firms experienced in foreign operations. To illustrate, consider the recent investments of the French automaker Renault. Recognizing that its factories in France were old and inefficient, and hoping to expand sales outside of France, the company sought to diversify its products and production facilities. During 1999 and 2000, Renault purchased a 37 percent share in Nissan (of Japan), a 51 percent share in Dacia (of Romania), and a 70 percent share of Samsung Motor (of Korea). With these investments, Renault expected to be able to coordinate production and operation facilities throughout much of the world.[27] It remained for a board of directors meeting in Paris to later decide which of the facilities in Japan, Korea, and Romania might eventually be closed, expanded, or merged with others.

When a subsidiary of the Diageo Corporation builds a brewery in Africa or Renault purchases an automobile factory in Romania it entails Foreign Direct Investment (FDI). The current definition of FDI, according to the International Monetary Fund, requires the purchase of at least 10 percent of the equity of the firm receiving the funds.[28] That criterion is employed to assure that the foreign investor will have a voice in the management of the company. The ownership of most large transnational firms is spread among thousands of small, separate investors. A holding as small as 10 percent is often sufficient, therefore, to accord a single owner a substantial amount of control.

Since about 1970, the worldwide volume of FDI has multiplied many times over. To be exact, total investment abroad by transnational corporations was less than $50 billion in the early 1970s. By the late 1990s it exceeded $350 billion, and over the past quarter century, it grew much faster than other components of the world's gross domestic product, providing another reflection of increased internationalization.[29] In recent decades, there have been two major flows of FDI. The first has gone from firms in economically advantaged nations, such as the United States and the United Kingdom, to firms in less economically advantaged countries. Most of the latter have been located in either Asia (notably Cambodia and Vietnam) or Latin America and the Caribbean (notably Columbia, Trinidad and Tobago). In addition, a growing proportion of FDI to these nations has tended to exceed the 10 percent criterion and, in fact, results in majority control for the foreign investors. The second major FDI flow has occurred among firms within economically advantaged nations, and has been less likely, than the first flow, to result in majority control for the investing firm.

Table 4.4 describes nations and cities according to the sum of FDI flowing outward from firms within them. The first column indicates the total amount of such funds invested in 1996, and shows that the United States, and to a lesser extent, the United Kingdom were in their own categories, that is, without equals. Moving down the first column to lower levels of investment, the number of more or less similar nations increases in number. When a number of na-

TABLE 4.4   FDI Outflows and Multinational Headquarters

Billions Invested (U.S.$)	Nations	Cities with at Least 10% of Top Global Firms	Cities with Between 1% and 5% of Firms
Over 80	United States	New York	Chicago, Los Angeles, San Francisco
Over 50	United Kingdom	London	
20–30	France	Paris	
	Germany		Dusseldorf, Frankfurt, Munich, Stuttgart
	Hong Kong*		Hong Kong
	Japan	Tokyo	Osaka
	Netherlands		Amsterdam
6–10	Belgium		
	Canada		Toronto, Montreal[†]
	Italy		[††]
	Switzerland		Zurich
3–5	Korea		Seoul
	Singapore		Singapore
	Sweden		Stockholm
	Taiwan		Taipei

* Hong Kong is an "administrative region" of Mainland China with its own economy. Almost all of its population resides in Victoria, the capital of Hong Kong Island.

[†] Unlike other cities within nations that are presented alphabetically, Toronto is presented first to call attention to the fact that it has more corporate headquarters than Montreal and scores higher on all of the other economic indicators.

[††] Both Milan and Rome barely missed inclusion.

tions are in the same category (column two), they are presented alphabetically because from year to year small increases or decreases in their FDI change the rankings among nations within (but not between) these categories. Columns three and four indicate the cities in these nations in which the transnational corporations making the bulk of foreign investments are located. Specifically, column three notes the major headquarter cities, each of which houses 10 percent or more of the top global firms. The final column includes the next largest set of headquarter cities, each of which houses between 1 percent and 5 percent of the leading firms in the world. There were no cities or metropolitan areas in which between 6 percent and 9 percent of the top global firms were located. This absence of intermediate cases suggests the fruitfulness of placing cities into these two categories, as in Table 4.4, rather than trying to view them along a continuum.

In the table, the investments noted in column one pertain to nations, and these figures are straightforward. Obtaining information about the nations' cities in which the investing firms are located is more difficult. Two kinds of information can be used. First, there are a number of listings of leading international corporations. Some rankings, such as *Fortune's* Global Five Hundred, are based solely on the firm's total revenue for the preceding year. To use this list to indicate city locations, one must assume that a firm's total revenue reflects its volume of nondomestic activity, which is true more often than not, but not necessarily the case. Another type of measure attempts to focus more specifically on firms' degrees of internationalization. For example, Ietto-Gillies has combined the percent of a firms' total assets, sales, and employment that are foreign into a single index, and then employed this index to identify the one hundred most transnational firms. Despite a few differences in the corporations that are included with each measure, the urban areas in which either set of firms are located are remarkably similar. Columns three and four in table 4.4 rely on both of these indicators.

Whether cities are in the higher (10 percent) or lower (1–5 percent) categories in terms of FDI outflows is a function of their nation's urban configuration and FDI volume. The total FDI outflows from the United States are so large that the nation can contain one major world center of corporate headquarters, New York, as well as three secondary world centers, in Chicago, Los Angeles, and San Francisco. France, in contrast, has only one major world center, following a classic primate city pattern in which a single metropolitan area, Paris, dominates as the nation's headquarters for transnational corporations. Although Paris has historically been its nation's most dominant city, its share of France's international economic activity increased over the last quarter of the twentieth century, mostly at the expense of Lyon and Marseilles.

In other nations, such as Canada and Germany, there is a more even distribution of headquarters locations among two or more metropolitan areas. In Germany there are two sets of cities that have expanded into important conurbations: the Rhine–Maine conurbation, with Frankfurt as its "global urban flagship,"[31] and the Rhine–Ruhr conurbation, in which no one city stands out. Even though these nations score relatively high in FDI outflows, they contain no single urban area among the world's top headquarters cities—which would not be the case if they followed the primate city pattern.

CORPORATE SERVICE FIRMS

As economic activity became more global, the scale and complexity of transactions increased, prompting the growth of specialized service firms to provide diverse types of assistance to corporate headquarters. Decision making in the home offices of multinational corporations requires diverse expertise in international banking and finance, advertising, accounting, and law. The firms that provide these services to the headquarters of multinationals provide the infrastructure necessary to run "the advanced corporate economy."[32] They do not, of course, provide entirely new services that suddenly appeared with globalization. What has changed is the increase in demand for such specialized services and it has led to enormous growth in their scale and scope. Because service firms bill resource-rich home offices, they have been particularly profitable and are able to afford desirable office space near the center of midtown Manhattan, the City of London, and elsewhere.[33] In fact, by the turn of this century, service firms accounted for about 40 percent of all employment in the central business districts of many global cities.

In recent years corporate service firms have tended toward increasing scale to accommodate the multinational corporations whose accounts are large, hence highly valued. The service firms have had to reorganize to prevent the appearance of conflict that could arise if they maintained as clients companies that competed with each other. For example, when a manufacturing company buys a retail food chain, the law firm that has been billing the manufacturing company would likely want the business of the food chain as well. In fact, not handling the food chain's legal matters could threaten the loss of the parent (manufacturing) company's business. But what if the law firm previously accepted a retainer from a rival food chain? Each client might be uncomfortable if the law firm attempted to represent the other. The same potential problems arise for firms providing accounting, advertising, and other services.

To illustrate how service firms have realigned themselves to handle potential interclient conflicts, consider True North Advertising. One of the top-ten ad agencies in the world with a roster of huge clients, in 1999 it moved all of its component parts into one of two renamed agencies, Bozell and FCB. To enhance their image as separate agencies, separate management teams were put into place. Bozell was able to service the Bank of America account, while FCB handled Chase Manhattan, and neither client had reason to object; Bozell then took Bell Atlantic Mobil, while FCB serviced AT&T, and so on.[34]

To better understand how large corporate service firms have expanded around the world, the research of a group of geographers at Loughborough University in England is illuminating. For the past several years, this research group (known as GaWC for "globalization and world cities") has been tracking the growth and connections among corporate service firms. Focusing upon the intercity linkages of the firms is on strong grounds theoretically, given the widespread conception that globalization entails an increasingly dense network of cities and that the command and control functions of world cities is best expressed via exchanges among cities.[35]

In one study, the GaWC group examined large U.S. law firms. Such firms clearly represent a specialized, knowledge-based producer service, though national jurisdictions over legal codes have somewhat discouraged the transnational growth of law firms. They were almost always local until around 1965, when they began to follow their multinational clients across national boundaries, despite the fact that most legal systems remained state based. The firms were still able to offer clients information and advice unavailable in most places and they hired local lawyers to complement their international specialists.

Many of the largest of the law firms are now found in several principal cities of the world. Baker and McKenzie, originally a Chicago firm, is the largest in the world and the most global. It provides foreign investment advice to 150,000 clients and employs 1,800 lawyers outside of the United States. Baker and McKenzie now denies that Chicago, or anywhere else, is its headquarters. It has become global to the point of becoming "homeless." As one might expect, New York is the U.S. city in which the most law firms with foreign offices are located. It is home to a third of these international U.S.-based firms. (Chicago is a distant second.) The foreign city in which these law firms are most likely to be present is London, followed by Hong Kong, Paris, and Tokyo.[36]

Of particular relevance to our interests here, the GaWC research group studied sixty-nine major multinational firms in four sectors: law, advertising, accounting, and banking and finance. Within each of the four sectors, cities were given scores ranging from 0 (no office was present) to 3 (meaning it was the corporate headquarters). Intermediate scores (i.e., 1 or 2) reflected the size and importance of nonheadquarter, affiliated offices. Summing across all sectors, city scores ranged from 0 to 12 (i.e., scores of 3 on each of the four sectors). Cities in the three highest categories—involving scores of 12, 10, and 9 (no city had a score of 11)—are presented in Table 4.5.[37] Only four cities had perfect scores (i.e., 12), and they are the same cities that were found at or very near the top of all of the previously considered world economic indicators. Most of the cities in the second and third groups (i.e., scores of 10 and 9, respectively) are also in familiar positions on global economic hierarchies. The GaWC research group's findings also suggest a fourth tier of cities with significant numbers of global service firms, but fewer than those noted in Table 4.5. Included in the fourth tier are Brussels, Madrid, and Washington, D.C.

The importance of basing ratings on multiple indicators is reinforced by the observation that some cities that scored highly on the other economic measures did not score highly on service firm locations. Especially notable is Osaka, the sight of a major stock exchange and home to a concentration of the world's largest banks. Its service firm score is only 6, however, putting it in a category that includes Jakarta, Prague, Santiago, and a number of other cities that do not score highly on any world economic indicators. If one relied solely upon the GaWC index, the international economic standing of Osaka would be seriously underestimated. That is also true for other cities, such Stockholm (which scored 5, even lower than Osaka). On the other hand, several cities had much higher scores on this linkage measure than any other economic indicator.

THE ECONOMIC HIERARCHY

Our objective now is to combine the four specific indicators discussed in this chapter into a single index that can be used to describe the global urban eco-

TABLE 4.5   Cities with Highest Concentrations of Global Service Firms

Service Firm Scores	Cities
12	London, New York, Paris, Tokyo
10	Chicago, Frankfurt, Hong Kong, Los Angeles, Milan, Singapore
9	San Francisco, Sydney, Toronto, Zurich

nomic hierarchy. Any city's score on this composite index may be interpreted as providing the best measure of that city's place in the global hierarchy. To combine indicators it is helpful to assign numerical values to the cases (i.e., cities) because they can readily be added. We will proceed by assigning a score of 10 to cities that were placed at, or near, the apex of any indicator. Cities in the next highest group will be given a score of 7, and cities in the third tier will be given a score of 4. Those other cities noted in addition to the leading cities will be given a score of 1. To illustrate, Table 4.1 described the location of the world's largest stock exchanges. New York, in the highest category by itself, receives a score of 10 on this indicator. Frankfurt and three other cities in the second rung each receive a score of 7. Hong Kong is the first of five cities in the next category, and each of them receives a score of 4. Finally, Chicago, Madrid, and Sydney were noted as three cities with sizeable stock exchanges, but below the leading cities included in Table 4.1. Each is given a score of 1. This is, of course, an arbitrary set of numbers. One could just as readily assign cities scores of 80, 40, 20, and 10, for example, or 4, 3, 2, 1. It is important, therefore, not to exaggerate the significance of small differences between cities' scores.

Table 4.6 presents, in column one, all the cities among the world's leaders on any of the economic indicators discussed in this chapter. The next four columns present all of the cities' scores on each of the indicators. (A dash indicates that the city was not among the world leaders on that indicator.) The final column shows the total scores on the composite index.

New York (with a total of 40) has the highest score. It could be placed alone at the apex because it was the only city that received the maximum score on every indicator. On the other hand, the difference between New York and London, Paris, and Tokyo, all of which had scores between 34 and 37, may be too small to treat as significant. Therefore, an equally plausible argument could be made for placing these four cities in the same category and regarding all of them as the leading cities in the global economy. The latter interpretation, as noted in the introduction to this chapter, is what most analysts have done. It was behind this top group that we saw a lack of consensus. Indeed, we noted that the different indicators employed here sometimes produced very different rankings. Frankfurt, with a score of 28, has the next highest score on the composite index. It seems too far behind the leading cities to be included with them in the top category. On the other hand, there are no cities immediately behind it. Thus, Frankfurt is a unique economic center in a class by itself, but closer to the top category than to the group below it.

Below Frankfurt, with composite scores of 15 or 16, are four cities that may be regarded as comprising the second tier of cities in the global economy. Included here are Chicago and Osaka, historically "second cities" in their nations, and Hong Kong and Zurich. Then there are six cities with scores between 8 and 12 that may be considered tertiary cities in the global economy. This category includes Los Angeles, Milan, Munich, San Francisco, Singapore, and Toronto. The entire hierarchy is summarized in Table 4.7.

At the bottom of the hierarchy are seven cities with scores of 4 or 5. All of their scores are primarily due to the fact that they housed significant numbers

TABLE 4.6 Global Cities Composite Economic Index

City	Stock Exchanges	Banks and Financial Institutions*	Multinational Corporations	Services Firms	Total
Amsterdam	—	1	4	—	5
Beijing	—	7	—	—	7
Brussels	—	—	—	1	1
Chicago	1	4	4	7	16
Dusseldorf	—	1	4	—	5
Frankfurt	7	10	4	7	28
Geneva	—	1	—	—	1
Hong Kong	4	—	4	7	15
London	7	10	10	10	37
Los Angeles	—	—	4	7	11
Madrid	1	—	—	1	2
Milan	4	—	1	7	12
Montreal	—	—	4	—	4
Munich	—	4	4	—	8
New York	10	10	10	10	40
Osaka	4	7	4	—	15
Paris	7	7	10	10	34
Rome	—	—	1	—	1
San Francisco	—	—	4	4	8
Seoul	—	—	4	—	4
Singapore	—	—	4	7	11
Stockholm	1	—	4	—	5
Stuttgart	—	—	4	—	4
Sydney	1	—	—	—	1
Taipei	—	—	4	—	4
Tokyo	7	10	10	10	37
Toronto	4	—	4	4	12
Washington, D.C.	—	—	—	1	1
Zurich	4	4	4	4	16

of multinational corporations. This was the "weakest" of the four indicators in that more of the cities in Table 4.6 received a positive score for multinational corporations than for any of the other indicators. Only six of the twenty-nine included cities failed to receive any points for multinational corporations, and five of the six were among the cities with the lowest scores on the composite index. Thus, we can surmise that housing multinational corporations may often be the first step toward becoming an economically important global city. The indicator with the next greatest number of positive scores is the location of professional services firms, and it would make theoretical sense to think of a progression in which cities become entry-level nodes in the global economy by virtue first of housing multinational corporations, and that these corporations

TABLE 4.7 The Global Economic Hierarchy

Score	City
40	New York
34–37	London, Paris, Tokyo
28	Frankfurt
15–16	Chicago, Hong Kong, Osaka, Zurich
11–12	Los Angeles, Milan, Singapore, Toronto
7–8	Beijing, Munich, San Francisco
4–5	Amsterdam, Dusseldorf, Montreal, Seoul, Stockholm, Stuttgart, Taipei

then attract professional service firms, thereby enhancing the global significance of the city.

In Chapter 7 we will present a different composite index based on whether the world's cultural industries are headquartered in a city. In Chapter 8, the economic hierarchy presented here and the cultural hierarchy presented in Chapter 7 will be compared, and it will then be possible to further differentiate among global cities according to whether they house economic or cultural concentrations, or both.

In addition to thinking about global cities arranged in an economic hierarchy, it is important to conceptualize them as a network within which information is exchanged, funds flow, and personnel are transferred. The relationships among many of these global cities is so well established that one city could drop out of the loop without necessarily disrupting the entire system because firms and activities located in other cities can be utilized as equivalents. The best case in point was provided in the immediate aftermath of the terrorist attack on the World Trade Center in New York. The large banks and specialized services firms that had been housed in the Twin Towers before September 11, 2001, were suddenly paralyzed. Many had satellite offices in other U.S. cities, such as Boston and Washington, but instead turned to their affiliates in London.

The investment firm of Cantor Fitzgerald, for example, was missing two thirds of its New York staff in the week following the terrorist attack. Its communication lines were also severed. (Those lines had been used to price over half of all trades in U.S. government bonds.) At the London office of the firm, employees worked around the clock for a week until they had Cantor Fitzgerald's electronic trading platform running smoothly. Traders and investors faced a time-zone gap as a result of New York's absence, though. In response, London employees extended their shifts until midnight, local time, when their colleagues in Tokyo could then take over (midnight in the United Kingdom is 9 A.M. in Japan). Thus, around-the-clock trading in securities was quickly reinstituted.[38]

POSTSCRIPT: SEPARATING PRODUCTS AND PLACES

Multinational corporations are, as we have seen, cornerstones of the world economy. The concentration of their headquarters in select cities contributes to a global structure in which wealth flows to the cities (and nations) at the top of the hierarchy, while influence and control emanate down. However, many multinationals have gone to great lengths to obscure their headquarters location in order to present themselves as "local"; in other words, to be seen as "genuine" parts of every place they are sold. The result is that people's mental images often do not correspond with the underlying economic structure.

We can begin with the obvious point that the products of large multinational corporations are necessarily "foreign" in most of the countries in which they are consumed. In order not to appear foreign, home corporations often attempt to identify their products with local icons. That is designed to increase sales, of course, but blending also helps to insulate the company from nationalistic backlashes against foreign domination. In advertising its beer products in the United States, for example, London's Diageo Corporation has often pictured their Guinness beer in the hand of the Statue of Liberty. To illustrate further, consider corporate advertising at Expo 2000, held in Hanover, Germany, in June 2000. As a World's Fair, the Expo had exhibits from many nations, but not from the United States. The U.S. Congress forbade the use of government funds, so the U.S. commissioner for the fair tried unsuccessfully to raise private funds for an American pavilion. U.S. corporations simply refused to contribute to a national site at the fair because they did not want to be associated with any particular nation. Coca Cola, for example, contributed $5 million in return for rights to advertise using the Expo logo, but did not want the logo to be connected to an American flag or under the roof of a building associated with the United States.[39]

When multinational corporations are able to separate their products from their locations in people's minds, the result is an amorphous conception of commodities that are not identified with real places or with the underlying interurban economic structure. A suggestive study of this effect was reported by Roper Polling in 1999. In thirty nations, representative samples of people were first asked to rate which products were best from among a large number of international brands that included Disney, McDonald's, Mercedes, Sony, and more. After people identified which they thought were best, the pollsters asked them the country with which they associated the best product. Most interesting from our perspective is the finding that nearly half of all the international respondents stated that the best brands did not belong to any country—they were simply regarded as global products, lacking any national connection. Among younger, better educated, and more traveled respondents, the percentage of respondents that tied the best products to the world rather than a specific nation was over 50 percent.[40]

CASE STUDY: McDONALD'S

McDonald's Corporation, headquartered in suburban Chicago, leads the world in number of franchises. Its golden arches may be the most widely recognized corporate icon in the world. For that reason, McDonald's could be a frequent target of antifranchise, anticapitalistic, or anti-American demonstrations. The "anti" sentiments are widespread, but do not lead to mobilization until they are galvanized. An interesting example is provided by the French farmer who led a group of protestors in an attack on a local McDonald's restaurant. Prior to mobilizing a band of followers, he had no organization, few long-term allies, and no real long-term strategy. However, his criticisms of McDonald's tapped into a widespread antagonism to the franchise in his country once he represented it as an agent of external intrusion ("McDomination") and many French citizens began to agree that fast food—both in its preparation and consumption—was decidedly out of place in their culture. One sociologist equated people's embarrassment at being seen coming out of a McDonald's in France with being "caught leaving an X-rated movie" in the United States.[41]

During the farmer's trial, thousands of supporters showed up: teenagers with green hair, middle-aged men with ponytails, and retirees, many wearing T-shirts with the slogan, "The world is not merchandise, and I'm not either."[42] This is the kind of mobilization—cutting across age, class, and lifestyle lines—that multinational corporations may most fear, and it provides an important part of the explanation for why corporations have often gone to great lengths to make themselves less conspicuous. The sporadic protests in France notwithstanding, McDonald's has been highly successful at blending with local settings.

The twenty-four McDonald's restaurants in India provide a good illustration of how the corporation weaves itself into any milieu. Most of the population in India is Hindu, hence they hold cows to be sacred and condemn their slaughter. Because they would never eat the meat of a cow, it is difficult to sell hamburgers in India. The restaurant's solution was the "Maharaja Mac," made of chicken and mutton. In every McDonald's in India a sign is posted stating, "No beef or beef products sold in this restaurant."[43] At the new McDonald's in Delhi, the Maharaja Mac is now popular with Indians on their way to the Taj Mahal. Once this flagship sandwich becomes connected in people's minds with an authentic aspect of local culture (such as the Taj Mahal), the blending is complete.

However, the McDonald's in the former Yugoslavia must surely provide the most dramatic example of how a corporation can fit in anywhere and become part of local culture. During spring 1999, American planes and bombs were conspicuously involved in NATO air strikes on parts of former Yugoslavia. (The bombing was designed to stop Serbian atrocities.) When air raids began, McDonald's franchises in Belgrade and other cities were vandalized by nationalistic protesters who smashed windows and scribbled insults on walls. The restaurants were targeted because they represented a conspicuously American icon. Even though every one of the franchises in the former Yugoslavia was entirely owned by McDonald's, the local head of operations launched a successful strategy to get Serbs to view the company as their own. Toward this end, the restaurants closed for a few days while they redesigned the familiar golden arches logo to include the traditional Serbian cap over one of the arches, and this redesigned logo was set against the colors of the Serbian flag. McDonald's printed thousands of banners and lapel buttons with the new logo and distributed them when the restaurants reopened.

As the NATO bombing continued, McDonald's passed out thousands of free cheeseburgers to the participants at anti-NATO rallies. They convinced Serbs that—in relation to bombs falling from the sky—they were all in the same boat. Hence, McDonald's was as Serbian as the dinar people used to pay for their fries. At McDonald's headquarters in suburban Chicago, a spokesperson argued that the local strategy should not be interpreted in national or international terms because it was the plan of the Yugoslav manager who was "functioning as a hamburger guy and not as a politician."[44]

NOTES

1. Brian J. Berry and John D. Kasarda, *Contemporary Urban Ecology* (New York: Macmillan, 1977).
2. Saskia Sassen, *Cities in a World Economy* (Thousand Oaks, Calif.: Pine Forge Press, 2000).
3. I have adopted this example from Chase-Dunn et al. They pose it as question at the beginning of their paper, however, while I have presented it as a statement, indicated by their results. See Christopher Chase-Dunn, Yukio Kawano, and Benjamin D. Brewer, "Trade Globalization Since 1795," *American Sociological Review*, 65, no. 1 (2000):77–95.
4. In addition to describing international financial markets, an insightful application of microsocial theories to the interactions among these electronically connected traders is presented in Karin K. Cetina and Urs Bruegger, "Global Macrostructures," *American Journal of Sociology*, 107(2002):905–50.
5. Janet L. Abu-Lughod, *New York, Chicago, Los Angeles: America's Global Cities* (Minneapolis: University of Minnesota Press, 1999). For further discussion of the limitations of demographic measures, see David A. Smith and Michael Timberlake, "Cities in Global Matrices," in *World Cities in a World System*, ed. Paul L. Knox and Peter J. Taylor (Cambridge: Cambridge University Press, 1995), 79–97.
6. Peter Hall, *The World Cities* (London: Werdenfeld and Nicolson, 1966).
7. John Friedman, "The World City Hypothesis," *Development and Change*, 17(1986): 69–84.
8. John Friedman, "Where We Stand: A Decade of World City Research," in *World Cities in a World-System*, ed. Paul L. Knox and Peter J. Taylor (Cambridge: Cambridge University Press, 1995), 21–47.
9. Figures from Sassen, *Cities in a World Economy*.
10. Klaus R. Kunzmann, "World City Regions in Europe." in *Globalization and the World of Large Cities*, ed. Fu-chen Lo and Yue-man Yeung (Tokyo: United Nations Press, 1998), 37–75.
11. For example, corporate services include finance, already included in banking, but three other specialized services are also included in this category (law, accounting, and advertising). So, the measures are only partially redundant.
12. Masahiko Honjo, "The Growth of Tokyo as a World City," in *Globalization and the World of Large Cities*, ed. Fu-chen Lo and Yue-man Yeung, 109–31.
13. For recent figures on market capitalization, see "Floating in the Air," *The Economist*, 26 May 2001, p. 11.

14. Janet Lippman Abu-Lughod, "Comparing Chicago, New York and Los Angeles," in *World Cities in a World-System*, ed. Paul L. Knox and Peter J. Taylor (Cambridge: Cambridge University Press, 1995), 171–91.

15. For further discussion, see Alfred Lewis and Gioia Prescetto, *EU and US Banking in the 1990s* (London: Academic Press, 1996).

16. Edmund L. Andrews, "Swiss Acquirer Has Had Plenty of Its Own Problems," *New York Times*, 13 July 2000, p. C4.

17. Sassen, *Cities in a World Economy*.

18. Laura M. Holson and Andrew R. Sorkin, "Telecommunications Powerhouse," *New York Times*, 13 December 1999, p. C10.

19. Leslie Wayne, "Elder Bush in Big G.O.P. Cast Toiling for Top Equity Firm," *New York Times*, 5 March 2000, p. 1.

20. Timothy L. O'Brien with Raymond Bonner, "Jury Charges 3, One a Bank Aide, in Russian Case," *New York Times*, 6 October 1999, p. A1. Edwards and her husband were also accused of looting assets from a now-defunct Russian bank by systematically transferring funds from that bank to BNY. Bloomberg News, "Bank of New York Suit Revived," *New York Times*, 15 January 2002, p. C7.

21. Jeff Gerth, "Under Scrutiny: Citibank's Handling of High-Profile Foreigners' Accounts," *New York Times*, 27 July 1999, p. A6.

22. Data on financial institutions are from Thompson/Polk, *Bank Industry Statistics* (Skokie, Ill.: Thompson Financial Publishing, 1998). Data on banks are from Sassen, *Cities in a World Economy*.

23. This information, and the following, about Diageo Corporation is taken from its *1998 Annual Review* (London: 1999). As of the summer 2001, Diageo was in talks to sell its nonbeverage holdings and purchase other companies in the beverage industry. However, its holdings were as presented here in summer 2002.

24. See the annual *World Investment Reports* prepared by the United Nations Conference on Trade and Development. Geneva: United Nations.

25. All figures in Table 4.3 are from Leslie Hannah, "Survival and Size Mobility among the World's Largest 100 Industrial Corporations, 1912–1995," *American Economic Review*, 37(1998), 19–31.

26. United Nations Conference on Trade and Development, *World Investment Report* (Geneva: United Nations, 2002).

27. John Tagliabue, "Volvo Buying Renault Truck and Bus Unit for $1.5 Billion," *New York Times*, 26 April 2000, p. C4.

28. International Finance Corporation, *Foreign Direct Investment* (Washington, D.C.: World Bank, 1997).

29. "World Investment Report 1997," *Transnational Corporations*, 6, no. 2(1997): 127–69.

30. *1999 Fortune Global Five Hundred*; (2000) New York: *Fortune* and Grazio Ietto-Gillies, "Different Conceptual Frameworks for Internationalization," *Transnational Corporations*, 7, no. 1(1998):17–39.

31. Klaus R. Kunzmann, "World City Regions in Europe," in Lo and Yeung, *Globalization and the World of Large Cities*, 41.

32. Saskia Sassen, "On Concentration and Centrality in the Global City," in Knox and Taylor *World Cities in a World System*, p. 63.

33. Sassen, "On Concentration and Centrality." These employment figures are for producer service firms, which also includes insurance and real estate.

34. Stuart Elliot, "Advertising," *New York Times*, 10 September 1999, p. C4.

35. This view is presented by David Meyer, "World Cities as Financial Centres," in Lo and Yeung, *Globalization and the World of Large Cities,* 410–32; and Sassen, "On Concentration and Centrality."

36. J. V. Beaverstock, Peter J. Taylor, and D. R. F. Walker, "United States Law Firms in World Cities," *Urban Geography,* 21(2000):95–119.

37. Peter J. Taylor, D. R. Walker, and J. V. Beaverstock, "Introducing GaWC," in *Global Cities: The Impact of Transnationalism and Telematics,* ed. Saskia Sassen (Tokyo: United Nations University, in press).

38. Suzanne Kapner, "Wall Street Runs Through London," *New York Times,* 26 September 2001, p. C1.

39. Roger Cohen, "A World's Fair Beckons; the Superpower Declines," *New York Times,* 29 May 2000, p. A4.

40. Diane Crispell, "McWorld?" *Public Perspective,* 12, no. 1(2001):18–21.

41. Suzanne Daley, "French See a Hero in War on 'McDomination'," *New York Times,* 12 October 1999, p. A4.

42. Ibid.

43. On the other hand, some critics insist that McDonald's will always represent "American patterns of consumption" and that its food will remain "Un-Indian." Nevertheless, there were twenty-four McDonald's in India at the end of 2000, and a total of eighty were planned. Luke Harding, "Lunch in India: A Big Mac, But Hold the beef," *Journal Inquirer,* 20 December 2000, p. 21. (Scripps Howard News Service, published in Manchester, Conn.)

44. Robert Block, "How Big Mac Survived NATO's Attack on Yugoslavia," *Wall Street Journal,* 3 September 1999, p. 3.

FIVE

Inequality

Since the 1980s, when studies began systematically to try to catalog the distinguishing features of global cities, one of the most emphasized characteristics has been differences in the wealth of the highest and lowest segments in these cities. Some analysts designated it income inequality while others referred to it as class polarization, but all were offering essentially the same diagnosis. After several decades in which the middle class had grown substantially, especially in the most economically advanced nations, observers believed it might be receding and that the highest and lowest classes were expanding. As a result, they hypothesized that the overall distribution of wealth, or income, in the global cities might be moving toward the shape of an hourglass. Friedmann and Wolff, in one of the earliest studies, used the metaphors of the "citadel" and the "ghetto" to describe the expanding classes at the top and the bottom.[1] They selected terms with an ecological referent to highlight the fact that they were not only describing strata within a hierarchy, but groupings that were segregated spatially from each other as well.

If the hypothesis about increased inequality being a concomitant of global city development turns out to be correct, it would portend serious future difficulties because inequality eventually results in multiple social and political problems. When there is a high degree of inequality in a city or nation, it can be difficult to maintain civic order and security, seek justice, provide needed welfare, and so on.[2] Of course there is nowhere, other than a fanciful utopia, in which everyone has the identical amount of whatever it is that people value. Some difference is ubiquitous. It is a high degree of inequality that creates special problems, as described later in this chapter's case study of São Paulo, Brazil.

In the following pages we will examine income inequality in both global cities and in nations. Although our primary interest is in cities, it is important to consider nations also because some of the inequality in any city is a result of national policies. The degree to which access to education is left to the marketplace, for example, will have a profound effect on opportunities for intergenerational mobility throughout a nation. The regressiveness of the nation's income tax and whether it similarly taxes wages, profits, and capital gains, to illustrate further, will have a large bearing on differences in everyone's net income. Inequality within nations and their cities will almost necessarily be correlated as a result of these national policies, but dynamics within cities can exacerbate or mitigate the income differences. From a measurement standpoint, however, it does not matter whether one is focusing on cities or nations. The techniques utilized to measure income inequality are the same.

MEASURING INCOME INEQUALITY

Inequality could pertain to any of the things that people value: wealth, prestige, power, and so on. If one wishes to compare cities or nations, however, it is best if whatever is selected can be measured in standardized units. That favors the use of income, which is probably why most of the comparative studies of inequality focus on it (or on earnings). Fortunately, other differences of potential interest—in people's health, life expectancy, educational opportunities, and so on—all tend to correspond closely with income inequality. Therefore, even though most of the studies we will review focus on income, their findings are suggestive with respect to other dimensions of inequality.

Despite its advantages, the use of income as an indicator is not without problems. The first issue to consider concerns the appropriate unit of analysis. Income is typically accumulated and spent on a family or household basis. There are strong reasons, therefore, to examine families or households—but which? While the two categories are often identical, they can diverge based on the definition of family that is utilized in a nation at any particular time. People of the same sex could always constitute a household, for example, but there are differences, over time and across societies, in whether they are officially considered a family.[3] Still further complexities are introduced if type of family, or life-stage, is considered. With the identical income, for example, a retired couple on Medicare with a paid-for home is probably much better off than a young, newly married couple. And a good deal of the income inequality in modern nations is a result of the growing difference between affluent dual-earner families and other types of families, such as single-parent and children households, adult child and widowed parent households, and the like.[4]

Regardless of whether the focus is on households or families, it is also important to take the size of the unit into account. If seven people have to live on an annual income of $20,000, they are probably a lot worse off than two people who live on the same amount. For this reason most studies calculate an average per person by dividing the total household income by the number of people in the household. For the calculation to be precise, one must assume that all members of the household have equal access to the household income, and that is unlikely, especially regarding children. In many societies, women are also disadvantaged with respect to access to household income, regardless of their age and marital status. Nevertheless, the average often seems to provide a workable estimate and it is preferable to ignoring household size.[5]

Still other studies do not place individuals into households or families. Instead, they divide some measure of a nation's wealth—such as gross domestic product, the value of all goods and services it produces—by the total number of people, or the number of adults in the labor force, to arrive at a per capita figure. Because calculations of inequality in different nations or cities are often based on different assumptions with respect to all of the issues mentioned, one must be cautious in making comparisons, and it is usually best not to attribute much significance to small differences.

Two principal statistics are used to measure income inequality among households, families, or individuals. The measures could be used to describe levels of inequality within cities, urban places, or any other geographical unit, but many more studies have focused on nations rather than cities (yet another indication of the world's attachment to the nation-state as a political form). The two most widely used statistics that measure income inequality are percentile shares and the Gini index. The calculation of each is described next, and both statistics are presented for a sample of twelve nations (circa 1996) in Table 5.1.

The percentile shares approach notes how much of an entire nation's income is associated with various deciles (tenths) or quintiles (fifths) of the population. If wealth were exactly evenly distributed, then each 10 percent (i.e., decile) of the population would possess exactly 10 percent of the total wealth. These figures are illuminating, but interpreting percentile shares can be cumbersome. Using deciles of the population, for example, would require examination of data for ten deciles to describe the entire society. Therefore, only the top and bottom deciles (or quintiles) are frequently presented, as in Table 5.1,

TABLE 5.1   Inequality Within Nations

Nation	Share of Income		Gini Index (%)
	Lowest 10%	Highest 10%	
Algeria	2.8	26.8	35.3
Brazil	0.8	47.9	60.1
China	2.2	30.9	41.5
Ghana	3.6	26.1	32.7
Honduras	1.2	42.1	53.7
India	4.1	25.0	29.7
Indonesia	3.6	30.3	36.5
Mexico	1.4	42.8	53.7
Russian Federation	1.4	37.4	48.0
Sweden	3.7	20.1	25.0
United States	1.5	28.5	40.1
Zambia	1.6	39.2	49.8

both for convenience and because deviations from equality are most likely to be pronounced at the top and bottom.

To illustrate how to interpret the figures in Table 5.1, consider the case of Brazil. The decile shares in column two indicate that its poorest 10 percent have less than 1 percent (i.e., 0.8 percent) of the nation's wealth. That is over twelve times less than they would have if there were no inequality. In contrast, the highest 10 percent of Brazil's population (column three) owns nearly half (47.9 percent) of all the income, which is almost five times more than would be expected in a completely equal distribution.

Remember also that inequality pertains to shares of income in various segments, and not to a nation's absolute wealth. To see the difference, think of each nation's wealth as a pie and suppose that each pie was cut into eight equal pieces. As a percentage of the pie from which it was cut, each slice would be the same, but if the circumference of one pie was larger than the other, a one-eighth slice from it would also be larger. Thus, even though the lowest decile in Mexico and the United States are seen in Table 5.1 to have similar shares of their nations' income (1.4% and 1.5%, respectively), the lowest decile in the United States has more income than its Mexican counterpart due to the greater wealth of the United States.[6]

The second statistic to measure income inequality is the Gini index, and its advantage is that it provides a single figure as a summary of how income is distributed among individuals, households, or families. The larger the value, the more uneven the distribution of income. The Gini index is typically expressed as a percentage that can vary from 0 (completely egalitarian) to 100 percent (one household, for example, has all of the society's income). Both extremes are really hypothetical because in actual societies Gini coefficients are rarely lower than 20 percent or higher than 60 percent.

The one-figure summary of the Gini index is convenient, though it does not disclose whether any degree of inequality is due more to the absence of wealth at the bottom, a concentration of wealth at the top, or the share of the middle classes. Thus, compare Sweden and Ghana in Table 5.1: the Gini index for Sweden is much lower, even though the lowest decile's share of wealth in both societies is almost the same (3.6 and 3.7). This suggests that Ghana's higher Gini index may be due to a greater concentration of wealth at the top, and that is borne out by the fact that the highest decile in Ghana does have a larger share of national income than its Swedish counterpart (26.1 vs. 20.1).

INEQUALITY IN GLOBAL CITIES

The expectation that inequality would increase within global cities was based largely on the presumed effects of labor force changes. John Friedmann and Saskia Sassen, whose influential early writings on global cities have been described in previous chapters, each focused on how increased inequality was a product of the distinctive labor forces of world cities.[7] And because global cities have globally oriented labor forces, occupational and earnings distributions are similar among them. Therefore, if inequality is a function of the composition of the labor force, all the global cities should have about the same degree of inequality—unless their cultural traditions make a difference.

The demands of global markets and the ethos generated by the occupational structure associated with globalization appear able to erode cultural traditions. Sweden's commitment to equality and welfare capitalism is instructive in this regard. To minimize inequality, Sweden historically maintained a variety of government and corporate policies, such as a prohibition on layoffs under normal circumstances. However, Sweden's major city, Stockholm, became headquarters for multinational corporations that became important instruments of change. Once the corporations had more employees outside than inside of their home nation, it put pressure on the Swedish government to permit firms to be more flexible in hiring and firing, promoting, and so on. The alternative usually threatened by the corporations was more foreign expansion, meaning less employment and tax revenue for Sweden. Some accommodations were forthcoming. Full-time employees remain protected from layoffs, for example, but the government permits the hiring of temporary workers, who have no such protection. By the start of the twenty-first century, Manpower, Inc., had 6,000 employees in Stockholm, and local temp agencies had thousands more.[8] Sweden's new entrepreneurial and deregulated culture, espoused by the Central Employers Association, publicly declares that generous welfare benefits, large public sector employment, and minimal inequality—the historic hallmarks of Sweden's welfare capitalism—are things of the past: "the 'Swedish model' is dead."[9]

Sweden's experience resembles that of many nations. Vying with each other to retain multinational corporations or lure those headquartered elsewhere into relocating, nations try to make themselves more attractive to these firms, which typically involves deregulation.[10] Thus, as the global reach of multinationals lessened the control of their home nations and increased internation competition, nations responded paradoxically by further relinquishing control.

The Dual-Service Sectors

With respect to labor forces, the global cities tend to contain the two fast growing, extreme poles of the service industries: the low-status end (fast food workers, janitors, security guards, and so on) and the high-status end (lawyers, computer programmers, accountants, and so on). Demand for the high-status service positions remained strong because of the growth of multinational business and financial services corporations in the global cities. The lawyers, executives, accountants, and the like were indispensable to corporate offices that were the command centers of global operations. Competition for scarce professionals with the requisite qualifications assured their high incomes.

The high-status service cohort, as discussed in Chapter 2, generates demand for low-status service workers. Studies in several metropolitan areas reported that increases in high-status producer service positions were associated with increases in permanent, full-time, extremely low-wage service jobs.[11] Some of the low-end jobs involve personal or household services provided to high-end, two-career families (jobs as nannies, cooks, and the like). Other low-end positions involve corporate employment (in maintenance or security, for example). However, the demand for low-status service workers has not translated into high wages because of the abundant supply of available labor (majority and minority women, immigrants, and racial minorities). Because the pool of labor that qualifies only for the low-end service positions disproportionately consists of people who tend to receive lower wages, even when they do the same work as majority males, the wages paid to the low-status service workers are especially low. Differences between the top and bottom segments of the labor force are therefore exaggerated.

Washington Post columnist David Broder saw the inequality generated by the two types of service positions in human terms when he met striking janitors outside a large office building in downtown Los Angeles. The janitors were picketing to back their demands for a $1 per hour raise. At the time (spring 2000), they were paid between $7 and $8 per hour by a producer services firm to clean office building bathrooms after most of the employees had gone home for the night. Each of the top executives whose facilities they cleaned was on average making well over a million dollars per year, or as much as about a hundred janitors. One question this raises is: How does that magnitude of difference affect interaction between people? Or, as Randall Collins asks about all abstract models of stratification, how do the hierarchies play out situationally?[12] An answer came one evening when a colleague of Broder's watched a late-working male executive walk into a just-cleaned bathroom without in *any* way acknowledging the female janitor who stood there with her equipment cart. "Whole human beings can be rendered invisible."[13]

While the top and bottom poles of the occupational hierarchy were expanding, the middle was contracting. In postindustrial societies, many middle-income positions—from factory workers to managers—lost relative income, security, or both. Massive layoffs became commonplace in occupations where they had previously been rare. In just over a two-year period at the start of this century, for example, Ericsson (a Swedish firm that makes wireless network equipment) reduced its workforce from 107,000 to 65,000, and Lucent Technologies (a U.S. company that makes telephone equipment) reduced its workforce from 106,000 to 50,000.[14] In both firms, most of those who lost their jobs were technicians, clerks, lower and middle managers, and the like. Cutbacks in these realms have made it difficult for many families to maintain middle-class lifestyles, even with two (or more) wage earners.

Metropolitan Area Profiles

Susan Fainstein has reviewed several published and unpublished studies of inequality in many of the leading global cities and their suburban regions, and

summarizes that research as supporting many, but not all, of the original inequality hypotheses.[15] The most consistently congruent finding concerned the
top group's increasing share of national wealth. Less consistent was the diminution of the middle class, and the growing poverty of the bottom group, although
widespread, was not always due to the growth of low-end service positions. Because results varied somewhat from place to place, it is best to begin with brief
summaries of inequality patterns in several of the leading global cities.

London Studies that focused on the distribution of household income showed
a marked tendency for polarization between 1979 and the mid-1990s. Studies
that examined individual earnings showed a similar trend, but it was less pronounced because only the household data could show the effects of multiple
wage earners in some households versus none in others. (Relying on household
data was similarly found to magnify inequality indices in Paris and other
global cities.)

The most marked change during this time period was in the group at the
top. For example, the number of people in London whose incomes in 1993
would have put them in the highest income quarter in 1979, adjusted for inflation, increased fifteen-fold. In terms of quintile shares, the highest 20 percent
increased its percentage of London's wealth from 26 percent to 33 percent.
(Neither the rate of increase in the number of people at the top nor their share
of wealth was as large in the rest of Britain, outside of London.)

As anticipated, the increased share of the top quintile in London was due
in large measure to the gains of professionals, managers, and others in the high
end of the service category. The expected increase in the number of low-status
service workers did not occur, though; their relative size, in fact, slightly declined in London. The bottom segment became increasingly made up of people
excluded from the labor force (i.e., nonemployed) and their share of the wealth
declined. In sum, there was greater polarization in London, but due only in part
to growth at the high and low ends of service occupations.

New York During the 1980s and 1990s, the bottom quintile's share of New
York's income, while always small, nevertheless fell markedly. In 1979 the lowest 20 percent of the metropolitan area's residents had a 4.9 percent share; by
1997 it was only 2.3 percent. The top quintile, in contrast, during the same time
period, increased its share from 44.6 percent to 56.1 percent. Much of the top
group's gains were at the expense of the middle class, and especially the lower
middle class, many of whom became "the working poor."

Census figures for New York City, published after Fainstein's summary,
compared the late 1990s to the late 1980s and showed that the percentage of all
families with children living below the poverty line in New York increased
from 29 percent to 32 percent. Especially surprising was the increase in the proportion of household heads in the below-poverty households who had completed at least some college; this segment more than doubled, to 23 percent.
There were also sharp increases in the proportion of below poverty families

with two parents, at least one of whom was working. In other words, these were people who, until the 1990s, would have been considered safe as far as the risk of living in poverty was concerned. They worked as security guards, warehouse personnel, janitors, cashiers, and so on, but they could not earn an adequate living. The problem, according to the author of the New York study, was that "we are telling people to climb out of poverty on a downward-moving escalator."[16]

The growth of poorly paying, low-status service jobs provides part of the explanation for the increased polarization in metropolitan New York. However, Fainstein notes that the bottom quintile's loss of income was also due in large part to city, state, and national welfare "reform" and retrenchment, and this reduction in benefits was not connected to globally induced changes in the city's labor force.

Tokyo Over the past two decades there is evidence of somewhat increased inequality, especially in central Tokyo rather than the larger region. The underlying cause follows the original hypothesis, namely growth in the top and bottom sectors of the service economy while mid-level jobs were declining. Some differences in the computation of statistics make it difficult to compare overall inequality in Tokyo to most other global cities; but it appears that even in central Tokyo inequality remains lower than in the global cities in most other nations, even though it is higher in Tokyo than it was in the past.

In Japan, a progressive income tax and steep inheritance taxes have for many years been intentionally utilized to level incomes. In addition, corporate policies of lifetime employment with small wage differentials tied to seniority also suppressed income disparities. Several of Japan's largest multinational corporations innovated changes, however, when they found it difficult to attract professional people whose talents were in short supply. The firms argued that they could not adhere to traditions if they were to compete internationally. At Sony Corporation in Tokyo, for example, despite some grumbling within the employee ranks, management more closely linked pay to performance and wage differentials increased. Management shrugged off the criticism with the explanation, "It is dictated by the market."[17]

In neighborhoods within central Tokyo a similar "revolution" has been occurring among small businesses that were passed on from generation to generation. The "mom and pop" convenience stores and small restaurants that maintained customers through long-term personal relations and found ways to share markets with each other have in recent years been confronted with an influx of domestic and foreign chains, like 7-Eleven and Starbucks. The franchises aggressively market their products and offer discounts and sales to attract more customers. This business style is foreign to the owners of the small independent shops, which have been unable to compete. By the spring 2002, six to twelve shops per month were changing hands in central Tokyo neighborhoods where one or two changes annually were typical just a few years earlier.[18] As a result, there are more employed, low status clerks and fewer middle class owners.

In sum, increased inequality occurred within the leading global cities discussed here, plus several others, providing clear support for the centerpiece of the theory. There was also a strong tendency for the top segment's share of the wealth to expand along the hypothesized lines. Changes in the middle and lower groupings were only partially congruent with the theory, though. Specifically, while the share of the middle class did tend to constrict, it was often not sufficient to produce the hourglass distribution associated with extreme polarization, and the decreasing share of the wealth in the bottom segment was due as much to their exclusion from the labor force as to underpayment in low-end service jobs.

Before leaving the issue of inequality within global cities it is important to further reflect on the impact of fertility differences. As noted, when inequality within global cities was examined at the household level, Gini indexes or disparities in percentile shares were usually more pronounced than when individual earnings were examined. Class-related fertility differences are the main reason the income gaps are larger at the household than individual level. Further insight into how birth rate differences affect household income is provided by two Swedish researchers, Bjorn Gustafsson and Mats Johansson, who examined inequalities in sixteen economically advanced nations. Although the study examined differences within nations rather than global cities, the sample type does not alter the principle to be deduced from the researchers' analysis.

Gustafsson and Johansson found that differences in inequality within the sixteen nations were associated with a number of globalization-related variables, such as the decline in manufacturing positions and the percentage of the labor force that was unionized. They also found that the proportion of the population under age fifteen was an important variable, even after all other economic and labor-force variables were held constant. The greater the relative number of youngsters, the greater the degree of income inequality.[19] The researchers explained that when there were more young people, the fiscal resources of families had to be split more ways, reducing everyone's share of the household income. In addition, because higher birth rates are associated with reductions in women's labor-force participation, the high birth rates in the lowest segments result in fewer working women able to contribute to family incomes. At the same time, lower birth rates in the upper segments translates into more labor-force participation by women, enhancing their household income and thereby further increasing income differences between the top and bottom groupings. (Later in the chapter we examine how inequality on a global scale, that is, across nations, is also increased by class differences in fertility.)

SPATIAL REFLECTIONS

Global city analysts have long assumed that increased economic inequality would have spatial consequences; that is, vertical economic polarization would be reflected in horizontal spatial segregation. The bottom segment in many global cities combines minority status and low income. These two characteristics interact, especially where housing is concerned. Studies in several major U.S. cities indicate that when minorities (who are frequently African in origin) are also poor, there is a tendency for their residential segregation to be greater than would be expected based solely on race or income alone.[20] This same pattern also appears to be common in large cities outside of the United States, and is particularly apparent in the development of housing complexes, such as Les Bosquets, on the outskirts of Paris. This high-rise complex is home to thousands of black residents, originally from former French colonies in Africa and the West Indies. It is a uniformly poor area, with unemployment at about 50 percent, lacking in recreational amenities, and suffering from high rates of crime and delinquency. It is also socially isolated from the rest of the city; for example, despite the city's extensive subway system, the closest commuter train into the center of Paris is a twenty-minute bus ride away for residents of Les Bosquets.[21]

The wealthiest segments of global cities also tend to be separated from the rest of the metropolitan area, though their separation (often symbolized by gates and guard houses at the entrances to their communities) is intentional. Even in London, where different social classes have historically been less widely dispersed than in many other global cities, the wealthy have tended to cluster in particular sections of particular boroughs, remaining apart from other classes.[22]

Across all of the standard metropolitan areas in the United States, Craig St. John found that the greater the degree of overall income inequality, the higher the rate at which high-income whites live in neighborhoods of concentrated affluence. He defined such neighborhoods as those in which at least half of all residents' incomes are at least four times greater than the poverty level for a family of four. (In 1999, for example, that poverty threshold was $17,029. So, in 1999, the affluence cutoff would have been $68,116.) Given the high inequality that is characteristic of global cities, one would therefore expect to find highly concentrated affluence in their suburbs. Indeed, four of the nation's five highest rates of concentrated affluence were in suburbs of New York; the one not in metropolitan New York was in suburban Chicago.[23]

Because there are relatively few moneyed black households, St. John notes, they cannot readily form enclaves segregated by race and class. In order to live in an affluent neighborhood, privileged black families must often live in predominantly white communities. Therefore, for high-income nonwhites, the probability that they will live in an affluent neighborhood is a function of the degree to which well-off black households are not segregated from well-off white households in their metropolitan area.

The growing polarization of income and space in U.S. cities is viewed with alarm by the Fannie Mae Foundation. This private agency, which supports housing-related research and urban renewal, contends that various forms of segregation in urban areas will increase unless the trend toward greater income inequality is reversed. The prosperous elite may further isolate themselves in gated suburban communities and the affluent living in central cities may (as described in Chapter 2) continue to use special tax districts and the privatization of public services to isolate their gentrified neighborhoods from the ghettos that surround them.[24] Thus, the Foundation fears that income disparities will lead urban life to further evolve into a patchwork of increasingly separate and isolated social spaces.

CASE STUDY: SÃO PAULO

São Paulo, Brazil, is an especially interesting city because economically, among urban areas in the latter half of the twentieth century, it was probably the most upwardly mobile; that is, it moved further than any other urban area from the periphery toward the center of the world economy. São Paulo became a notable, if not leading, global city. However, its economic gains were accompanied by a stretching of the already large differences between the city's rich and powerful residents and its poor and powerless ones.

Through the 1980s, Brazil experienced high inflation and struggled with a large foreign debt. The International Monetary Fund and the World Bank provided Brazil with about $50 billion in loans during the 1990s, but they required that the government begin to privatize almost all sectors of the economy and that the privately owned firms operate without subsidies or protective tariffs. Government divestment had an almost immediate impact on São Paulo's financial services sector as new foreign owned banks opened in the city's financial district. In addition, substantial shares in established São Paulo banks were purchased by banks headquartered in Austria, New York, Switzerland, and other foreign countries. Some officials expressed concern that too much of Brazil's banking was foreign owned, and that these corporations would not consider Brazil's interests when they made financial decisions. However, the former president of Brazil's central bank shrugged off the criticism and attributed it to local bankers' desires to avoid competition. "Ask the consumer if he prefers a foreign or Brazilian bank," the ex-president stated, and the consumer will tell you, "the one which provides the best service."[25] In the global marketplace, this banker believed, efficiency was the only criterion.

Those segments that became most able to compete internationally benefitted from Brazil's post-1990 movement to a market economy, while those that were most dependent on the constraints of the traditional economy were adversely affected. To illustrate, Lorenzo Bertini once owned a profitable factory in São Paulo that produced artificial flowers for domestic consumption. As the government's tariffs on imported artificial flowers fell from 73 percent to 16 percent, Bertini slowly reduced his number of employees from 120 to 10. He explained the effect of the tariff reduction by asking, "You know how a wave wipes out a castle made of sand?"[26] In 1996, Bertini finally closed his doors for good, and his factory became another of the many in São Paulo to be abandoned in the 1990s.

About half of the population of São Paulo lives in desperate poverty as a result of scarce regular employment and meager welfare benefits. The many years in which São Paulo neglected its poorest neighborhoods, combined with the steady incoming streams of poor migrants, resulted in a large percentage of the population living in extremely substandard housing. The poorest of the poor—an estimated 10 percent of the city—live in concentrations of tiny shacks lacking both electricity and running water, with make-do roofs that do not keep out the rain. Another 25 percent are estimated to live in "corticos": old dwellings subdivided into small cubicles to house forty to fifty families, all of whom share a single bathroom and kitchen.[27]

The unregulated growth of these self-constructed shantytowns near the city's reservoirs has lead to a high level of pollution in the three major rivers and the reservoirs that provide water to São Paulo. During the winter months, when there are usually heavy rains, these rivers and reservoirs are prone to flooding, and it is the city's slum dwellers who are most affected because many of them live in low-lying sections—areas considered unsuitable for housing by people who are better off.[28]

Families in these lower class enclaves push thousands of children into the streets of the city. Some are banished by parents who cannot afford to keep them, others choose to leave, finding the street better than a crowded shack with an abusive parent. They are joined on the street by children from rural areas, who are lured to São Paulo by promises of a better life, but instead wind up homeless. On the street, the children get by however they can: by begging for food, robbing tourists and each other, mugging commuters, selling drugs, becoming prostitutes. A 1997 survey conducted by the University of São Paulo estimated that there were 4,500 homeless children on the streets of São Paulo, 85 percent of whom used drugs, 86 percent of whom were sexually active, and the number of street children infected with the AIDS virus was increasing by 30 percent each year.[29] Until 1990, "death squads"—typically comprising off-duty policemen—beat and murdered street children with impunity. To São Paulo's upper classes, the street children were a menace, and they (at least implicitly) supported the death squads. Over the past decade, however, there has probably been some decline in violence against street children as a result of 1990 legislation and subsequent monitoring of death squads by church organizations.[30]

Prior to the government's divestment, many white-collar, middle-class jobs were in government-run phone companies, banks, railroads, and so on. These jobs offered security, good benefits, and opportunities for upward mobility. However, private management resulted in substantially reduced workforces. Hundred of thousands of clerks and managers lost their jobs. Middle-class unemployment increased, as did under-employment (i.e., people working part-time rather than full-time or at positions for which they are overqualified). In the long term, new positions that offer middle-class amenities may be created, but, in 2000, the largest purely private employer in São Paulo was MacDonald's. The demand for jobs comparable to those previously available is illustrated by the way people responded to an advertisement by a large bank that was still run by the government. The ad announced that over the next few years the bank would offer 10,000 entry-level jobs with benefits and that it would begin to accept applications right away. Within a few weeks the bank received nearly a million applications.[31]

At the top of São Paulo's social scale is a wealthy elite. They stroll down Rua Oscar Freire, São Paulo's most elegant mile of boutiques, to shop for the latest fashion from New York, Milan, and Paris. In Brazil, the wealthiest 10 percent of the population owns nearly 50 percent of the nation's wealth. The wealthy mostly live in communities of concentrated affluence, such as Alphaville, an enclave that is entirely surrounded by an electrified fence and patrolled by a private security force numbering over 1,000. Many in this elite group are top executives of multinational corporations; others are venture capitalists, investing in the high-tech sector emerging in São Paulo; and some possess hereditary wealth. They are an "affluent few in a sea of poverty" that circumvent São Paulo's crowded and sometimes dangerous streets by flying helicopters to their high-rise offices, their beach homes, even to religious services.[32] At any time of day, hundreds of privately owned helicopters fly above the buses and cars that jam São Paulo's streets and freeways.

Because of an increase in kidnapping and mugging by small gangs that roam São Paulo's streets, local newspapers and magazines warn those who cannot afford a helicopter against driving flashy cars, and recommend varying the route taken between office and home. Nevertheless, at least 251 people are known to have been kidnapped for ransom in São Paulo in 2001. The city became the "kidnapping capital," according to a professor at the University of São Paulo because of the pronounced income inequality: "the excluded are no longer willing to be docile while an elite enjoys the fruits of a globalized economy."[33]

GLOBAL INEQUALITY

We have reviewed a substantial amount of research showing that growing inequality within global cities is due, at least in large measure, to the concentration of multinational corporations that produce a labor force characterized by dichotomized service positions. However, the inequality that has been generated within the global cities is only part of a much larger story. The multinational corporations that are headquartered in these cities reach around the world: extracting natural resources, setting up subsidiaries, and employing cheap labor. Some analysts are convinced that the international operations of these firms have also increased inequality in two other ways:

1. within other nations that are linked via investments from multinational corporations headquartered in global cities,
2. between the rich and poor nations of the world.

We will review the evidence for each contention separately.

Inequality Within Nations

An optimistic view of the future of nations with high levels of inequality, like Brazil, is that disparities will be reduced as foreign investments help the countries modernize their economies. In the past, analysts have observed some tendency for inequality initially to increase as a nation's economy develops, then to level off and eventually decrease. The pattern resembles an inverted "U", originally described by economist Simon Kuznets, and frequently referred to as the Kuznets curve. At the same time, there is a good deal of variation in the paths nations have followed, especially in the recent global era. Therefore, although the inverted "U" describes a historically common pattern, it provides only a rough approximation for many contemporary nations.[34]

Direct evidence of the effect of global investment flows on inequality within nations comes from an analysis of eighty-eight diverse nations, between 1967 and 1994, reported by Alderson and Nielsen. Their objective was to assess whether Foreign Direct Investment (FDI) inflows had an impact on inequality when other potentially confounding variables (such as birth rate, school enrollment, region of the world, and so on) were held constant. Alderson and Nielsen found that it did. When they subsequently looked only at the wealthiest nations, foreign investment's impact on inequality disappeared, but its effects remained strong in the other nations. Thus, inflows of foreign investment, one of the major ways in which economically less developed nations are attached to the global economy, add a significant boost to the level of income inequality in these nations.[35] The dependence on foreign capital seems to boost inequality because it is associated with the presence of foreign multinational corporations. These companies pay relatively high wages to select segments of the host nation's labor force—those who have the requisite financial, legal, computer, or other skills. Meanwhile, the other jobs in these nations provide limited earnings for everyone else.

This pattern creates a quandary for government officials trying to promote their nation's economic development without increasing inequality. On one hand, if the nation attempts to distance itself from the world system, it is difficult to find alternatives to a continuation of stark poverty. It is not easy indigenously to create well-paying jobs. There is also some evidence to suggest that the economies of economically less developed nations that are more open to foreign trade grow faster than those that are closed to trade.[36] On the other hand, if these nations are receptive to multinational corporations, external trade, and outside capital, they may face the prospect of foreign domination and greater inequality. The dilemma is clearly illustrated in Manila, the capital of the Philippines, a city with a metropolitan population of over 9 million people.

About a third of the nation lives in poverty, surviving on $1 per day or less. Thousands of Filipinos have emigrated, many to the United States, in search of better opportunities. Many of those people who remained moved from rural villages to Manila, believing the urban area offered better prospects, but there were few good jobs to be found. One site that has attracted thousands of the poorest Filipinos is a shantytown with the anomalous name Promised Land. It is, in fact, a mountain of garbage: 5 stories high, covering 74 acres, produced by the 10,000 tons of trash from Manila that are dumped there every day. The poorest migrants in Manila, often working in family units, comb through the refuse looking for plastic bottles, cardboard boxes, broken toys, and the like. They sell whatever they find to local middlemen who work out of the Promised Land. It is a foul-smelling, illness-infested place to work, and dangerous to boot, because mountainous piles of trash and waste periodically collapse. The worst collapse to date occurred in July 2000, when as many as 800 adults and children may have perished in a particularly ferocious landslide (the many never-recovered bodies made an exact count impossible). The day after the avalanche, even as rescue workers were searching for survivors, the scavengers were back at work. "They had no choice. They had to live," explained the priest who served the shantytown.[37]

A few miles away from the Promised Land, at the former Clark Air Base outside of Manila, is the America Online (AOL) service center. When AOL subscribers in most of the world, including the United States, have a technical problem or a question about their bill, they go online to this service center, not realizing they are connected by fiber-optic cable under the Pacific Ocean. The AOL center employs 900 young Filipinos. Their jobs pay triple the minimum wage (which is what most employees at local firms earn), plus they receive health benefits and free Internet phone and Web access (valued benefits because many employees do not have phones at home). There is a long waiting list for these jobs. Those people who have them feel fortunate and consider the jobs a ticket to a better life. *New York Times* columnist Thomas L. Friedman talked with the AOL employees and suggested that the people who regularly demonstrate against globalization and multinational corporations listen, too. "Yo, protesters!" he wrote, "Ask the Filipino techies what they think about globalization. . . . Trust me, you've got mail."[38]

We conclude our discussion of within-nation inequality by examining the consequences of foreign investments for the cities and nations from which they emanate. A major claim associated with trade unions and the political parties with which they are allied has been that Foreign Direct Investment (FDI), especially involving manufacturing, has been funneled from high-wage to low-wage nations. Inexpensive employment in the recipient countries has expanded, as a result, while the absence of domestic investment has resulted in fewer manufacturing jobs in global cities and their nations. The rebuttal, from investors, large corporations, and the political parties allied with them, has stressed that deindustrialization in economically advanced nations actually began ten to fifteen years before FDI increased in the early 1970s. The loss of factory jobs was, therefore, destined to occur anyway.

In a direct assessment of FDI and manufacturing employment, Arthur Alderson has shown that an increase in outward FDI, by itself, significantly accelerated the decline in manufacturing employment in the United States, the United Kingdom and sixteen other nations that formerly had high levels of manufacturing employment. Focusing on the 1968 to 1992 time period, Alderson found that the greater the volume of investment flowing outward from these nations, the more employment in domestic factories declined. Alderson was sensitive to the fact that some decline in factory jobs was going to occur anyway over this quarter century as mature economies entered a postindustrial era. How much of the labor-displacing effect attributed to FDI was exaggerated as a result? To reflect on this question Alderson tried a hypothetical statistical experiment. He began by noting that the average employment in manufacturing among his sample of countries declined by 8.7 percent between 1968 and 1992. Next, Alderson removed the effects of FDI from his analytic model and noted that the average number of industrial jobs would still have fallen by 5.8 percent. Thus, about two thirds of the manufacturing employment that was lost would still have been displaced, even if there were no FDI outflows during the twenty-five-year period.[39]

It must be emphasized that the imaginary experiment, while instructive, is hypothetical. In addition, even if only about 3 percent of the lost manufacturing employment is properly regarded as an FDI casualty, that still translates into thousands of jobs in hard-hit nations, such as Australia, Belgium, Sweden, the United Kingdom, and the United States. The service economy that expanded as manufacturing declined in the formerly highly industrial nations tended, as we have described, to offer high-end and low-end jobs. Overall, the people that had been recruited into factory work had limited formal education, but respectable working and middle-class lifestyles, with union benefits, were still possible with most industrial employment. However, this segment of the population could usually qualify only for the low-end positions in the new service economy, so they could not duplicate the relatively high wages associated with the disappearing manufacturing jobs. The result: greater levels of income inequality within the deindustrializing nations, and their global cities in particular.[40]

The effects of these changes in employment on inequality in the United States are illustrated in Figure 5.1. Note that the Gini index hovered in a narrow band between the late 1940s and the early 1980s, then it began a steady increase. In the United States, greater inequality was due both to a decreased share for the lowest quintile and an increased share for the highest quintile.

Inequality Across Nations

Prior to examining inequality *across* nations, it is important to note it is quite different from inequality *within* nations. Across, or between, nation analyses focus on how much divergence there is among the averages of different nations. How each nation's income is internally distributed is not assessed. Given this difference in how the two types of inequality are examined, it should be apparent that they do not necessarily follow the same trends. To illustrate, consider the hypothetical possibility that for a period of twenty years inequality decreased within every nation, but to varying degrees. The nations would be more different from each other at the end of this twenty-year period than at the

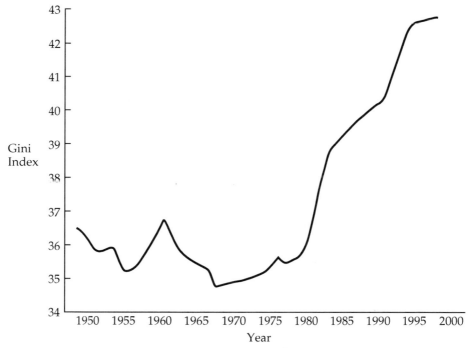

Figure 5.1   Income Inequality in the United States.[41]

onset because of their uneven rates of change. Thus, there would be greater inequality across nations, even though inequality fell within each of them.

We begin by noting that different rates of economic growth that accumulated over several centuries have resulted in enormous differences between the wealthiest nations and the poorest ones. By the close of the twentieth century, people in the wealthiest nations, such as the United States and Japan, had average per capita annual incomes that were well over $20,000. In the poorest nations of the world, most of which were in Africa, per capita annual incomes were no more than about $500.[42] Our central question concerns the effects of globalization over the last decades of the twentieth century: Did the growth of multinational corporations, FDI, and external trade (all of which mushroomed in the closing decades of the twentieth century) further increase inequalities across nations?

Most writing on globalization's effect have followed either of two different perspectives. The first emphasizes convergence. As espoused by officials of agencies such as The World Bank and International Monetary Fund, and by some social scientists, the wealth of all nations will rise as their ties to the world economy are strengthened. The superiority of the wealthiest nations, according to this view, has been based primarily on technical and administrative expertise. By connecting more closely to the world economy, the formerly less wealthy nations will more rapidly assimilate the technological and administrative abilities they have lacked, and their income and that of the wealthier nations will converge. The alternative perspective stresses divergence. It was initially derived from World System Theory, which assumed that the wealthy nations that controlled the capitalistic world economy would continue to exploit the economically less developed nations by paying meager wages to their labor forces to enhance profits, by paying less than their natural resources were worth, and so on. The more the poorer nations engaged in these inherently unequal exchanges, the worse off they would likely become.[43] Thus, in 2002, when the leaders of the wealthiest nations convened a conference in Monterrey, Mexico, to address inequality, protesters outside the meeting were cynical. One involved student summed up the protesters' view when he said the differences between rich and poor countries were growing. To reconcile the divergence the student believed he was observing with the pious statements of world leaders, he concluded that, "The conference is theater and the actors are the presidents of the developed countries."[44]

A good deal of data were assembled that initially appeared to provide support for divergence rather than convergence views. For example, increased divergence was indicated by calculations of each nation's gross domestic product (GDP), the value of all goods and services it produces, on a per capita basis. Using this measure, almost none of the twenty poorest nations in the world,

Figure 5.2 The annual meetings of the World Trade Organization and the International Monetary Fund have been routinely disrupted by demonstrators. (Pictured are demonstrations in Washington, D.C., in 2000.)

around 1960, improved much during the rest of the century, and some actually declined. In contrast, over the same time period, wealth on a per capita basis grew in the twenty wealthiest nations. The per capita GDP of the twenty wealthiest nations doubled relative to the twenty poorest between 1960 and the late 1990s; specifically, the wealth ratio increased from 15:1 to 30:1.[45]

However, comparing changes in inequality across nations is complex, and investigators' methodological decisions can have a substantial effect on their findings. The most consequential decision is whether or not to weight nations according to their population size. When studying the world, with its units defined as nations, a case could be made for treating each nation the same, mirroring, for example, their equality as nations in votes of the U.N.'s General Assembly. Alternatively, differences in nations' size could be taken into account by weighting each according to share of the world's population. If nation A is fifty times larger than nation B, then the contribution of nation A to inequality in the world is calculated to be fifty times greater than nation B's.

There is no absolute rule concerning whether the nations included in a sample ought to be weighted. It depends, at least in part, on an investigator's theoretical framework. If the nations in a sample are thought to represent the people of the world, then weighting them by size would seem important. If, on the other hand, the nations are regarded as depicting the universe of nations, then it might seem more important to include large and small nations, wealthy and poor ones, but conceptually it would seem less imperative to weight them by size.[46]

Whether nations are weighted has enormous consequences for the conclusions studies reach. Specifically, increased inequality across nations is only likely to be observed if samples of nations are not weighted.[47] The reason, according to Firebaugh, is that the slower population growth of the wealthy nations offsets the income divergence that was generated by uneven rates of economic growth. Suppose population growth rates had not varied among nations, Firebaugh speculated, and to pursue the possibility he statistically removed dependents from within the nations in his sample and looked only at income per worker. This eliminated most of the children under age fifteen, seen to be an important antecedent of inequality *within* nations in the preceding analysis. Following this statistical modification, the increase in inequality across nations that had been observed when they were not weighted disappeared. Firebaugh concluded that "per capita income ratios *are* diverging, but the divergence is *population induced* . . . from the . . . more rapid population growth of poorer nations."[48] Thus, higher fertility rates are strongly implicated in increased inequality both within nations (where lower segments are poorer because of their higher birth rates) and across nations (where poor nations are made poorer by their high birth rates).

INEQUALITY CONCLUSIONS

What has happened to inequality in the world, regardless of whether it arises from nations' internal distributions or the divergences across nations? Has the global economy, and all that entails for cities and nations, led to an increase in *total* inequality? An answer to these questions comes from an analysis of ninety-three nations reported by Brian Goesling. Using data from the World Bank, Goesling was able to compare and combine the effects of the two types of inequality between 1980 and 1995. He reported that total inequality decreased during the time period because the differences across nations (weighted by population size) decreased. The magnitude of that decline was moderate, about 18 percent. Goesling also found, as did the studies reviewed here, that inequality within nations increased substantially, by about 40 percent. However, total inequality is about three times more dependent on across-nation than within-nation differences. In other words, across-nation inequality indexes are about three times larger in size than within-nation inequality indexes. Therefore, a modest decline in across-nation inequality was sufficient to more than offset a substantial increase in within-nation inequality.[49]

For anyone concerned with the magnitude of inequality in the world, Goesling's findings present a quandary. The global economy has apparently reduced inequality across nations. In this respect, it has acted just like advocates of free international trade though it would, and it has generated a modest push toward convergence. For the future, as nations become more strongly linked to the global economy, one may optimistically project that the inequalities across them will continue to decline. At the same time, however, globalization appears to have been associated with markedly increased inequality within nations. If that pattern continues—and it certainly may, given the rather robust increases that occurred over the last decades of the twentieth century—then many nations will face a daunting set of intractable predicaments. And the most intense social problems will be especially likely to occur where the inequalities are greatest: the global cities.

APPENDIX

The World Bank and International Monetary Fund

A number of supranational organizations have been explicitly created to try to manage the world economy. Two are of special importance here. The first is the Bank for Reconstruction and Development, which is actually one of several banks that comprise The World Bank Group, but it alone is typically referred to as the World Bank (TWB). The second is the International Monetary Fund (IMF). Established in 1945 and headquartered in Washington, D.C., the IMF and the TWB are among more than a dozen specialized, self-governing agencies associated with the United Nations. Countries affiliate with (i.e., support and oversee) these sister lending agencies on a voluntary basis, entirely separate from their membership in the United Nations. Each of the agencies has a board, representing member nations, and it appoints directors who manage day-to-day operations.

The primary missions of the IMF are to facilitate international trade and assist member nations when they face short-term balance-of-payment, or cash flow, problems. In addition to money, the IMF provides technical support and advice. That is also true of TWB in conjunction with its primary objective (to further economic development). In recent decades, this has frequently involved helping formerly socialist or communist nations make a transition to "free market economies" (i.e., capitalism) and addressing problems such as poverty and disease in nations that are sometimes termed "developing," but that the bank tends to describe as not yet integrated into the world economy.[50]

For people who think that global economic interdependence has gone too far and is destroying trade unions, promoting sweatshops, degrading the environment, and leading to greater inequality among and within nations, these agencies (along with the World Trade Organization) are the most visible culprits. As a result, when the directors of these agencies have met in recent years there has usually been some type of large-scale demonstration at the meeting site. In September 2000, in Prague, for example, thousands of demonstrators forced the annual World Bank–IMF conference on aid to close ahead of schedule. Protesters in downtown Prague smashed the glass storefronts of franchises such as Kentucky Fried Chicken and Dunkin' Donuts. About a hundred people were injured in two days of skirmishes between protesters and police. One demonstrator, wearing a black mask and preparing to run into a line of police, explained, "To fight them for me is symbolic of fighting the IMF."[51]

The standoffs between police and demonstrators can be seen as a microscopic reflection of a north–south division of the world. Working closely with TWB and IMF has been the G-7 and G-8, affiliations of the wealthiest nations that are also the agencies' major supporters. The G-7 includes Canada, France, Germany, Italy, Japan, the United Kingdom, and the United States. The G-8 includes the G-7 plus adds Russia. Their finance ministers meet regularly to analyze the world's economic situation and to review how well the agencies are promoting economic development.

Representing the southern hemisphere, and attempting to counter the G-7, is the Group of 77. This group includes representatives of the less developed countries, mostly in Africa and Latin America, that contain nearly 80 percent of the world's population. (The group had 133 member states in 2000, but continues to refer to itself as G-77, the number of member states when the organization formed in 1964.) The G-77 complains that global economic policies, dictated by the rich nations and backed with funds from IMF and the TWB, have locked them into cycles of debt and poverty, perpetuating the differences between rich and poor nations, while forcing them to follow the dictates of these global organizations. Thus, while representatives of the G-7 generally condemn protestors for trying to disrupt TWB and IMF meetings, spokespeople for the G-77 frequently praise demonstrators for calling attention to the deleterious policies of the agencies.[52]

In return for sometimes massive loans, the TWB and IMF have generally required that nations remove most of their tariffs and subsidies to facilitate both imports and exports. In some instances that can provide widespread benefits to the population. In the Republic of Mozambique, on Africa's southeast coast, the TWB demanded that the country markedly reduce its large export tax on raw cashew nuts. Roughly 5 million small farmers grew cashews in this former British colony and, before the agency made new loans contingent on the reduction of this tax, they were pressured to sell their cashews to a small number of politically influential processing plants that were foreign owned. The export tax on unprocessed cashews had been so high that the Mozambique farmers could not sell their products on the world market. The corporations that owned the factories were economically hurt by TWB's position because they had to pay more for raw cashews after export sales became a viable alternative, and some of the 10,000 or so people who worked in the factories lost their jobs. Critics of the agency made much of its adverse effect on Mozambique's processing plants.[53] However, the costs paled in comparison to the benefits to the 5 *million* poor cashew farmers whose incomes increased as a result of TWB's action.

On the other hand, when trade barriers are removed there is often a rush of imports that leads to high rates of business failure among domestic companies who lack experience in competing with imports. Fearing this consequence, India has tried to protect many of its domestic industries, such as chicken production. American producer Perdue tried to export dark meat, which sells poorly in the United States, to India, where it is more in demand. To protect its domestic industry, however, the Indian government raised the tariff to 100 percent, effectively doubling the price of imported chicken. Perdue raises its own chickens, then takes them to highly mechanized plants where a chicken is placed on a conveyer belt, then never again touches human hands. It is mechanically plucked, boned, placed in plastic, and stamped with a retail price. One plant can process 250,000 chickens per day. By contrast, in a New Delhi slaughterhouse, one man sits and slices off a chicken's head, hands it to another who tears off the feathers, then to another who cuts it into pieces. Other workers stand by to shoo away swarms of flies. As the head of one of India's hatcheries explains, "Without the tariff, we would be in a big soup."[54]

From the perspective of the international lending and monitoring agencies, the businesses that fail when markets are opened are less efficient, hence unavoidable casualties of a nation's better integration into the world economy.[55] However, business failures and unemployment obviously exacerbate any economy's problems and often lead nations to seek repeated loans. Critics of TWB and IMF policies contend that poor nations are thereby prodded into a cycle of ever-increasing debt from which they cannot emerge. Furthermore, once their debt becomes high, the lending agencies have to provide more loans because they cannot afford to let the poor nations default. Hence, poor judgment by debtor governments and banks might actually be rewarded.[56]

On the other hand, there has been growing awareness and concern over the amount of debt that is burdening some nations. Debt relief has been a major issue of protesters at IMF and TWB meetings, and when protesters were joined by religious leaders and popular entertainers, the pressure was sufficient to push European and U.S. officials to endorse the principle of debt reduction. In 2001, they agreed to provide up to $90 billion to lessen the burden on forty-one of the most indebted nations. The amounts being considered were literally drops in a bucket because one large debtor nation, Turkey, by itself, owed $104 billion.[57]

NOTES

1. John Friedmann and Goetz Wolff, "World City Formation," *International Journal of Urban and Regional Research*, 6(1982):69–84.
2. This position is elaborated on in the essays included in Andrew Hurrell, Ngaire Woods, and R. Albert Berry, eds., *Inequality, Globalization and World Politics* (New York: Oxford University Press, 1999).
3. For a discussion of how practices differ among nations, see Anthony B. Atkinson, "The Distribution of Personal Income," in *The Personal Distribution of Income in an International Perspective*, ed. Richard Hauser and Irene Becker (Berlin: Springer, 2000), 56–71.
4. See Gary Burtless, "Effect of Growing Wage Disparities and Changing Family Composition on the U.S. Income Distribution," *European Economic Review*, 43(1999): 853–65.
5. Calculating these averages also eliminates some of the methodological problems that are created in trying to disentangle individual and group effects. This has been the approach of the Luxembourg Income Study, one of the most ambitious analyses of income inequality among nations. See Peter Gottschalk and Timothy M. Smeeding, "Cross National Comparisons of Earnings and Income Inequality," *Journal of Economic Literature*, 35(1997):633–87.
6. Figures are taken from The World Bank, *World Development Indicators* (Washington, D.C.: The World Bank, 1999).
7. For early statements of their positions, see John Friedmann, "The World City Hypothesis," *Development and Change*, 17(1986):69–84; and Saskia Sassen, *The Global City* (Princeton, N.J.: Princeton University Press, 1991).
8. Edmund L. Andrews, "Sweden, the Welfare State, Basks in a New Prosperity," *New York Times*, 8 October 1999, p. A1.
9. Gregg M. Olsen, "Re-Modeling Sweden," *Social Problems*, 43(1996):15.
10. For further discussion, see Richard J. Barnet and John Cavanagh, *Global Dreams* (New York: Simon and Schuster, 1994).
11. For further discussion of this relationship, see Saskia Sassen, *Cities in a World Economy* (Thousand Oaks, Calif.: Pine Forge Press, 2000).
12. See Randall Collins, "Situational Stratification: A Micro-Macro Theory of Inequality," *Sociological Theory*, 18(2000):17–42.
13. Quoted in David S. Broder, "Of Janitors and Billionaires," *Washington Post*, 16 April 2000, p. B7.
14. Alan Cowell, "Ericsson Battens Down Its Hatches," *New York Times*, 23 April 2002, p. W1.
15. The following profiles, except where otherwise indicated, are taken from Susan Fainstein, "Inequality in Global City Regions," in *Global City Regions*, ed. Allen J. Scott (Oxford: Oxford University Press, 2001), 285–98.
16. Nina Bernstein, "Poverty Found to Be Rising in Families Considered Safe," *New York Times*, 20 April 2000, p. B1.
17. Stephanie Strom, "Tradition of Equality Is Fading in New Japan," *New York Times*, 4 January 2000, p. A6.
18. Howard W. French, "Mom-and-Pop Stores' 'Hello' Becomes a Goodbye," *New York Times*, 26 April 2002, p. A4. To further promote an entrepreneurial culture, the Japa-

nese government reduced its progressive income tax rates and reduced its extremely high inheritance taxes, another major tool for redistributing wealth in the past.

19. Bjorn Gustafsson and Mats Johansson, "In Search of Smoking Guns," *American Sociological Review,* 64(1999):585–605.

20. For further discussion, see Camille Zubrinsky Charles, "Processes of Racial Residential Segregation," in *Urban Inequality,* eds. Alice O'Connor, Chris Tilly, and Lawrence D. Bobo (New York: Russell Sage Foundation, 2001), 217–71.

21. The political views of residents are described by Suzanne Daley, "France's Non-whites See Bias in Far Rightist's Strength," *New York Times,* 30 April 2002, p. A4.

22. See Chapter 4 in H. V. Savitch, *Post-Industrial Cities* (Princeton, N.J.: Princeton University Press, 1988).

23. Craig St. John, "The Concentration of Affluence in the United States, 1990," *Urban Affairs Review,* 37(2002):500–20.

24. Robert Fishman, *The American Metropolis at Century's End* (Washington, D.C.: The Fannie Mae Foundation, 2000).

25. Simon Romero, "Brazil Having Second Thoughts About Foreign Bank Inroads," *New York Times,* 4 January 2000, p. C4.

26. Simon Romero, "Brazil Still Embraces Globalization," *New York Times,* 2 December 1999, p. E-4.

27. Gilberto Dimenstein, *Brazil: War on Children* (London: Latin America Bureau, 1991).

28. For further information on São Paulo's water, see Celso N. Oliveira and Josef Leitmann, "São Paulo," *Cities,* 11(1994):10–14; and Milton Santos, "São Paulo," in *The Mega-City in Latin America,* ed. Alan Gilbert (Tokyo: United Nations University Press, 1996), 224–40.

29. Associated Press, *More Street Children in São Paulo,* 18 March 1997.

30. Paul Jeffrey, "Life Changes Slowly for Brazil's Street Children," *New World Outlook,* May–June, 1997, p. 8–11.

31. There is also comparable demand for unskilled labor positions. When the government of São Paulo advertised 50,000 openings for laborers to sweep streets, water public gardens, and the like, nearly a half million people applied. See Simon Romero, "Brazilians Eagerly Seek a Big Bank's Entry-Level Jobs," *New York Times,* 16 August 1999, p. C4.

32. Simon Romero, "Rich Brazilians Rise Above Rush-Hour Jams," *New York Times,* 15 February 2000, p. A4.

33. Simon Romero, "São Paulo Becomes the Kidnaping Capital of Brazil," *New York Times,* 13 February 2002, p. A3.

34. Francois Nielsen and Arthur S. Alderson, "The Kuznets Curve and the Great U-Turn," *American Sociological Review,* 62(1997):12–33.

35. Arthur S. Alderson and Francois Nielsen, "Income Inequality, Development and Dependence," *American Sociological Review,* 64(1999):606–31.

36. In fact, the economies of peripheral nations that were open to trade actually grew slightly faster than those of core nations, but these percentages can be misleading given the much smaller base of the peripheral nations' economies. See Alberto F. Ades and Edward L. Glaeser, "Evidence on Growth, Increasing Returns and the Extent of the Market," *Quarterly Journal of Economics,* 114(1999):1025–46.

37. Seth Mydans, "Before Manila's Garbage Hill Collapsed," *New York Times,* 18 July 2000, p. A6.

38. Thomas L. Friedman, "Under the Volcano," *New York Times,* 29 September 2000, p. A27.

39. Arthur S. Alderson, "Explaining Deindustrialization," *American Sociological Review*, 64, no. 5(1999):701–21.

40. This pattern is described in the United States by David Brady and Michael Wallace, "Spatialization, Foreign Direct Investment, and Labor Outcomes in the American States, 1978–1996," *Social Forces*, 79(2000):67–97.

41. Figures are from Table 1 in U.S. Census Bureau, *Income Inequality* (Washington, D.C.: Government Printing Office, revised December, 2000).

42. For a variety of statistics illustrating differences in world wealth, see United Nations Development Project *Human Development Report 1998* (New York: Oxford University Press, 1998).

43. World System Theory contended that for several hundred years a small group of nations in Western Europe (later joined by the United States) formed the core of the world economy, first as colonial powers and later as the dominant centers of world capitalism. By setting the conditions under which all nations' economies had to operate, the core was able continuously to keep the periphery (the economically undeveloped nations) engaged in unequal exchanges. The core and the periphery were the key sectors in a division of labor among nations that, once put into motion, reproduced itself over time through these unequal exchanges. Thus, once a nation was in the core or the periphery, it tended to remain within the same stratum. It was assumed by World System theorists that the newest phase in world capitalism, involving FDI, would not materially alter the worldwide division of labor among nations. Through FDI, and its consequences for the recipient nations, the core would continue to dominate the periphery. See Immanuel Wallerstein, *The Modern World-System III* (New York: Academic Press, 1989).

44. Tim Weiner, "Monterrey's Poor Sinking in Rising Economic Tide," *New York Times*, 21 March 2002, p. A8.

45. Economic Policy Group and Development Economics Group, "Does More International Trade Openness Worsen Inequality?" *Briefing Paper* (Washington, D.C.: The World Bank Group, April, 2000).

46. A second consequential decision an investigator must make concerns how to compare income across nations. To simply calculate per capita shares of GDP is not adequate because such measures do not take purchasing power into account. Therefore, most researchers agree that income must be related to purchasing power, but the knotty question concerns whether it ought to be calculated in relation to local prices or exchange-rate prices. Some researchers argue that focusing on local prices produces the better measure of people's relative well-being; others insist that it is important to take exchange rates into account because the "same" basket of goods and services does not cost the same in different nations. See Roberto P. Korzeniewicz and Timothy P. Moran, "World-Economic Trends in the Distribution of Income, 1965–1992," *American Journal of Sociology*, 102(1997): 1000–1039.

47. For further discussion of these measurement alternatives, see the commentary and debate involving Roberto P. Korzeniewicz and Timothy P. Moran, "Measuring World Income Inequalities," and Glenn Firebaugh, "Observed Trends in Between-Nation Income Inequality and Two Conjectures," in *American Journal of Sociology*, 106(2000):209–21.

48. Glenn Firebaugh, "Empirics of World Income Inequality," *American Journal of Sociology*, 104(1999):1622. For a comparison of weighted and unweighted inequality indexes see Table 2 in Firebaugh.

49. Brian Goesling, "Changing Income Inequalities Within and Between Nations," *American Sociological Review*, 66(2001):745–61.

50. These were the agencies' stated goals, as presented to the Committee on Banking, Finance, and Urban Affairs, U.S. House of Representatives, November 21, 1994. Serial No. 103–173 (Washington, D.C.: Government Printing Office, 1995).

51. Joseph Kahn, "Protests Distract Global Finance Meeting," *New York Times*, 27 September 2000, p. A8.

52. John W. Anderson, "Poor Nations' Leaders Back Washington Protesters," *Washington Post*, 16 April 2000, p. A31.

53. It is interesting to note that the Web site of one of the leading critics of the World Bank uses the Mozambique case as an example of how the bank "destroyed" the nut processing industry in Mozambique. See Paul Krugman, "A Real Nut Case," *New York Times*, 19 April 2000, p. A23.

54. Celia W. Dugger, "Market Economics," *New York Times*, 14 June 2000, p. C1.

55. Alassane D. Ouattara, "Better Integration in an Increasingly Globalized World," *IMF*, Geneva, 7 June 1999.

56. Robert J. Barro, "The IMF Doesn't Put Out Fires, It Starts Them," *BusinessWeek*, 7 December 1998:46–47.

57. Douglas Frantz, "Turkey Floats Currency, and It Falls 25%," *New York Times*, 23 February 2001, p. E1.

SIX

Global Culture and the Cultural Industries

The cultural industries are the major topic in this chapter and the next. This chapter provides theoretical background, examining culture in a world that has become increasingly global, then focusing on the cultural industries from dual perspectives: as important agents of global cultural change and as crucial parts of modern economies. This chapter also examines how mergers and acquisitions have led to entertainment conglomerates that dominate the world in sales of feature films, syndicated television shows, recorded music, books and magazines, and the like.

Chapter 7 examines how several of the most significant cultural industries became transnational in their reach and describes their headquarters concentration in global cities. The decisions made in those headquarter cities, which are at the top of the global hierarchy, have enormous consequences for people everywhere. A comparison of leading cities, based on their rankings in the cultural industries hierarchy and the previously described economic hierarchy, is presented in Chapter 8.

The cultural industries include mass media, as conventionally defined (newspapers, television, movies, and the like), plus other cultural goods (such as CD players) and cultural services (such as museum preservation or arranging live concerts).[1] These consumer goods and services are overtly intended to inform or entertain, but they simultaneously present ideas, values, and symbols. The secondary discourse imbedded within the overt content subtly conveys images about people and relationships.[2]

The cultural industries are significant sociologically because of the important part they play in establishing people's beliefs and aspirations as well as setting popular styles. The various mediums of this industry are unsurpassed in providing models and symbolic forms for people to use in interpreting the significance of public and private events in their lives and in deciphering the meaning of their social relationships.

GLOBALIZATION, CULTURE, AND IDENTITY

People from across the world are now simultaneously exposed to the same movies, music, and related products. A few years ago, when the movie *Titanic* was extremely popular, people across the world were humming the song from the movie ("My Heart Will Go On"), wearing shirts and caps adorned with the *Titanic* logo, and reading books on the making of the film and the original sinking. Despite the irony of being encouraged by a movie celebrating a naval disaster, the film led record numbers of people throughout the world to decide that cruises made the ideal vacation.[3]

To understand the full effects of the global reach of the cultural industries, it is helpful to consider two views of culture. The traditional view focuses on an indigenous "way of life" organized about symbolic classifications. Symbols, such as a crucifix or a skull and crossbones, divide the world into categories, such as sacred-profane or edible-inedible, and provide norms that guide people's behavior within these categories. According to the traditional view, the symbols more or less fit together so a culture can be a reasonably integrated whole, providing a behavioral "road map" for people who acted in accordance with cultural expectations without much reflection.[4]

During stable periods in a society, the traditional view of culture may be most applicable. However, globalization has brought change and disruption, which prompts a second view of culture, as a pastiche of information and identities that are available to people everywhere. Anthropologist Gordon Mathews describes contemporary societies as offering a "global cultural supermarket."[5] Viewing culture as a supermarket comes into play when the symbolic parts of a society no longer fit together well. A people's way of life then becomes moot. Mathews makes the point when he asks, What is Japanese culture today? He implies there is no real answer as he notes that rock musicians in Tokyo may share more in common culturally with rock musicians in Seattle than with their own grandparents.

An interesting illustration of Mathews's thesis is provided by the growth in Tokyo of a large and growing Katakana vocabulary, consisting of words imported from Western languages, especially English. A few examples include *negoshieishon* (negotiation), *intarakutibu* (interactive), and *mootaa* (motor). These words are parts of a vocabulary used almost exclusively by teenagers and young adults. In Tokyo's clothing stores that cater to young people, for example, almost everything is written either in English or Katakana. This creates a cultural gulf between age groups because most members of the older generation do not even try to understand the imported words.[6]

The juxtaposition of the traditional and supermarket views of culture is especially pronounced with regard to the shaping of people's identities. Viewed according to the traditional way of life, symbolic categories—gender, race, class, marital status, and so on—convey labels, and both the person to whom they are affixed and others respond to the labels in the same way, thereby establishing social identity. Thus, a person may think of himself as a young, married, middle-class man, and others may similarly regard him. How people think about themselves and their relationships to others are not open to much negotiation. People may hardly be aware of, or consider, alternatives. The supermarket view, by contrast, presents people with an array of possible choices concerning the values they want to live by and the identities they wish to cultivate. As people within the same society take different paths, culture as a coherent way of life becomes unrecognizable.

The capacity of the global media to penetrate traditional cultures and create changes that set groups of people apart from each other is clearly reflected in African conceptions of beauty. Voluptuousness has traditionally described the ideal black woman in Africa. In southwestern Nigeria, for example, brides to be were sent to "fattening farms" before their weddings. At the same time, in Lagos, Nigeria's major city, people were seeing an American model of beauty from American movies and television shows on M-Net, the satellite channel from South Africa. In Lagos in 2001, when selecting Nigeria's representative to the Miss World Contest, the judges chose a slender woman, 6 feet tall, who looked—to the dismay of some Nigerians—like "a white girl in black skin."[7] When the contestant went on to win the Miss World Contest, however, her televised victory promoted a new slender image of the ideal African woman among teenage girls in Lagos. Like their counterparts in Western cities, Lagos girls vowed to exercise and diet to emulate the new symbol of beauty.

We must emphasize, however, that choices from the cultural supermarket are not entirely unrestricted. As Mathews comments, people who are more affluent, better educated, or live in a large city have more access to the cultural items offered in this modern supermarket. At an opposite pole, consider women in lower (i.e., scheduled) castes in villages in rural Indian districts. The lack of technology in their village limits their exposure to the global media, and their subordinated status restricts their access even to the limited items that may be available. The women also lack the social space in which to explore alternatives and, in any case, there are few significant others they could approach to validate new identities.[8] Regardless of social stability or change, culture is always more of a global supermarket for people in privileged positions.

Tool Kits and Toggle Switches

As a general rule, how much cultural components (such as the cultural industries) influence people's actions and values may be a function of the degree to which society is experiencing rapid and widespread social changes. When profound transformations are unsettling people's lives, Ann Swidler writes, they are most likely explicitly to seek symbols, rituals, and guides to action from the cultural repertoire. The past few decades have involved particularly significant transformations in the way work, gender, and family have been organized, and the incursions of the global economy have sometimes dramatically altered traditional ways of life. We would expect, as a result, that people in societies undergoing significant changes would be particularly reliant on the cultural

industries to construct new styles or strategies of action, to decide which rituals and beliefs were still relevant to their lives, and to determine which objectives remained worth pursuing. Viewed in this way, Swidler proposes that
culture (and the cultural industries) provide a kind of "tool kit."[9]

The question that arises next concerns how to reconcile the metaphor of the
tool kit with the influential image of classic theorist Max Weber. Writing nearly a
hundred years ago, Weber proposed that culture be regarded as a "toggle switch"
or a "switchman" that could alter the direction and rate of societal change. Weber
employed this parable to express the capacity of ideas or values to guide the
bearing of social change, even when its impetus originated in the economic
realm. He wrote, "ideas have, like switchmen, determined the tracks along which
action has been pushed by the dynamic of interest."[10] This is, of course, a highly
abstract argument. A more concrete illustration is provided by a recent study reported by Inglehart and Baker, who examined changes in sixty-five highly diverse societies between 1981 and 1998. They found a direct correlation between
changes in the economies of nations and differences in the modernity of their citizens' values and beliefs. As nations became wealthier, more people expressed
tolerance of criminals and homosexuals, and more people supported women's
rights and other modern values. Despite the pervasive changes that appeared to
be economically driven, however, the cultural heritage of nations continued simultaneously to shape its citizens' values. In nations with a Protestant heritage,
for example, people continued to be more tolerant and modern in their values
than in historically Catholic or Orthodox nations, even when each nation's degree of economic development was held constant. Thus, traditional values continued, independently, to guide the rate of change that occurred in societies.[11]

In examining Weber's use of the toggle switch metaphor, Judith Blau points
out that Weber believed the ability of culture to influence social change was
most pronounced when there were discrepancies or inconsistencies among the
ideas and world views people held.[12] Such contradictions are, of course, most
likely to arise during periods of great flux, when people are exposed to a diversity of ideas and values, none of which seems unambiguously legitimate.
The ongoing tool kit role of culture may, therefore, be supplemented by the
toggle switch function when traditional cultures are transformed into global
supermarkets.

ROOTLESSNESS VERSUS MULTIPLE IDENTITIES

Some analysts are highly critical of societies offering people opportunities to
shop in a global supermarket because it connotes a separation of identity and
place. These observers note that people were once locally attached. Approximately two generations ago (circa 1940) in cities, the media most important in
people's daily lives—newspapers and radios—were primarily local in ownership and coverage. They provided their audience with an immediate sense of
place and helped to make the local area salient to people. Being a New Yorker
or a Parisian mattered to people's sense of self.

The contemporary social world as cultivated by the global media, in contrast, does not provide its audience with much sense of place. Rather, it is a world imagined by people who are moving—as tourists, immigrants, exiles, and guest workers—or who hold fantasies of moving. They are the engineers from India living in Houston, the refugees from Sri Lanka working in Geneva, the college students in Boston waiting to graduate so they can move to London. Much of the world's population (or at least its more privileged segments) has as a result become essentially rootless, comprised of people who see themselves as citizens of the world rather than as belonging to any one place.[13]

Most of these world citizens spend a great deal of time in the commercial habitations "imagineered" by the cultural industries: in front of a television screen or in a mall, movie theater, or fast food restaurant. What are they doing and thinking? According to Benjamin Barber's observations, these world citizens are absorbed in the images on a screen, buying some licensed product, or thinking about a promotion for a movie tied to the fast food franchise in which they are eating. They spend much less time involved with a community service center, library, or other local facility that could promote an attachment to a real place. So, Barber concludes, they are "inhabiting an abstraction. Lost in cyberspace."[14]

A decline in attachment to communal and civic groups was at the heart of the thesis put forward by political scientist Robert Putnam in his critique of the postindustrial United States. Americans have become, he claimed, less likely to join the Elks or the Masons, a PTA, labor union, or bowling league. Putnam entitled his essay "Bowling Alone" to capture the trend toward social isolation he was trying to describe.[15] In major media centers there seemed to be a lot of support for Putnam's ideas, which were widely disseminated. However, a good deal of survey data pertaining to the entire nation suggested that people might actually have become more inclined to join communal groups and civic associations than in the past. How can the divergence be reconciled? An interesting perspective came from journalist, Nicholas Lemann, who was mulling over the heated controversy that Putnam's essay provoked. This journalist had lived in a number of different types of cities, from Austin, Texas, to Washington and Boston, and he related Putnam's descriptions to his own experiences. Lemann wrote that he found social life in the more global cities to be highly constrained; community meant a professional peer group, not a neighborhood. "To people living this kind of life," the journalist wrote, "the 'bowling alone' thesis makes sense, because it seems to describe their own situation."[16] So, as with most postmodern trends, global cities may be ahead of the curve on social isolation.

An unlikely source of support for Putnam's contention comes from anecdotal observations by the owners of funeral parlors, some of whom have noticed changes in people's commitments as reflected in epitaphs, specifically in the items the deceased want included in their obituaries. One funeral parlor owner remarked on how times had changed in this regard when he noted that in the past, people "joined organizations and got involved," and their obituaries acknowledged the importance of their membership in the Lions Club or a bowling league.[17] Now it is media figures, chat rooms, and Web sites to which people are attached. Correspondingly, people are asking to be remembered in new ways: as fans of professional and college sports teams, for example, even if the team played hundreds of miles from their home and they were connected to the team only via the media (e.g., watching games on television).

The rootlessness of people "lost in cyberspace," according to critics, creates more demand for popular programming that is severed from any real locale, which further erodes place attachments. The tendency for popular movies, television shows, and the like to explicitly situate their programs in specific places that provide the names for the series or films is not really a contradictory force because these local setting are typically portrayed in a selective way that makes them look and feel like everywhere else; hence, nowhere. The irony is that television series such as *Boston Public, NYPD Blue,* or *Providence* could be filmed anywhere—and they are, in fact. Many of the street scenes portrayed in episodes of *NYPD Blue* were actually filmed in Toronto, Canada.

Multiple Identities

On the other hand, to attribute contemporary rootlessness to the global media may involve seeing only a small part of the larger picture. Most urban analysts would probably agree that the decline of distinct neighborhoods and associated place attachments actually began with the development of modern cities—decades before the media became global. In rural areas a variety of activities encouraged or facilitated social bonding: common harvesting, for example. In addition, there were limited friendship choices in the countryside; that is, people either chose their neighbors as friends or no one. In cities, by the middle of the twentieth century, there were many more alternatives and basic activities, such as work, were typically removed from neighborhoods. Thus, entire cities or metropolitan areas became modern communities, in a sociological sense, and component neighborhoods lost some of their significance as places of attachment.[18] Globalization, from this perspective, merely extended a trend that actually began decades earlier.

Furthermore, to assume that being a New Yorker, a Parisian, or the like no longer matters to residents of these cities is almost surely an exaggeration. A dramatic counterexample is provided by the 10,000 travelers who were stranded at the Vancouver, B.C., airport on September 12, 2001. That was the day after the New York World Trade Center attacks, and most air traffic was grounded across North America. Complete information about the catastrophe, for those who understood English, was available to the people stuck in the airport from CNN and Vancouver newspapers. However, even English-speaking travelers wanted their hometown newspapers. The airport hotel had the technology to print exact copies of newspapers from across the world, and the stranded passengers were eager to pay a surcharge for copies of the *New York Post, Boston Globe, London Financial Times,* and so on. A hotel spokesperson explained that the hotel made a variety of newspapers available, but people kept asking for newspapers from their own cities.[19] This is a telling example because the attacks of September 11, 2001, were a world concern, covered by the world media, but people who were away from "home" continued to want a local approach to the news.

The theories of classical German sociologist Georg Simmel sensitize us to a different interpretation of the effects of the global supermarket. Perhaps the global span of the modern cultural industries should be viewed as enhancing people's ability to shift among numerous identities, rather than with the absence of an authentic (i.e., place-based) identity. The travelers in Vancouver, from this perspective, may have had both local and global identities.

Simmel's interesting approach to the question of identities was historical and comparative. He described a preurban form of association as characterized by a single network of people with whom one interacted. Familial and all other bonds were layered over each other in the immediate locale, creating overlapping sets of relationships that were closed to outsiders. One's kinship status and gender largely determined who one was, not only in the family, but in political, religious, and other arenas as well. The result was that each person had a circumscribed number of highly congruent identities. By contrast, modern urban forms of association, according to Simmel, involve a variety of networks, only some of which intersect, and even then only to a limited degree.[20] One's work group, church group, and family, for example, may have no overlapping members.

Associated with the distinct social networks of an urban setting are different identities, any of which can be salient, depending on circumstances and situations. To illustrate, consider an Egyptian immigrant in Scotland in front of her television. She might regard herself as Glaswegian while watching a local Scottish station, British when she switches over to the BBC, an Islamic Arab expatriate when she turns to the satellite service from the Middle East, and a citizen of the world when she surfs over to the CNN channel.[21] She may also belong to different (and nonoverlapping) networks of people associated with these identities (e.g., a parent-teachers association connected to her children's local school, an organization of Egyptian exiles living in the United Kingdom, and so on).

In conclusion, the capacity of people exposed to modern media to shift among multiple identities is different from lacking identity, and the absence of a single dominant identity should not be confused with rootlessness. That said, we can also acknowledge that the more pessimistic view of the global media is not without some foundation, especially when one is examining less privileged people in economically less developed nations. The Mexican peasant wearing a Los Angeles Dodgers baseball cap and a Disneyland Tee-shirt and watching reruns of *Friends* may have been rendered rootless (and perhaps estranged from his local setting) by the global cultural industries.

CULTURAL INDUSTRIES AND THE ECONOMY

There is a long tradition in the social sciences of separating the cultural and economic realms. It probably emanates from Weber's criticism of Marx's economic emphasis, and his own preference for explanations that placed more stress on values and ideas (i.e., cultural considerations). We are following this tradition solely for convenience in presenting global economic and cultural hierarchies in separate chapters because, as one examines culture, the cultural industries, and the global economy, it is their interpenetration that stands out. The distinction between the economic and cultural realms may even be another of the industrial era categorical distinctions that are now imploding as "the economic is becoming cultural and the cultural is becoming economic."[22]

With respect to the spatial organization of world cities, the culture–economy overlap is certainly clear. Museums, galleries, Disney stores, and theaters are interspersed among the high-rise office buildings in virtually every major global city's financial district. The size of a city's museums or orchestras also became viewed as a direct reflection of the vitality of its financial center.[23] Thus, to persuade executives of the Boeing Corporation that Chicago offered the right business setting in which to relocate, city officials invited Boeing executives to dinner at the Chicago Art Institute, complete with a string quartet.

The spatial blending of culture and high-rise finance has also resulted in "hybrid" projects that cannot really be classified as one or the other. Consider the Sony Wonder Technology Lab (in the Sony Building in New York), the Petronas Science Center built by the Petronas Petroleum Company (on the ground level of its corporate headquarters in Kuala Lumpur), or the television history display built in São Paulo by the Globo Media Group. Are they corporate exhibits or museums? Are they designed to sell products or to inform and entertain? Neither set of alternatives fits well. The blurring of demarcation lines that makes these questions difficult to answer further argues against the exaggerated separation of cultural and economic dimensions.

Cultural diversions have become vital to the economies of global cities because they help fill convention centers and hotels, and theaters and restaurants—and contribute to each city's overall image. That image, promoted by the cultural industries, is critical in attracting not only tourists, but footloose business enterprises looking to relocate. Because of its potential economic consequences, a city's image has became a valuable, but difficult to quantify, asset—and an arena of intense intercity competition. That seems to be the only way to account for the decision by the city of Osaka, Japan, in 2001, to invest over a billion dollars to build a Universal Studios theme park (like the one in Orlando, Florida). Even though almost all of the theme parks in Japan had lost money over the previous decade, Osaka went forward because its major Japanese economic rival, Tokyo, had a Disneyland. Osaka's business community concluded that to compete successfully with Tokyo for businesses, tourists, and image, they would have to build a theme park.[24]

We may also note that the lifestyles and symbols espoused by the cultural industries and the economic exchange of *all* types of commodities have become increasingly integrated. In other words, we can say that the symbolic and value-laden aspects of culture have increasingly suffused objects and exchanges in which the cultural component was formerly more limited. The enor-

Figure 6.1   Warner Brothers Studio Store in downtown Tokyo is among the global entertainment industries found in the center of the city. (Pictured in 2000.)

mous sales increases of athletic footwear that began during the 1980s provides a ready illustration. The profitability of shoe companies was enhanced by their ability to take advantage of changes in the world's economic structure: reduce manufacturing costs by building plants in South Korea, for example, then establish efficient global distribution systems. Apart from these business considerations, the companies also benefitted enormously from the growing mass popularity of running, conditioning, and physical fitness, trends that were promoted by the cultural industries.[25] People who never ran or exercised still felt constrained at least to try to look as though they did. Athletic footwear sales increased because wearing these shoes enabled people to convey a desirable picture of themselves.

As a result of the stronger interplay between the cultural industries and the rest of the economy, characteristics that once distinguished cultural markets seem to be blurring. Specifically, one of the most defining features of cultural markets has been the tendency for the choices made by other buyers to exert an especially strong influence on individuals' decisions. Sheer popularity can more readily overwhelm the attributes of the product being purchased or consumed when cultural products are involved. Thus, people feel pressured to see a particular movie while everyone is talking about it or to watch a popular television show at night lest they feel left out of conversations the next day. Popularity begets popularity. As a result, small differences among movies, recordings, or the like are associated with huge differences in their economic success. Because only a few movies, recordings, or the like reap enormous profits while others languish, these cultural goods have been described as involving "winner-take-all markets."[26] However, as the cultural industries have been employed to sell more of the world's commodities, this once-distinguishing feature of cultural markets has increasingly come to characterize all markets. Thus, tiny differences in athletic footwear, one particular logo on the side of a shoe otherwise like every other brand, lead to large differences in sales and the enormous profitability of a small number of firms.

ENTERTAINMENT CONGLOMERATES

One objective in this and the next chapter is to examine recent changes in the organization and distribution of the cultural industries over the last few decades, noting how each became a more global form of entertainment. In analyzing the cities in which the cultural industries are located, we will be sensitive to a distinction between the sheer volume of activity and decision-making influence on a broad scale. Global activity pertains to the number of CDs, feature films, or the like that are produced by studios in one location, then played or shown in other parts of the world. Cities in which the most active studios are located are important nodes in the global cultural hierarchy. However, the most important indicator of a city's global rank involves whether it houses the parent companies whose decisions determine which cultural goods or services will be produced or offered, and how they will be marketed and distributed. It is the location of the latter that entails the greatest global influence.

It is in the headquarters of global conglomerates that the most consequential decisions are made. To clarify, there is a great deal of recording *activity* on Nashville's "Music Row," especially involving country music. Through a dispersed network of sales and distribution offices, the recordings made in Nashville's numerous studios are played in many parts of the world. However, most of the recordings on Nashville labels are made in studios that are parts of corporations with headquarters elsewhere, particularly New York City, but also London and Los Angeles. The Nashville labels' major decisions—whether to sign new artists to single or full-album deals, whether to invest a half million dollars on radio station tours to promote album sales—are likely to be made at the headquarters location. Even if these decisions are made in Nashville, they are generally made in accordance with guidelines and criteria that come out of the corporate parent office. The fact that many of these companies are headquartered in New York means that firms in New York exert enormous influence over the world's country music market, even though many of the recording studios are in Nashville. (Interestingly, many of these decisions may also be made by executives in New York who personally dislike the genre.)[27] Based on the locations of activity and corporate headquarters, we would place Nashville well below New York with respect to influence over the world's recorded music industry.

The placements of cities must usually be regarded as approximations, however. Judgments about the current worldwide reach of any studio can be confounded by the temporary popularity of one particular artist. Further, in deciphering the arrangements among units of a cultural industry, there are typically some difficult to specify considerations, such as how much autonomy the Nashville recording companies or Los Angeles movie studios have in making key decisions. Mergers and joint ventures have become increasingly common in the cultural industries, and they introduce a fluidity to these interunit relationships. In numerous instances, the revised corporate hierarchy following a merger was not fully implemented before still another merger occurred.

One result of mergers that has made it difficult to infer the relationships among units of a cultural conglomerate is "title inflation." Traditional conceptions of an organization's hierarchy imply a single chief executive, the CEO. However, after mergers, rank-sensitive former chief executives do not want titles that imply they are now subordinate to someone else. In addition, relationships with local clients can be compromised if the head of a unit in a specific geographical area (that reports to a headquarters located elsewhere) does not have a lofty title. It may seem illogical to employ the title of chief executive when the person reports to another corporate official, but firms are reluctant to use titles like "division chief" for the person in charge of operations in major territories, such as the United States or Germany. The News Corporation, the parent of media companies like Fox Televison and Twentieth Century Fox film studios, has eight "chief executives" under the top chief executive, Rupert Murdoch. Bertelsmann, another media giant, has an even greater number of chief executives throughout the world, but the company is unsure of the exact number (a spokesperson explained that it was not possible to state the precise number of Bertelsmann chief executives in all of the company's various divisions and subsidiaries because its structure was too complex).[28] It can sometimes be difficult, therefore, to examine a particular unit of a conglomerate and decipher how autonomously it operates from the title of its unit head.

Most of the major forms of popular entertainment—recorded music, theme (amusement) parks, video games, television, and movies—are owned or controlled by one of only seven corporations in the world. Shares in most of these companies are widely held by thousands of investors, each of whom owns an extremely small percentage of the company. A purchase of between 10 percent and 30 percent of these shares by a single firm is ordinarily sufficient to provide it with a controlling interest, or a controlling interest that it shares with another firm that holds a similar percentage. (Recall that this issue was discussed in Chapter 4.) Throughout the world, these same parent companies also own or control large publishing companies, many major daily newspapers and radio stations, and a number of professional sports teams. They are entertainment behemoths created by an intensified rate of corporate purchases and mergers at the close of the twentieth century. By 1997, for example, the total volume of these seven largest companies equaled the volume of the fifty largest companies in 1993.[29] Purchases and mergers continue to occur with regularity within

the cultural industries, making the summary of the conglomerates presented in
Table 6.1 subject to change in detail, though the overall outlines of the global
entertainment industry are unlikely to be modified very much.

Of the seven conglomerates, three (AOL Time Warner, Disney, and Viacom)
are located in the United States. Collectively, they account for over half of the
world's audiovisual entertainment sales. Most of the other half is shared by
four other firms headquartered in Sydney, Australia (News Corp.); Paris,
France (Vivendi); Gutersloh, Germany (Bertelsmann); and Tokyo, Japan (Sony).
The conglomerates are presented in Table 6.1 according to total revenue in 2000,
with the highest at the top.[30]

Note that Table 6.1 presents a highly selective overview of the enterprises
these superfirms own in entirety or of those in which they have a controlling
interest. A complete listing of their entertainment and communications companies would run several pages in length; hence, the table is only intended to provide an idea of the magnitude of these conglomerates' holdings.[31]

TABLE 6.1   World's Major Entertainment Enterprises and Selected Principal
Component Companies

Corporation Headquarters	Record Labels	Television Networks	Feature Film Companies	Print Publications	Other Entertainment
AOL Time Warner (D.C.-New York)	Warner Music Atlantic	HBO, CNN, TBS, TNN	Warner Brothers, New Line Cinema	Time, Little, Brown	Warner Brothers Stores, Atlanta Braves
Walt Disney (Los Angeles)	Lyric, Disney Hollywood	ABC, ESPN, A&E, Lifetime	Disney, Buena Vista	Disney, Hyperion	Resorts, theme parks, Anaheim Angels
Viacom (New York)	Famous Music Publishers	CBS, MTV, Nickelodeon	Paramount, United International	Simon & Schuster	Paramount Parks, Blockbuster Video
Vivendi (Paris)	Decca, Verve, MCA, Motown	Universal TV, Canal Plus*	Universal Pictures	Havas Magazines†	Universal Studios, Cendant Software
Bertelsmann (Gutersloh, Germany)	BMG, Jive, Arista, RCA	CLT-UFA,‡ RTL Television	—	Random House, Bantam Dell	Media Systems, Doubleday Club
News Corp. (Sydney, Australia)	Mushroom Festival	Fox Broadcasting British Sky	20th Century Fox, Blue Sky	HarperCollins, TV Guide	L.A. Dodgers, National Rugby League
Sony (Tokyo)	Sony, Columbia, Epic, Nashville	Game Show Network, Telemundo	Columbia TriStar, Sony Pictures	—	PlayStation, Loews Cineplex

* Canal Plus is the largest pay-television operator in Europe.

† Havas is the top publisher of magazines in France, and third largest distributor of health care information
in the world, first in the United States.

‡ CLT-UFA is the dominant television and radio network in Europe.

To better grasp the size of these enterprises, examine Disney in a little more detail. As indicated in Table 6.1, Disney was second in the world in media revenue during 2000. What were the major components? In broadcast television in the United States, its ABC network had a 12 percent share of prime-time viewers; Lifetime, A&E, the Disney Channel, and ESPN added about 5 percent more. In worldwide visitors, Disney's amusement parks drew more than twice as many visitors as the second-place set of parks, Six Flags. In worldwide revenue, Disney was first in the world in licensing revenue (for clothing, Mickey Mouse toys, and so on). Its film companies, led by Buena Vista, had a better than 10 percent share of box office revenue in the United States and Canada. In addition, Disney's Web sites were among the ten most visited; then there was recorded music, a major league baseball team, and so on.[32]

A number of cultural and technological changes contributed to the increased global conglomeration among media corporations, as did two important business considerations. The first consideration is horizontal integration, which involves ownerships of multiple types of media companies.[33] The advantages of horizontal integration become apparent when different media are used to enhance each other. For example, a company introduces a fictional character in a feature film, then records the movie's soundtrack on its own label, sells the related merchandise in its own studio stores, and utilizes the invented characters in its own theme parks. To supplement such advantages of horizontal integration, there are horizontal economies of scale: if you are going to sell books to retail stores, you might as well represent five publisher's imprints rather than one (or, if you are Bertelsmann, more than twenty major imprints, including Crown, Delacorte, Fodor's Travel, and Vintage). The president of one of the seven major conglomerates illustrated this point when he mused over the most important factors in the success of his television empire. He finally concluded: "At the end of the day, scale is king." The bigger the network, the better. "If you can spread your costs over a large base, you can outbid your competitors for programming."[34]

The efficiency of vertical integration provides the second reason for conglomeration. It entails ownership of companies that span production and distribution. By owning companies along this type of chain, the parent corporation can reap profits at several points. Such efficiency is illustrated by a complex built in 2000 by the Sony corporation in San Francisco. The complex was the first of a number of planned ventures designed to take advantage of Sony's ownership of Columbia TriStar and Sony Pictures, plus Loews Cineplex theater chain. The fifteen-screen theater in San Francisco is enclosed within a larger marketplace that includes several stores selling Sony electronics and recordings, an amusement park, and four IMAX theaters showing Sony's multidimensional films.

The line between a commercial broadcast and an infomercial can blur when horizontal or vertical integration is carried to an extreme. For example, the evening of June 23, 2000, the American Broadcasting Company (ABC), owned by Disney, presented a special "Walt Disney Concert." The concert was set at Magic Kingdom and other Orlando amusements owned by Disney, and it featured songs from Disney movies, whose soundtracks were available on Disney recordings. Between musical numbers the singers talked about their favorite rides at Disney's theme park. How many of the millions of viewers who watched the program realized the degree to which the network's corporate parent was promoting its diverse interests?

The conglomerates are also striving, almost continuously, to extend their geographical reach, and thereby permeate all the cultures of the world. To illustrate, Disney expects to open its third theme park outside of the United States, in Hong Kong, in 2005. (The other two parks are near Paris and Tokyo.) It took over a year for Disney executives to work out an agreement with Chinese officials that would make it possible to bring Mickey and Minnie to China, but the large population that could potentially be lured to the park made protracted negotiations worthwhile for Disney. The park will, Disney hopes, attract visitors not only from China, but from throughout Southeast Asia.[35] In addition, when Disney films have been released in China they have not usually done well at the box office. Might exposure to Disney characters in a theme park improve demand for Disney films, and vice versa?

As horizontal and vertical integration within media conglomerates have increased, and corporate global reach has simultaneously expanded, related types of firms feel pressure to grow in size and expand geographically. Advertising agencies are an excellent example. The world's marketers have increasingly demanded that agencies create campaigns in many different media, in many different nations. In response, the agencies have followed an acquisitions–merger strategy that parallels the entertainment conglomerates. According to 2001 revenues, the largest agency in the world was the Omnicom Group (in New York). Formed by the merger of two relatively small companies in 1986, Omnicom acquired five other companies between 1993 and 1998. Close behind Omnicom was the Interpublic Group (also in New York), which, in order to keep up, acquired four agencies between 1996 and 2001. The third largest firm, the WPP Group (located in London), made four large acquisitions between 1987 and 2001. London, Paris, and Chicago were the locations of the greatest number of agencies merged with or acquired by the three principal companies. No other advertising agencies were close to the top three in revenue or size, leading industry analysts to predict that the remaining independent firms would have to merge or be acquired to survive in any form at all.[36]

CONCLUDING GENERALIZATIONS

The process of conglomeration as described for the cultural (and related) industries is not unique to that segment of the economy. It can readily be seen in other industries, from discount department stores to credit unions to fast foods. At first there is a competitive market involving a substantial number of firms, none of which dominates the market. The larger organizations have an advantage in terms of resources and are more likely to survive, and often wind up gobbling up the smaller organizations along the way. Once this process begins, an analysis by David Barron suggests, it is often self-accelerating. The larger organizations that survive take over the resources of the failed organizations, and their ability to continue to prosper is further enhanced.[37] The resources that are taken over by the survivors vary according to the type of industry involved. In fast foods or discount department stores, it is outlets; in the movie industry, it is talent (e.g., actors and directors) and investors.

Despite the extensive resources accumulated by the large organizations that survive, they rarely become entirely self-sufficient. The "resource dependence" model of organizations sensitizes us to the fact that even huge firms will still sometimes need external resources: personnel, finances, and so on. Each organization must, therefore, make a series of strategic decisions involving other firms, such as when to compete and when to cooperate.[38]

The eventual economic success of products of the cultural industry is difficult to predict. In addition, the products are frequently expensive to produce and it can be a long time before they pay any return on the investment: expensive films are sometimes box office failures, DVDs may be slower than expected to catch on, and so on. In response to these risks, large firms minimize potential vulnerability by engaging in many cooperative activities. In the movie industry, this results in a lot of joint ventures, movies co-produced by studios associated with two of the conglomerates. (*A Beautiful Mind*, which won several Oscars in 2002, was jointly produced by Vivendi's Universal Pictures and Dreamworks, discussed in the next chapter.) In other realms, it results in joint ownerships: AOL Time Warner and Sony share ownership of Columbia House Music Club; Viacom and Vivendi are joint owners of the Sundance Channel; and so on.

Apart from minimizing everyone's risks, cooperation among these companies is also facilitated by the circulation of many of the same executives among the firms. For example, after the merger of AOL and Time Warner in 2001, the company hired as the chief executive of their television division a former president of the Fox Network (News Corp). He reports at AOL Time Warner to the former head of MTV, owned by Viacom. At roughly the same time, Fox hired as the head of its television division a former top executive of Universal Pictures (owned by Vivendi). The possibility that one may soon be working for a rival can blunt competition and encourage cooperative ventures. At the least, it is easier to work together when you know your counterpart at another company from past employment. One media analyst has concluded that competition between the giant firms is sometimes publicized, "but that the new media leaders compete only over marginal matters."[39]

Within capitalistic societies, maximum competition and lowest prices are expected when many small firms compete, and none has a significant market share. In principle, this form of competition will also produce more diverse products as firms try to find a niche for themselves. By contrast, when a small number of firms dominate an industry—McDonald's and Burger King, or a few national movie theater chains—there is little pressure to lower prices or be innovative. Consumers pay more for goods and services and must select from a smaller and less diverse array than if there was more competition in the marketplace. In other words, as a result of concentrated ownership, the products of the cultural industries have become more homogenous: movies, television shows, and recordings all tend to follow "formulas" in which successful formats are continuously imitated. If a "reality" program draws a television audience, try another and another. There is the overt appearance of competition, but consumers really have a narrow range of choices.

Furthermore, because of minimal competition, the firms tend to compete with each other more on promotions and advertising than on price, and the minimal competition enables them to pass the cost of the promotions and advertisements on to consumers in the price of the product. The profits of the small number of firms that dominate a market can reach enormous levels, resulting in huge salaries for leading figures (chief executives, actors who draw large audiences) and large dividends for the corporate shareholders. To illustrate, when AOL and Time Warner merged in 2000, the CEO of the newly expanded company received a raise to $163 million in annual salary, bonuses, and options. The CEOs at Viacom and Walt Disney each received over $70 million, and none of the CEOs of the seven giant entertainment conglomerates received less than $40 million in annual salary, bonuses, and options in 2000.[40]

The enormous profitability of the few firms that dominate a market does not, by contrast, do much for ordinary workers. The film industry, for example, has increasingly relied on big stars to draw audiences. This leads to competition for their services, which drives up the salaries they can demand and leaves little for the "middle-class" actors, who get small parts in movies and television shows and try to supplement their income by making commercials. The Screen Actors Guild estimated that, during 2000, about 70 percent of its members earned less than $7,500 a year. As illustrative of how the dual-wage system operates, consider Joe Howard, a professional actor for thirty of his fifty-two years. In 1993, he played the minor role of a pharmacist in *Grumpy Old Men,* starring Jack Lemmon and Walter Mathau. Howard earned $750 for each day he was in a scene that was filmed. In the sequel two years later, the big money went to the stars, and Howard was offered even less, specifically a per-day rate of $450. Further, he was told he would have to pay his own airfare from Los Angeles to Minnesota, where the movie was being filmed. It was too big a risk for Howard to take because it was possible that his scenes might never be shot. He would not be paid under those conditions, so he declined the part.[41]

To illustrate further, at the same time that AOL Time Warner's CEO became one of the five highest paid executives in the nation, to make the newly merged company more efficient, management laid off several thousand workers: clerks, customer service representatives, market analysts, and so on. Because many industries are characterized by the same trends—domination by a few giant firms that reward chief executives with huge salaries while cutting mid-level positions—one consequence is that there are more marked income differences, with the attendant problems we explored in Chapter 5.[42]

NOTES

1. The distinction between cultural goods and services has important practical implications because they are treated differently in various international trade accords. However, technological changes can make it difficult to distinguish clearly between them. Should online books, for example, be regarded as virtual goods or as services? See UNESCO, *Study of International Flow of Cultural Goods Between 1980 and 1998* (New York: United Nations, 2000).
2. For further discussion of this primary-secondary distinction, and an application to advertising, see William O'Barr, *Culture and the Ad* (Boulder, Colo.: Westview Press, 1994).
3. David Croteau and William Hoynes, *The Business of Media* (Thousand Oaks, Calif.: Pine Forge Press, 2001).
4. For further discussion of the structure of culture from a sociological perspective, see Ann Kane, "Analytic and Concrete Forms of the Autonomy of Culture," *Sociological Theory*, 9(1991):53–69.
5. Gordon Mathews, *Global Culture/Individual Identity* (London: Routledge, 2000), p. 11.
6. Howard W. French, "To Grandparents, English Word Trend Isn't 'Naisu'," *New York Times*, 23 October 2002, p. A4.
7. Norimitsu Onishi, "Globalization of Beauty Makes Slimness Trendy," *New York Times*, 3 October 2002, p. A4.
8. For further discussion, see Mangala Subramaniam, "Whose Interests? Gender Issues and Wood-Fired Cooking Stoves," *American Behavioral Scientist*, 43(2000):707–728.
9. Ann Swidler, "Culture and Social Action," *American Sociological Review*, 51(1986): 273–86.
10. Max Weber, *The Protestant Ethic and the Spirit of Capitalism* (New York: Scribner's, 1958), p. 280.
11. Ronald Inglehart and Wayne E. Baker, "Modernization, Cultural Change, and the Persistence of Traditional Values," *American Sociological Review*, 65(2000):19–51.
12. Judith Blau, "The Toggle Switch of Institutions," *Social Forces*, 74(1996):1159–77.
13. For further discussion of deterritorialization and sense of place, see Arjun Appadurai, "Disjuncture and Difference in the Global Cultural Economy," *Popular Culture*, 2, no. 2(1990):212–234.
14. Benjamin R. Barber, *Jihad vs. McWorld* (New York: Times Books, 1995), 99.
15. Robert D. Putnam, "Bowling Alone," *Journal of Democracy*, 1(January 1995), 65–78.
16. Nicholas Lemann, quoted in Everett C. Ladd, *The Ladd Report* (New York: Free Press, 1999), 9. In this book Ladd presents a great deal of data indicating that, at least outside of global cities, there is a trend toward joining more communal and civic organizations.
17. Pat Seremet, "Sports Fans," *Hartford Courant* 5 April 2000, p. 17.
18. Claude S. Fischer, *The Urban Experience* (New York: Harcourt, Brace, 1984).
19. Sabrina Tavernise, "A Technology Delivers the Dailies to Some New Doorsteps," *New York Times*, 7 January 2002, p. C4. The non–English-speaking travelers were able to obtain newspapers from Madrid, Moscow, and elsewhere.
20. This description of networks and identities follows Simmel's insights, initially presented in Georg Simmel, *Conflict and the Web of Group Affiliations* (New York: Free Press, 1955). For a creative extension of Simmel's ideas, see Bernice A. Pescosolido and Beth A. Rubin, "The Web of Group Affiliations Revisited," *American Sociological Review*, 65(2000):52–76.
21. This example is taken from chapter one in John Sinclair, Elizabeth Jacka, and Stuart Cunningham, eds., *Global Television* (New York: Oxford University Press, 1996).

22. Roland Robertson, "Globalization Theory 2000+," in *Handbook of Social Theory*, ed. George Ritzer and Barry Smart (London: Sage, 2001), 458–71.

23. Sharon Zukin, *The Culture of Cities* (Oxford: Blackwell, 1995).

24. Miki Tanikawa, "Japanese Theme Parks Facing Rough Times," *New York Times*, 2 March 2001, p. W1.

25. For further discussion of Nike, in particular, see Miguel Korzeniewicz, "Commodity Chains and Marketing Strategies," in *Commodity Chains and Global Capitalism*, ed. Gary Gereffi and Miguel Korzeniewicz (Westport, Conn.: Greenwood Press, 1993), 231–258.

26. For further discussion, see Robert H. Frank and Philip J. Cook, *The Winner-Take-All Society* (New York: Penguin, 1996).

27. For further discussion of country music's claim to "authenticity," and the taste preferences of the corporate executives who promote it, see Richard A. Peterson, *Creating Country Music* (Chicago: University of Chicago Press, 1997).

28. Jonathan D. Glater, "At Title-Happy Companies Its a Chief per Bottle Washer," *New York Times*, 11 April 2001, p. A1.

29. Some of this change is due to an increase in the total volume of business in the cultural industries, but there is still no denying the increasing scale of these companies. For further statistics, see "European Audiovisual Observatory," *The Economist* (November 1998), 12–13.

30. Specifically, it is total revenue for the year ending June 2000. If one focuses solely on the media portions of revenue, the rankings change somewhat, although AOL Time Warner remains first by a large margin with any calculation. "A New Titan," *New York Times*, 15 December 2000, p. C6.

31. The information about these corporations presented in Table 6.1 is taken from their Web pages and from their annual reports (1999) to shareholders.

32. These figures pertain either to the 2000 calendar year or the first five months of 2001. Seth Schiesel, "Where the Message Is the Medium," *New York Times*, 2 July 2001, p. C1.

33. Croteau and Hoynes, *The Business of Media*.

34. Saul Hansell, "Murdoch Sees Satellites as Way to Keep News Corp. Current," *New York Times*, 16 June 2000, p. C7.

35. Mark Landler, "After Protracted Talks, a Disneyland Will Rise in Hong Kong," *New York Times*, 1 November 1999, p. C1.

36. Figures on advertising agencies' revenue and further discussion of mergers and trends are presented in Stuart Elliot, "3 Ad Competitors Unite to Conquer," *New York Times*, 8 March 2002, p. C1.

37. These effects of organizational size are described in empirical and simulation findings by David N. Barron, "The Structuring of Organizational Populations," *American Sociological Review*, 64(1999):421–45.

38. The most influential statement of the resource dependence model was Jeffrey Pfeffer and Gerald R. Salancik, *The External Control of Organizations* (New York: Harper and Row, 1978).

39. Ben Bagdikian, *The Media Monopoly* (Boston: Beacon, 1997), xi.

40. These salary figures are presented in Jill Goldsmith, "H'Wood's High-Priced 'Suits'," *Variety*, 23–29 April 2001, p. 1.

41. Barbara Whitaker, "Actors' Talks Center on Journeymen Shortchanged by Pay of Stars," *New York Times*, 18 June 2001, p. C7.

42. For further discussion of the income inequalities this generates in capitalistic societies, see especially the Foreword by Paul M. Sweezy in Harvey Braverman, *Labor and Monopoly Capital* (New York: Monthly Review Press, 1998).

SEVEN

The Global Cultural
Industries Hierarchy

When compared to the extensive literature on the place of cities in the global economy, there is meager research that systematically examines the cities that are the major headquarters of the global cultural industries. The cultural research is limited because, as discussed in Chapter 4, there has been a theoretical emphasis on the role of fiscal-economic considerations in shaping the world urban system, which may have led to an underappreciation of the importance of the industries that disseminate cultural values and ideas. The studies that have been reported have typically examined cities in relation to a single type of cultural activity, such as publishing or television, and have focused on patterns of influence among cities in limited geographical areas, such as Western Europe or the Middle East.[1] As a result, we cannot begin this chapter by reviewing previously developed global hierarchies of the cultural industries. However, it would not be surprising to find many of the same cities atop the world's cultural hierarchy that were previously found to be at or near the apex of the global economy.

A number of theoretical perspectives—including the writings of Karl Marx, World System Theory, and some variants of the Cultural Imperialism thesis—lead to the expectation that the cultural industries will reflect and reinforce the global economic structure. However, these theories tend to suggest a subordinate role for culture, in general, and the cultural industries, in particular, that we do not mean to imply. In addition, as noted earlier, the cultural industries can be viewed as representing one specific type of economic activity. Why should cultural industry location not correlate with that of other measures of economic activity?

The approach in this chapter mirrors that followed in Chapter 4 for reviewing several indicators of the place of cities in the world economy. However, the focus in this chapter is on indicators of a city's place in the cultural hierarchy, based on headquarters locations of the principal cultural industries.

Specifically, we will discuss three of the most important forms of the global entertainment industries: recorded music, movies, and television. In relation to each of these subindustries, we will describe some of the key changes that led to increased globalization, then examine the headquarters locations of the principal firms. At the end of the chapter we will present a ranking of cities produced by combining the three indicators of the cultural industries into a single index. The overall cultural and economic hierarchies are compared to each other in Chapter 8.

RECORDED MUSIC

When rock 'n' roll began in the early 1950s, primarily in the United States, few recordings were international hits. There were not even a lot of national hits. Many recordings were bestsellers only in some geographical regions; for example, the popularity of country and western songs was largely confined to the South. And many U.S. cities—including Chicago, Memphis, New Orleans, Philadelphia, and San Francisco—had local markets in which performers who lived in the city made recordings for local record labels whose distribution outside of that city was limited. Thus, national and local markets coexisted.

Television played an important part in the transition from local to national markets, and a key figure was Dick Clark. In the 1950s, he became the first truly national disc jockey with *American Bandstand* on the ABC television network. Clark was apparently also ahead of his time in forging horizontal and vertical integrations, according to a U.S. House of Representatives inquiry. Specifically, Clark was charged with having financial interests in varied movie, recording, and distributing companies, and using his televised show to promote artists from which his companies would benefit. Although Clark claimed the government's charges were false, he could not produce financial records to prove it. He was eventually forced to divest many of his holdings at a loss, by his account, of millions of dollars.[2]

By the late 1950s, most of the independent record companies that initially promoted rock 'n' roll had either gone out of business or been purchased by one of the major record companies associated with a film studio, publishing company, or television network. Columbia Pictures, United Artists, ABC-Paramount, and other large companies already in the entertainment business set up a number of subsidiary recording companies that proceeded to sign contracts with most of the leading performers. The headquarters of almost all of these major recording studios, by the end of the 1950s, were in New York. Most recording companies also had an affiliate in Los Angeles, to be close to the movie industry, because rock 'n' roll singers—such as Elvis Presley and Pat Boone—were becoming movie stars as well. Many of the major studios also had an office in Nashville, for the country and western market, which the major labels dominated. However, Nashville facilities were operated quite separately from main offices because at the time few songs and few performers crossed over from country to popular charts and it was unusual for a country record to sell more than 100,000 copies.[3] While Nashville has remained the major record-ing and performing site for country music—which is now more mainstream, with international markets—the recording studios and television networks as-sociated with Nashville's country music continue to be headquartered else-where, especially in New York.

The situation confronting black performers in the 1950s is especially no-table. Most black artists recorded for small, independent labels and, when their songs appeared to be hits, the major studios "covered" them with white vocal-ists and then out-distributed the small company with the original record. "Just Walking in the Rain," for example, was a hit in 1953 in Memphis when recorded for local Sun Records by an African American singer, Johnny Bragg, backed by a group called the Prisonaires (inmates at the Tennessee State Penitentiary). Months later it became a national hit when recorded by a white singer, Johnie Ray, for the major label Columbia. The limited distribution of local labels led black performers to aspire to contracts with the dominant national labels, but these labels typically forced singers to make "lifestyle" versus career decisions. For example, the black singers and musicians who were involved in the civil rights movement, beginning in the late 1950s, were avoided by the major (i.e., "white") studios. Al Hibler, who had the first vocal hit of "Unchained Melody" in 1955, is an interesting example. A former big-band singer, Hibler signed with a major company, Decca, in the early 1950s, and had several hit records. How-ever, he began marching with civil rights protesters in the South and after he and hundreds of other marchers were arrested for civil disobedience in 1959, the major labels avoided him, and it was the virtual end of his recording career.[4]

In this social context, Motown was a distinctive label. Formed in 1960 in Detroit ("motor-town," shortened to motown), it was the first studio with effective national distribution to feature mostly black performers, such as Michael Jackson, Diana Ross and the Supremes. Motown's founder, Berry Gordy, claimed that his label was intimately tied to the inner city and expressed black ghetto life, "its rats, roaches and soul."[5] In 1970, however, Motown left Detroit for Los Angeles to be closer to the film and television studios, and it later became part of the Vivendi conglomerate (see Table 6.1).

Worldwide, the most significant development in popular music during the 1960s was the Beatles. Their success, and that of other British groups that fol-lowed, significantly increased the internationalization of the music market. Be-fore the Beatles there were only a few international connections in the music industry, notably between London and New York. Companies in each city had previously arranged numerous cross-Atlantic tours of musical performers. Singing movie stars affiliated with the recording companies' film studios had also regularly appeared, live and in movies, on both sides of the Atlantic since the 1920s. In addition, New York and London were each the headquarters of numerous record companies that had affiliates in the other. However, when "Beatlemania" struck, first in England then in the United States, the London–New York link intensified. By connecting to that link, recording companies from other European nations found the fast track to international markets in the late 1960s and 1970s. Especially notable were the Dutch company Philips (Dusty Springfield's label) and the German company Polydor (the Bee Gees label), who set up British and American divisions and sold the same recordings in both nations and, to a lesser extent, across the continent. By the early 1970s, the Beatles had also contributed directly to the vertical integration of the international music business. They had their own recording company, arranged their own worldwide tours, and controlled several movie projects.[6]

Through the 1980s and 1990s, telecommunication and transportation developments enhanced international music sales and distribution, and an increasingly international youth culture provided a broad market. During this period there were steady increases every year in world trade in music, part of an overall trend toward more global exchange of all cultural goods: magazines, films, recorded music, and so on. Specifically, in 1985 the world trade of all cultural goods was valued at less than $125 billion (U.S.). By 1999, it was nearly $400 billion (U.S.).[7] Recorded music accounted for about 10 percent of the cultural goods total across this time period; correspondingly, world music sales were approximately $39 billion (U.S) in 1999.

To further illustrate how international the music industry had become, consider the five top-selling albums in the world around the first of June 2000. They are listed in Table 7.1, which also displays sales rank in a sample of eight nations.[8] (Where a dash appears, the album was not on the nation's top-twenty list that week.) Note that every one of these five leading albums was recorded for a label that was owned or controlled by one of the megaconglomerates described in the Chapter 6.

Not shown in Table 7.1 are a number of albums that were popular in only one or two nations, although most of them were also recorded on a label attached to one of the seven conglomerates. Language differences were, of course, involved in regional sales. For example, in June 2000, Doe Maar's album *Klaar* was a top-ten seller only in the Netherlands; Los Nocheros had two top-ten albums in Argentina, but did not make any charts in the United States, Europe, or Asia. So, there remains a noninternational music market, though it continues to shrink relative to the international market. On the other hand, there are international, but not national, hits to be considered: performers whose primary popularity lies outside of the nation in which they live and record their music. An interesting example is provided by Carl Craig, Kenny Larkin, and other Detroit performers whose electronic music is known as "Detroit techno." These artists record CDs for twenty-five different independent record companies in Detroit, and 85 percent of their sales are international. Detroit techno is an obscure form of music to most people in Detroit and the United States, but it is popular across Europe and Asia where it is regularly featured in music stores and on MTV-Europe. Most of the broadcasters who attended a 2000 festival of techno music in Detroit were from Paris, London, and Tokyo; and the concert was broadcast live only on national radio networks outside of the United States.[9]

Recorded music, like all cultural goods, conveys values, symbols, and ideas about ways of life. America's long-standing dominance in the international

TABLE 7.1 Most Popular Albums in the World (June 2000)

Artist (Title)	Label (Conglomerate)	Australia	France	Germany	Italy	Japan	Netherlands	U.K.	U.S.
					Sales Rank of Album by Country				
Britney Spears (*oops . . . I did it again*)	Jive (Bertelsmann)	7	1	1	6	18	1	3	2
Santana (*Supernatural*)	Arista (Bertelsmann)	—	3	6	1	—	5	9	12
Whitney Houston (*Greatest Hits*)	Arista (Bertelsmann)	13	—	4	10	3	—	1	9
Pearl Jam (*Binaural*)	Epic (Sony Corporation)	3	—	9	2	—	7	14	13
Eminem (*The Marshall Mathers LP*)	Web/Polydor (Vivendi Universal)	—	—	3	—	—	2	2	1

recording market is associated with its cultural hegemony in many parts of the world. For example, there are five times more annual translations of published materials from English than translations from any other language. French and German are the next most translated languages, but they are far behind in absolute numbers of translations.[10] This dominance is especially impressive because English is widely spoken and read in many parts of the world, making translations from English less necessary than from other languages.

The observations of a visitor to the Philippines are illustrative of America's musical-cultural influence in many parts of the world. The visitor made his way around bars and nightclubs and noticed that every performer, amateur and professional, impersonated American singers. At a sing-along pub, for example, he watched a young Filipino woman from the audience put on a tape, with backup instrumentation, and then deliver a perfect version of a Madonna hit, down to the last pause. Across the street he watched professional singers simulate not only the sounds, but ways of moving their eyes and twisting the microphone in perfect impersonations of Bruce Springsteen, Kenny Rogers, and other American singers. Both the musical arrangements and the feelings that accompanied the performances seemed borrowed to the observer, which seemed odd in a nation that took great pride in its musical abilities. The anomaly disappeared, however, when a Filipino friend explained that every young Filipino dreams of growing up to be an American. American music culture is so ingrained, the observer concluded, that even when Filipinos want to rebel against its influence, they wind up writing down their insurgent strategies in a notebook that has Michael Jackson's picture on the cover. Or, when a Manilla newspaper editorialized in favor of closing the U.S. base in the Philippines, it was under the headline, "Bye, Bye, American Pie."[11]

America's international music influence is also illustrated by the popularity in Iran of recordings made at several of the Persian-pop labels located in Los Angeles. Government censors try to block their distribution, but many cassettes made in studios in Los Angeles are nevertheless bootlegged into Iran. Most people in Tehran, Iran's principal city, dismiss the government-approved singers who remain in their city as mere "sound-alike artists" who imitate the *authentic* Iranian singers who are in the United States in the city they call "Los Tehrangeles."[12]

Principal Headquarters Cities

In this section we examine the locations of the firms that most control activities within the world's music industry. Of the seven major conglomerates described in the Chapter 6, four own labels with large shares of the world's recording business. These four are AOL Time Warner, Bertelsmann, Vivendi and Sony. In a typical year, the affiliated labels of the four conglomerates account for about two thirds of the world's recorded music sales. (In the U.S. market, the world's largest, they account for nearly three quarters of all music sales.) In addition to tape and CD sales, these four firms also own or control many other parts of the

recorded music industry. To illustrate, Bertelsmann owns music-related manufacturing and digital technology businesses and has an alliance with Napster
(the music Web site); Vivendi owns MP3.com, a leading online music platform
with nearly a million songs; and a joint venture between Vivendi and Sony created Duet, an online music subscription service to rival Napster.

The cities that house the corporate headquarters of the major conglomerates are centers of the world's music industry. Remember that these conglomerates serve as beacons, also attracting to the city people and firms in related
activities, such as advertising and talent management firms. The leading cities
and the headquarters they house are as follows.

New York is corporate headquarters to:

1. Bertlesmann's BMG division. All of Bertelsmann's music business is
   conducted under BMG Entertainment. Although BMG is completely
   owned by Bertlesmann, a decentralized German firm, its world headquarters is in New York.

2. AOL Time Warner. The company's world headquarters, as of 2002, is in
   New York's Columbus Circle, consolidating corporate activities pertain-
   ing to AOL (formerly headquartered in suburban Washington, D.C.) and
   Time Warner (always located in New York).

3. Viacom does not have any record labels, but it does own a major music
   publisher and the most important television networks in the world for
   recorded music: MTV (and its global affiliates) and VH1 (and its global
   affiliates). These activities make it a significant company in the world's
   recorded music industry.

No other city in the world matches New York as a headquarters for major
conglomerates in the recorded music industry. Following New York, in the second tier, are three other cities that house previously introduced conglomerates
and one other city that houses a major firm in the recorded music industry that
is not connected to any of the entertainment conglomerates. Included in this second tier are Tokyo, home of Sony; Paris, home of Vivendi; and London, home of
EMI, the one significant recording and music publishing company not connected
(as of this writing) to any of the entertainment conglomerates. EMI is the contemporary offspring of the Gramaphone Company, which began recording in
London in 1898. EMI's affiliated labels include Virgin, Capital, Priority, Sparrow,
and others. Although its revenues were nearly $4 billion (U.S.) in 2000, its princi-
pals considered it too small to compete with the entertainment behemoths, and
over the next twelve months tried to merge it first with AOL Time Warner and
then with BMG Entertainment. European regulators blocked both deals in 2000
and 2001, arguing that they would have stifled competition in the music industry. EMI may yet became part of a larger entity, but as of this writing it remains
independent, and is the fifth largest corporation in the world's music industry.

From the discussion of principal headquarters cities, it is apparent that New
York is at the apex of the world's music industry hierarchy. It would be the lead-

ing city no matter how one chose to weight different types of corporate locations. Although the rest of the cities can be placed into categories according to the influence of the world music corporations headquartered within them, it is also important to recognize the intense interconnections among activities in three cities: New York, Los Angeles, and London. Thus, EMI's principal office outside of London is in New York; Los Angeles contains a principal office of New York's BMG; and London is Viacom's European headquarters of MTV.[13] In addition, most of the largest talent management, publicity, and public relations firms in the music industry have primary offices in either New York, London, or Los Angeles, and large affiliates in the other two cities in which it is not headquartered. These three cities therefore constitute a *core network* and among them there is a seamless movement of performers, agents, publicists, and related activities, even though they can also be hierarchically ordered. (The complete recorded music hierarchy is summarized later, in column one of Table 7.4.)

Other Centers

The two conglomerates not yet discussed in this section—Disney and News Corp—both own several recording labels (see Table 6.1). Neither's share of world music sales is sufficient to make its headquarters a major center, but both of their corporate headquarters warrant inclusion as tertiary centers. Included here are Los Angeles, home of Disney, and Sydney, home of News Corp. In addition, based on housing a combination of corporate recording activities and independent studios, two other cities deserve inclusion in this category: Nashville, home to recording companies associated with BMG, the Universal and Warner Music Groups, and a number of independent studios; and Toronto, the Canadian headquarters for Universal Music Group and Sony of Canada, plus host to several independent labels.

Two additional cities warrant mention on a different criterion, namely because they house organizations that have important regulatory impacts on the world's major music markets, thereby greatly affecting the entire industry. First is Brussels (Belgium), which, as the capital of the European Union, has been a center of trade agreements involving recorded music in Europe, the world's second largest market. Brussels is also the principal site of "Platinum Europe," the preeminent music awards show and ceremony for albums that sell a million or more copies in Europe. The second city is Washington, D.C. A variety of regulatory decisions affecting the music industry in the United States (the world's largest market) are made in the nation's capital, and the city is also home to RIAA, the dominant trade association of the American recording industry.

MOVIES

In the summer of 2000, a huge French corporation, the tenth largest in Europe, Vivendi S.A., bought the Seagram Corporation of Canada. One of the large Seagram companies that then fell under Vivendi's control was Universal Studios, the producer of numerous television shows (*Law & Order, Jerry Springer*) and a long list of extremely popular movies. It is instructive to look back over Universal's corporate history because it encapsulates many of the major trends in the motion picture industry.

Universal was founded in 1912 in Chicago, when pioneers in the movie industry were opening studios in a number of U.S. cities. In 1915, it was among the first studios to relocate near Hollywood, and it was the first to turn movie making into a recreational attraction. For 25 cents one could purchase a bleacher seat on the studio's back lot and watch movies being made. *All Quiet on the Western Front* won Universal's first Academy Award in 1929, and over the next few decades a series of Frankenstein movies and Abbott and Costello comedies were the major sources of the studio's profits. In 1958 Universal was sold, but its ownership remained in the entertainment business. The new owner was MCA (Movie Corporation of America), a theatrical talent agency that, coincidentally, also began in Chicago. Soon after MCA's purchase, the recreational facilities at the Hollywood studio were expanded and became the first Universal Studio Theme Park. During the 1970s, Universal enjoyed some of its most spectacular successes when it hired a young director named Steven Spielberg, who began a long string of hits with *Jaws* and *ET* and permanently altered the way movies were made.[14] In addition, Spielberg's movie characters became integrated into rides and other popular attractions at Universal's theme parks in Tokyo, Orlando, and elsewhere.

In 1991, Universal's parent, MCA, was purchased by a Japanese conglomerate, Matsushita Company, and Universal became the first major Hollywood studio whose owners were not based in the United States. (Shortly afterward, another Japanese corporation, Sony, bought Columbia Pictures.) However, Universal's management ran the studio with virtually no external intrusion from Matsushita. The former chief executive stated that, "During the Japanese era, they never made one decision as to what movie got made or didn't get made."[15] Matsushita's tenure was brief, though. In 1995, Seagram (of Montreal) purchased MCA, and took control over Universal, but it too continued to permit the management in place to run the studio with great autonomy. Then, in 2000, Vivendi bought Seagram, and Universal's new owners had a Paris address. And one of Vivendi's first post-purchase announcements was that it planned to make no significant changes in Universal's top management.

American Dominance

Where Hollywood movie studios are concerned, corporate culture may provide a degree of insulation from changes in ownership—but that is probably contingent on the studio also being successful. For example, after a half-dozen expensive-to-produce 20th Century Fox movies did poorly at the box office in 1999 and 2000, the head of the Fox studio was apparently forced to resign by Rupert Murdoch, the chief executive of Sydney-based News Corp (which owned Fox). However, when a Hollywood studio is successful, no new directions may be apparent to corporate owners given Hollywood film studio's dominance in the international movie industry. To illustrate that dominance, consider the top grossing films of spring 2000: *Gladiator* and *Erin Brockovich*. Between March 25 and May 24 2000, they were the two leading movies in U.S. box office receipts. During this period, either *Gladiator* or *Erin Brockovich* was also the leading film in Argentina, Australia, Brazil, Germany, Hong Kong, Italy, Mexico, Norway, South Africa, Sweden, Turkey, and the United Kingdom. Furthermore, in most of those countries, the two movies ranked first and second in box office receipts.[16]

The success of U.S. films in France—a nation with a distinguished history of filmmaking—is particularly illustrative of America's dominance. France continues to have a major movie industry: the number of new releases with total or majority French financing increased during the 1990s, and the number of movie theater patrons also increased in France. However, the French productions' share of their own market declined (to 27 percent) while the American share increased (to 63 percent).[17] France's leading films, in terms of box office sales for 1999, are shown in Table 7.2, with U.S. productions in boldface italics.[18]

The French Ministry of Culture has been described as working hard to protect French culture from total submersion, but also pessimistic about the prospects of escaping America's influence. The head of the Cannes Film Festival explained the fear that Hollywood movies were actually a Trojan horse for American culture. Once France opened its gates, he warned, these films would also bring Disneyland, fast food chains, and free advertising for American clothes, rock music, and the like. "America is not just interested in exporting its films," he said, "it is interested in exporting its way of life."[19]

One lifestyle aspect intimately associated with movies that has clearly been exported is the megascreen theater complex connected to a retail shopping mall. AMC Entertainment, the company that pioneered multiplex theaters in the United States, recently completed twenty-screen complexes in malls in France, Spain, and Italy. The multiplex, viewed as a distinctively American style, has

TABLE 7.2   Leading Movies in France

Title	Gross (in millions)
Asterix & Obelix vs Caesar	59
Star Wars: Phantom Menace	56
Tarzan	31
The Matrix	31
Notting Hill	29
Mon Pere, Ma Mere	23
Au Coeur du Mensonge	20
Enemy of the State	20
I Still Know What You Did . . .	20
Wild, Wild West	19

threatened the grand "movie palaces" built in European cities during the 1920s and 1930s. In Paris, the mayor had to turn to the Ministry of Culture for assistance in preserving La Pagode, an elegant old theater that was one of the city's landmarks, but was finding it difficult to compete with the multiplex.[20]

French and other European observers fear that multiplex theaters will not only overrun grand old movie halls, but that they will be overbuilt, as they have been in the United States. Almost all of the cinema chains are in bankruptcy, or on the brink, because excessive construction in the United States dramatically lowered earnings per screen. Funding for multiplexes in malls was readily available during the 1990s because, combined with food courts, they extended mall hours of operation from twelve to eighteen hours per day. However, too many multiplexes were built, leading to the closing of over 10 percent of the theaters, with more likely to follow. The closing of the theaters produces a "blight" because they are usually deep structures with little mall frontage, not easily converted to other purposes. Thus, closed theaters tend to leave unsightly empty buildings attached to malls.[21]

The success of American films has suppressed film production across much of the rest of the world. It has had this adverse effect by depressing sales for domestic films and by reducing the demand for exports from any nation except the United States. Across Europe, the success of American imports has been particularly devastating for domestic film studios. The Barrandov Film Studios in the Czech Republic, for example, had been among the largest in Europe. Until the mid-1990s, the studies produced about twenty-five films per year, and many of their productions were top-grossing films in the Czech Republic, Poland, and elsewhere in Eastern Europe. By the mid-1990s, however, over 90 percent of the films shown in Eastern European theaters were American films, and the Barrandov Studios production fell to about five films per year.[22] To illustrate further, through the middle of the twentieth century, Japan imported a wide variety of films from Italy, Russia, France, Sweden, and other nations. The United States accounted for about a quarter of the imports. The U.S. share began to increase around 1970, and by the 1990s it exceeded 80 percent of all imports and American films claimed over half of the entire Japanese market.[23] However, some of Japan's American "imports" are from Columbia TriStar, a Los Angeles studio that is owned by the Sony Corporation of Tokyo. (*Bicentennial Man* and *The Bone Collector* are recent examples of Columbia TriStar films that were large box office successes both in the United States and in Japan.)

Another way to see the influence of Hollywood is to examine the movies with the all-time highest box office receipts. Because admission prices continue markedly to increase and worldwide demand continues to grow, any compilation of top-grossing films tends to be dominated by recent releases made in the United States. Table 7.3 presents the twelve all-time leading movies at the box office as of May 2000. It also shows date of release and box office receipts in the United States and the rest of the world.[24]

All twelve of the all-time hits are products of Hollywood studios, and most have the Hollywood trademarks: lavish, spectacular movies with extensive

TABLE 7.3   Top Movies at the Box Office (in millions of U.S. dollars)

Film (Year)	U.S. Receipts	Rest of World
Titanic (1997)	601	3,059
Star Wars: Episode I: The Phantom Menace (1999)	431	1,414
Jurassic Park (1993)	357	1,483
Independence Day (1996)	306	1,316
Star Wars (1977)	461	1,135
The Lion King (1994)	313	1,223
E.T. The Extra-Terrestrial (1982)	400	1,010
Forrest Gump (1994)	330	1,030
The Sixth Sense (1999)	294	968
The Lost World: Jurassic Park (1997)	229	1,000
Men in Black (1997)	250	924
Return of the Jedi (1983)	309	836

special effects, a good deal of violence, and fairly simple plots to ensure mass appeal. In many ways, they express the Los Angeles approach to popular culture. As one industry observer described the entertainment industries in Los Angeles, their objective is, "pumping out audience-tested dreams to please the world: what is the point of making a movie or music, runs the logic in Tinseltown, if it isn't created in the most current style with the intention of entertaining the widest audience possible?"[25]

The growing international demand for Hollywood films can also be seen in Table 7.3 by examining the distribution of the receipts according to time of release. Three of the movies were released before 1990, and their total receipts in the United States were 28.2 percent of their receipts in the rest of the world. Three other films were released between 1990 and 1994, and their U.S. box office receipts were down to 21.1 percent of their world (minus U.S.) total. For those six top films released between 1995 and 1999, their U.S. total was still less, specifically it was 19.6 percent of their total in the rest of the world. As these figures illustrate, the source of the income generated by films made in U.S. studios has become increasingly international.

Most of the all-time top box office attractions, as displayed in Table 7.3, were produced by a studio associated with one of the seven major conglomerates. At any given time, about three quarters of the top-grossing films in the United States and nearly two thirds of the world's top grossing films are from one of the studios associated with these entertainment behemoths. The one studio that has had numerous movies among the box office leaders that is outside of this group is DreamWorks, formed by Steven Spielberg and two partners in 1994. Between 1997 and 2000, DreamWorks released twenty films. Two won Academy Awards (*Saving Private Ryan* and *American Beauty*) and their average box office gross was nearly $80 million. This average was more than 15 percent higher than any other studio. However, the high cost of film production led the company to co-produce films with other studios affiliated with the entertainment conglomerates. When you are sharing profits, just a few flops on your own are enough to push a studio into the red. In addition, as a "stand alone" studio, DreamWorks could not benefit from the horizontal and vertical integration utilized by the conglomerates. Thus, despite its artistic successes, DreamWorks reported a profit in only one of its first six years.[26]

Principal Cities

Two cities are home to corporate concentrations that place them at the apex of the world's movie industry. The first is New York, the corporate headquarters of Viacom (Paramount Studios) and AOL Time Warner (Warner Brothers Studios). Sony of America is also located in New York, but reports to its corporate parent in Tokyo. The second city in the top tier is Los Angeles, the corporate headquarters of Disney and DreamWorks. It also houses major studios connected to Vivendi (Universal) of Paris and Fox Corp (Fox Studios) of Sydney, as well as a number of smaller independent studios.

Supporting the view of New York and Los Angeles as the principal centers of the global film industry, these two cities are home to the two major international news weeklies that cover movies and related entertainments: *Variety*, published in New York, and *The Hollywood Reporter*, published in Los Angeles. One would expect specialized news weeklies to locate in what they have found to be the most important cities with respect to the activities they cover. (Similarly, the major international news weekly of music and related entertainment, *Billboard*, is published in New York.)

The studios located in Los Angeles produce the most feature films of anywhere in the world outside of Asia. (Unlike most Asian films, the movies produced by Los Angeles studios will usually have extensive worldwide distribution.) No other city is even close to Los Angeles in this type of studio activity. Los Angeles has also been the principal site of movies themselves, with New York a distant second. Of those films being shot in a single location in June 2000, for example, Los Angeles was that location more than twice as often as any other city.[27]

The specific area most often in the background of feature films is the 4-square-mile historic core of downtown Los Angeles. Until 1998, there were few residences in this area. As a result, production companies could set up lights, close off streets, and film throughout the night. There are now several thousand people living in once-vacant commercial buildings in this downtown core, however. The tenants in these recently converted residences have been complaining loudly about the way film crews are interrupting their sleep. For Los Angeles officials, it poses a difficult conflict because they want to revitalize the downtown area, and a residential presence is an important piece of the effort, but film production brings the city $30 billion annually.[28]

The repeated presence of New York or Los Angeles, or parts of these cities, in films makes the "Hollywood" sign or the Empire State Building immediately recognized icons anywhere in the world. That helps to attract foreign tourists, and New York City followed by Los Angeles are the U.S. cities most visited by foreign travelers.[29] Of course, the entertainment conglomerates own numerous local attractions to offer the visitors after they arrive, including Disneyland, the Los Angeles Dodgers, and Warner Brothers Studio stores. In addition, there is always the possibility that tourists will want to take in a movie, and the conglomerates own some of the largest chains of theaters in the world, including Loews Cineplex (headquartered in New York, owned by Sony of New York and Tokyo), and Famous Players (housed in Toronto, owned by Viacom in New York).

The corporate configuration, as noted, indicates that New York and Los Angeles are at the apex of the global film industry. There are also a variety of related service firms, such as talent management agencies and movie publicists, with primary offices in either New York or Los Angeles and major affiliated offices in the other city. These firms help to tie together film activities in the two cities. The generally close ties between New York and Los Angeles, transcending entertainment, are illustrated by the fact that New York–Los Angeles is the domestic U.S. airline route with the most annual passengers.[30]

There are three secondary centers in the global movie industry, cities in which the remaining entertainment conglomerates are located. Specifically, they are Paris (home to Vivendi, the corporate parent of Universal), Sydney (headquarters for News Corp and its Fox Studios division), and Tokyo (home to Sony and Sony Pictures).

Tertiary Centers

Five other cities house corporations that are important to the production and distribution of movies throughout the world. It might be possible to make distinctions among them, but recommending against that is the fact that the overall differences among the studios in these cities are small; further, their relative rankings vary somewhat from year to year. They are presented here alphabetically, with no distinctions implied.

Hong Kong studios produce a large number of action films, such as martial arts features, for both local and international film markets.

London houses regional offices of several major U.S. headquartered studios, and a number of active local studios not attached to any of the conglomerates.

Manilla studios produce diverse films for local and international markets. (Both Hong Kong and Manilla studios' movies are most popular in Asia, but have more penetration in European and U.S. markets than those from Mumbai, discussed next.)

Mumbai (India) studios led the world in the volume of movie production through the 1990s. Within the city there is a major agglomeration of studios, directors, and actors in a distinct district known locally as "Bollywood." (It was given this name when the city was still known by its former name of Bombay.) The Indian films tend to be romantic sagas, often musicals, with no explicit sexual scenes. They have large domestic audiences and are also popular among Indian expatriates across many parts of the world, but the Indian films have limited reach to non-Indian groups.[31]

Toronto is home to a number of independent studios whose total activity ranks behind only Los Angeles and New York (outside of Asia). It is also in third place in North America in audience size and as the locale of films. Studios in Toronto (and Montreal) have benefitted enormously from funding by Telefilm, funded by the Canadian government to promote Canadian movie and television programming. In movies, Telefilm has supported a large number of co-productions, and currently has agreements with fifty-four nations from around the world. The city also hosts one of the premier international film festivals in the world every September. The Toronto Film Festival is an important market in which producers and directors sell the rights to their films to international distributors. According to the president of Sony Pictures Classics, "Toronto has always been the best launching pad for a movie of any festival in the world."[32]

Movie studios headquartered in the ten cities described above, and placed into the three tiers in the global movie industry, produced about 60 percent of all the full-length movies in the world between 1988 and 1999, and a still higher proportion of all the films that were exported anywhere in the world.[33]

TELEVISION

When television first began to expand in the 1950s, radio networks provided much of the programming. Many of the earliest television shows were essentially former radio programs, mildly altered for a visual medium, and some of network radio's most successful shows became television's first hits. (U.S. examples include *Arthur Godfrey's Talent Scouts* and *The Jack Benny Show*.) The significant role played by radio networks in developing television shows meant that those nations with established radio entertainment, such as the United States, had a head start in television broadcasting. There was initially little exporting of television programs to nations that lagged behind, though, because most early television programs were broadcast live. Technical limitations and time differences basically confined their showing to domestic and "border" (e.g., U.S. and Canadian) audiences.

The advent of videotape in the late 1950s expanded opportunities for exporting programs both because videotaped shows could be shown in the same time slot despite time zone differences and because they could be more easily dubbed to transcend language differences. Through the 1960s, the export of U.S.-made television programs soared, and they became important parts of the television schedule in many parts of Latin America and Europe, and other English-speaking nations, such as Australia. With respect to the exchange of television programs, a UNESCO-sponsored study published in 1974 described the U.S. relationship to many parts of the world as resembling, "a one-way street."[34]

The next important technological innovation involved satellites. Beginning in the late 1970s satellite technology made distance irrelevant, and importantly, made it difficult for governments that wanted to remain "closed" to prevent other nations—notably the United Kingdom and the United States—from beaming their television signals across national boundaries. Thus, by the early 1980s, Americans were watching the same episodes of *Dallas* as television audiences in rigidly controlled Eastern European nations, such as Romania. The conniving and successful oilman J. R. Ewing (played by Larry Hagman in a cowboy hat), was one of the most recognized people in Romania, a nation whose regime was then so anticapitalist it outlawed the board game Monopoly.[35] The show was equally successful in Algeria, an Islamic nation that was hostile to American values and at the time had one, state-owned television station. Analysis of the crosscultural popularity of shows like *Dallas* stressed the openness of the stories to different interpretations, thus making them accessible to people who lived in various cultures and seemed quite different from the people portrayed in the series. However, the international popularity of such shows may seem less strange if one remembers the multiplicity of (situational) identities that characterize many people exposed to the global media.

Satellite technology also expanded the number of broadcast stations, triggering the demand for more programs to fill stations' schedules. The U.S. television industry was one beneficiary, but the same demand also encouraged the development of a number of non-U.S. broadcast companies that became important in limited regions. In addition, because language differences have always been more of a barrier to television than to movie markets, the world television industry's organization includes a larger number of important regional (i.e., language-group) cities than the world movie industry. Nevertheless, the leading cities in the global television and film industries necessarily overlap because many of the largest studios serve both industries. Thus, movie studios produce large numbers of television series, and there is growing interchangeability between movies made for television and those made for theatrical release.

The United States continues to be the world leader in the export of television programs, but its relationship to the rest of the world can no longer be described as a one-way street for a couple of reasons. On one hand, there are multiple "streets." In most regions of the world, active centers of television broadcasting provide much of the region's programming, plus there are exports from outside of the region coming from several sectors.[36] On the other hand, there is a more substantial flow of programming coming into the United States. Some of it is geared to special populations and will be discussed in the following pages. Other programs imported to the United States are specifically directed at the mainstream audience.

During the first years of this century, imported programming dominated the U.S. market. The highest rated show on U.S. television in 2000, *Who Wants to Be a Millionaire?*, was imported from the United Kingdom, as were two of Comedy Central's most popular series, *Absolutely Fabulous* and *Mirrorball*, and NBC's hit, *Weakest Link*, complete with the same British host. The most popular television series of summer 2000, *Survivor*, was a Swedish import, and its CBS follow-up, *Big Brother*, began in Holland and was picked up in Spain and Germany before coming to twenty other nations, including the United States (with the original Dutch producer, but without the Dutch series' camera in the bathroom). These imported shows subsequently became, with minor modifications, international hits. *Millionaire* (in Hindi) shattered television ratings in India and was a top-rated show in Hungary, Finland, Israel, and more areas. *Survivor* was sold to eighty countries and was an immediate hit in half of them. Before the U.S.-version of the *Weakest Link* series ever appeared in the United States, the show was sold to a dozen other countries, including the United Kingdom. In other words, the British watched an American version of what was initially a British show.[37]

Principal Cities

New York (again) sits alone at the apex, this time with respect to the global television industry. It is the only city in the world that headquarters two of the major entertainment conglomerates, and both are actively involved in international television programming. Specifically New York is home to AOL Time Warner, whose channels include Home Box Office (HBO) and Cinemax, rated first and second among premium cable channels in the United States. Through joint ventures, HBO and Cinemax reach 12 million subscribers in Asia, Central Europe, and Latin America. The corporation's CNN also broadcasts around much of the world. The second conglomerate headquartered in New York is Viacom, owner of MTV, the most widely distributed television network in the world, reaching over 300 million households. MTV has regional headquarters in London (for Europe), Miami (for Latin America), Moscow (for Russia), São Paulo (for Brazil), and Singapore (for Asia). Viacom also owns Nickelodeon, which offers customized channels in Australia, Brazil, Japan, Turkey, and elsewhere. The CBS unit syndicates television shows internationally; the Paramount Studios unit produces the series *Entertainment Tonight*, in China (in Mandarin), Germany, and the United Kingdom, and is a major supplier for French cable and satellite channels.

In the second tier are six cities that each house one of the entertainment conglomerates plus London, home of the BBC and several notable production companies. The global television activities of the corporations in these six cities are described next, and the cities are presented alphabetically so that no ranking among them is implied.

London does not housing any of the global entertainment conglomerates, but it is nevertheless a major world center for the television industry (as noted previously in describing the recording industry). The city's role is historically linked to the British Broadcasting System (BBC). Begun as a radio network in the 1920s, the BBC became a more international service in conjunction with its coverage of World War II. Hitler's propaganda chief later admitted that the BBC won the "intellectual invasion of Europe."[38] Today, the BBC operates multiple radio and television networks in the United Kingdom and over eighty other nations, though its coverage is most extensive in English-speaking nations, such as Australia and the United States (BBC America). In addition to its role as a network, the BBC is also a major producer of the programs (dramatic series, movies, news hours) shown on its networks, and many of its productions appear on other networks in other nations (such as Public Broadcasting Stations in the United States). In addition to the BBC, London is home to several other production companies, notably Planet 24 and Celador, that put together many of the British television programs that became international hits.

Los Angeles is home to the Disney Corporation, parent of the Disney Channel, with 30 million U.S. subscribers and 7 million outside of the United States. It also operates local Disney Channels in Australia, France, the United Kingdom, Spain, the Middle East, and elsewhere. Disney also owns ABC (the American Broadcasting Company, headquartered in New York), which distributes programs around the world, and ESPN (and ESPN-2), with over 150 million subscribing households.

Luxembourg is the headquarters of Bertelsmann, which owns CLT-UFA, the leading commercial station in Europe and one of the leading providers of pay television. CLT-UFA is also a major provider of films, sports, and other entertainment to European and American networks. (In joint productions, CLT-UFA has brought such shows as *Baywatch* and *The Price Is Right* to U.S. television.) The corporation also has significant holdings in television stations in: Brussels, Budapest, London, Paris, and across all of Germany.

Paris is home to Vivendi, which owns approximately half of Canal Plus (also headquartered in Paris), the largest pay-television operation in Europe, and of British Sky Broadcasting, a wide-reaching satellite service. Universal Television, owned by Vivendi, operates television networks in Brazil, France, Germany, Italy, Spain, the United States, and the United Kingdom. It is also a major producer of syndicated television shows (including *Jerry Springer* and *Law & Order*.)

Sydney is home to the News Corp, owner of the Fox Network (headquartered in Los Angeles), which is the single largest owner of television stations in the United States. Fox Worldwide broadcasts in forty countries in Europe and Latin America. News Corp's STAR TV (headquartered in Hong Kong) is the largest network in Asia, reaching 300 million people in Asia, India, and the Middle East. The corporation also owns 20th Century Fox Television (in Los Angeles), a major producer of network television shows (*The X-Files, The Practice,* and more). Sky Latin America (headquartered in Miami) also is owned by News Corp. and jointly broadcasts in Brazil, Mexico, and several smaller South American nations.

Tokyo is headquarters of the Sony Corporation, and its Sony Pictures Entertainment Unit (headquartered in Los Angeles) is the owner or major partner in television channels in Australia, Brazil, Poland, Spain, and elsewhere. Sony Japan produces numerous movies and shows for Japanese and other Asian television stations. Sony's Columbia TriStar Television (also in Los Angeles) is a leading supplier of prime-time series and produces *Jeopardy* and *Wheel of For-*

tune, which for many years were the two most watched game shows in the world.

Tertiary Centers

Four cities are included in the third tier. Each houses the corporate parent of a television network that has strong penetrations in only a few nations, or houses studios that produce programs that are widely syndicated in a single region. A brief profile of the activities in each of these cities follows.

Cairo is historically the movie and television center of the Arab world. Through a number of pan-Arab television agreements, it is the major provider of movies and variety and religious programming throughout the Arab portion of the Middle East, and to a lesser extent, to European nations with large Arab populations.[39]

Mexico City is home of Grupo Televisa, the leading broadcast stations in Spanish-speaking markets of the world. Via satellite, Televisa channels offer programs to Spain, parts of South America, and to U.S. cities with large Spanish-speaking populations, such as Los Angeles and New York. Televisa owns a large percentage of Univision, which has significantly penetrated the market in a number of U.S. cities. In the May 2000, Nielsen ratings in Los Angeles, for example, Univision's Spanish language station in Los Angeles had the highest 6 P.M. news audience of any station in the city, including the affiliates owned by ABC and NBC.[40] The national ratings of the Spanish-language stations in the United States are difficult to specify, however, because of the way Nielsen Media Research rates audiences. Executives at the English-language stations, which pay the brunt of the Nielsen surveys, want to limit the size of the Spanish-language sample. If it were expanded—proportional to the size of the Spanish-speaking population in many large cities, such as New York and Los Angeles—it would remove points from the estimated size of the English-language station audience; and each point reduced lowers the fee that stations can charge to advertisers.[41]

Rio de Janeiro is home of the Globo television group, which dominates in Portugese-speaking portions of the world, including Portugal. Globo's success in exporting programs to Portugal, the nation that once occupied Brazil, led one newspaper in Lisbon to describe the influence as "reverse colonization."[42] Globo's most popular programs, telenovelas that resemble American soap operas, are frequently dubbed and shown in Spanish-speaking nations.

Toronto, in part through the help of Telefilm (discussed in relation to global films), has nurtured a number of independent studios, the most successful of which may be Alliance Studios, a firm that has produced a number of programs and series for Canadian and U.S. networks that have also been syndicated across much of the world.

Finally, two other cities warrant mention as nodes in the global television industry, though they rank below all of those thus far discussed. The cities are *Miami,* which is a regional headquarters for several corporations (including Viacom and Fox) broadcasting into Latin America; and *Montreal*, which, through independent studios and joint productions with studios in Paris, is an important source of programming in French-speaking nations.[43]

THE CULTURAL INDUSTRIES HIERARCHY

In Chapter 4, multiple indicators of the place of cities in the global economy were combined into a single index. To combine them, a score of 10 was assigned to cities with the highest score on any indicator, followed by 7 for the second group of cities, then 4, and finally 1 was given to cities in the lowest tier. We will follow that some procedure here, though in this instance we are dealing with indicators of the place of cities with respect to the global cultural industries. All of the cities noted in any of the preceding tables (along their scores) are presented in Table 7.4.

Based on the total scores presented in Table 7.4, New York is unique. On two of the three indicators it was the only city to receive the maximum score (10), reflecting the fact that New York sat alone at the apex. Other indicators of media or entertainment concentrations not discussed here present a congruent view of New York's stature. For example, there are over 10,000 journalists, photographers, and editors working on the island of Manhattan, a media concentration that is unequaled in any other city in the world. This dense clustering

TABLE 7.4   The Cultural Industries Composite Index

City	Recorded Music	Movies	Television	Total
Brussels	1	—	—	1
Cairo	—	—	4	4
Hong Kong	—	4	—	4
London	7	4	7	18
Los Angeles	4	10	7	21
Luxembourg	—	—	7	7
Manila	—	4	—	4
Mexico City	—	—	4	4
Miami	—	—	1	1
Montreal	—	—	1	1
Mumbai	—	4	—	4
Nashville	4	—	—	4
New York	10	10	10	30
Paris	7	7	7	21
Rio de Janeiro	—	—	4	4
Sydney	4	7	7	18
Tokyo	7	7	7	21
Toronto	4	4	4	12
Washington, D.C.	1	—	—	1

TABLE 7.5   The Global Cultural Industries Hierarchy

Score	Cities
30	New York
18–21	London, Los Angeles, Paris, Sydney, Tokyo
12	Toronto
4–7	Cairo, Hong Kong, Luxembourg, Manilla, Mexico City, Mumbai, Nashville, Rio de Janeiro
1	Brussels, Miami, Montreal, Washington, D.C.

reflects New York City's cultural (and economic) preeminence, and it also gives activities in the city an exceptional access to the global media.[44]

The second tier following New York consists of five cities with composite scores between 18 and 21: London, Los Angeles, Paris, Sydney, and Tokyo. All five of these cities had some ranking on all three indicators. Only one other city also appeared on all three indicators, and that was Toronto. However, it consistently scored in the third tier, hence received a total score of 12, placing it, by itself, behind the five cities placed in the second tier cities.

In the next tier is a set of eight cities that were in the second or third categories on one of the three indicators. Their total cultural industries scores were between 4 and 7. Finally, there were four cities that placed in the lowest category on one indicator, hence have scores of 1. A summary of this entire hierarchy is presented in Table 7.5.

Most of the lowest scoring cities included in Table 7.5, especially those that scored between 1 and 4, could be described primarily as regionally important cities with respect to the cultural industries, as opposed to the more globally important cities in the higher rungs. Whether or not these cities are included in the cultural industries hierarchy depends on how one conceptualizes that hierarchy. If a truly global reach is emphasized, then they probably do not warrant inclusion. On the other hand, if one stresses the presence of any substantial degree of supranational influence, then the cities should be included in the lowest rung.

NOTES

1. See, for example, Hussein Y. Amin, "Broadcasting in the Arab World and the Middle East," in *World Broadcasting*, ed. Alan Wells (Norwood, N.J.: Ablex, 1995, 18–39); and Klaus R. Kunzmann, "World City Regions in Europe," in *Globalization and the World of Large Cities*, ed. Fu-chen Lo and Yue-man Yeung (Tokyo: United Nations University Press, 1998), 37–75.
2. Dick Clark and Richard Robinson, *Rock, Roll, and Remember* (New York: Crowell, 1976), 275.
3. For an excellent description of the early rise of rock 'n' roll and its urban roots, see Charlie Gillett, *Sound of the City* (New York: Pantheon Books, 1983).
4. Ben Ratliff, "Al Hibler, a Singer with Ellington's Band, Dies at 85," *New York Times*, 27 April 2001, p. C13.

5. See Gillett, *Sound of the City* (New York: Pantheon Books, 1983), 217.
6. See the insightful analysis of "The British Caravan" in *The Seventh Stream*, ed. Philip H. Ennis (Hanover, N.H.: New England Press of America, 1992), 86–99.
7. UNESCO, *Culture, Trade and Globalization* (New York: United Nations, 1999).
8. The data used to prepare Table 7.1 were taken from "Hits of the World," *Billboard*, 10 June 2000, p. 58.
9. Nichole M. Christian, "Introducing Techno Sound to the City that Spawned Motown," *New York Times*, 29 May 2000, p. A9.
10. UNESCO, *Culture, Trade, and Globalization*. There were nearly 29,000 translations from English, approximately 5,700 from French, approximately 4,700 from German. These data on translations are for the year 1994, but it was not an atypical year. Similarly, a survey in the European Union countries in winter 2001 found that over two thirds of the population in the Netherlands, Sweden, Greece, Italy, Germany, and France believed that everyone ought to be able to speak English. Reported in *The Economist*, 24 February 2001, p. 51.
11. Pico Iyer, *Video Night in Kathmandu* (New York: Alfred A. Knopf, 1988).
12. Neil Strauss, "Iran's Shadowy Tape Man, Spreading What's Forbidden," *New York Times*, 5 October 2000, p. E1.
13. Each of these three principal cities also contains affiliates of the major conglomerates headquartered elsewhere; for example, Los Angeles and London both contain important offices of Vivendi's Universal Music Group.
14. Andrew R. Sorkin, "Melding of Cultures the Next Step in Seagram Deal," *The New York Times*, 21 June 2000, p. C1.
15. Rick Lyman, "No Trace of Anti-Hollywood Bias in French Purchase of Universal," *New York Times*, 21 June 2000, p. C12.
16. International figures are from "International Box Office," *Cinema1*, 21 June 2000; and "International Box Office," *The Hollywood Reporter*, International Edition, 30 May–5 June 2000. The distribution of movies to different countries varies more in time than the distribution of recorded music, so it is less meaningful to compare all the box office leaders in many different countries at the same point in time. For example, the 1999 Academy–Award-winning *American Beauty* had left movie theaters and was already in home video in the United Kingdom and United States in May, 2000 before it was released in Japan, where it quickly became a major hit.
17. Alan Riding, "French Fume at One Another Over U.S. Films' Popularity," *New York Times*, 14 December 1999, p. E1.
18. John Tagliabue, "Now Playing Europe," *New York Times*, 27 February 2000, p. C1.
19. Editorial, "Culture Wars," *The Economist*, 12 September 1998, p. 12.
20. Tagliabue, "Now Playing Europe."
21. Norma Cohen, "Silver Lining for Silver Screens?" *Financial Times*, 1 May 2001, p. 28.
22. UNESCO, *Some Cultural Aspects of the Transformation in Central and Eastern Europe* (New York: United Nations, 1995).
23. Benjamin Barber, *Jihad vs. McWorld* (New York: Times Books, 1995).
24. "All Time Top 100 Movies at the Box Office," *Cinema1*, 21 June 2000.
25. Neil Strauss, "The Pop Life," *New York Times*, 15 June 2000, p. E 3. The literal domination of top box office hits by films made by Hollywood studios will likely end in the near future, given the recent completion of Fox Studios Australia, which opened in Sydney in 1998. However, its objective is to produce films like those of its Hollywood sisters: violent and spectacular with mass appeal. The large size of Fox Studios Australia also resembles studios in Hollywood.

26. Rachael Abramowitz, "Almost Famous," *New York*, 13 November 2000, p. 32.
27. Film production figures are from *The Hollywood Reporter*, International Edition, 30 May–5 June 2000. A number of films are shot in multiple locations and are not counted here. It should also be recognized that cities are sometimes substituted for each other; thus, parts of Toronto are frequently presented as being in New York. (The reason for the switch: production costs are lower in Toronto.) Nevertheless, this simple counting of sites does reflect the relative frequency with which cities, billed as themselves, provide the backdrop of a feature film. For further perspective on Los Angeles and the film industry, see Roger Keil, *Los Angeles* (New York: John Wiley & Sons, 1999).
28. "Lights, Camera, Action—Cut," *New York Times*, 23 September 2002, p. A18.
29. In 1998, 21 percent of foreign travelers visited New York City, 15 percent visited Los Angeles. Miami was third with 14 percent. This excludes visitors from Canada and Mexico. Data are from U.S. Department of Commerce, International Trade Administration (Washington, D.C.: Government Printing Office, 2000).
30. New York–Los Angeles carries nearly three quarters of a million passengers more than any other domestic route. Air Transport Association of America, *Air Transport 1998* (Washington, D.C., 1999).
31. For further discussion of Bollywood, see Lewis M. Simons, "Inside Bollywood," *Smithsonian*, 31(2001):46–57.
32. Rick Lyman, "Back from the Beach and Bound for Toronto," *New York Times*, 7 September 2000, p. E5.
33. UNESCO, *A Survey on National Cinematography* (New York: United Nations, 11 May 2000).
34. Kaarle Nordenstreng and Tapio Varis, *Television Traffic—A One-Way Street?* (Paris: UNESCO, 1974).
35. Roger Thurow, "Who Shot J.R.? It's All a Capitalist Plot by Russian Oil Guys," *Wall Street Journal*, 21 December 1999, p. 1.
36. Ibid.
37. Bill Carter, "Britons Revamp American TV," *New York Times*, 18 July 2000, p. E1.
38. Quoted from the BBC Web page (www.bbc.co.uk), "History of the BBC, the 1920s."
39. Hussein Y. Amin, "Broadcasting in the Arab World and the Middle East," in *World Broadcasting*, ed. Allan Wells (Norwood, N.J.: Ablex, 1995):128–149.
40. Melissa Grego, "Spanish B'Casting Strong in L.A. May Sweeps," *Variety*, 21 June 2000, p. 1.
41. Jayson Blair, "TV Advertising Drives Fight Over Size of Spanish Audience," *New York Times*, 17 July 2000, p. B1.
42. John Sinclair, Latin American Television (New York: Oxford University Press, 1999):59.
43. Atlanta could also be listed by virtue of having housed CNN; however, CNN operations have been increasingly moved to New York and it appears likely that New York will become CNN headquarters.
44. David Laventhol, "Ten Thousand Journalists Together on a Tight Little Island," *Columbia Journalism Review*, 40(March/April 2001): p. 2.

EIGHT

Some Final Thoughts

We are now ready to address, in a more precise way, some questions raised earlier in this book. Specifically, we began by describing how changes in the scale and scope of commerce, in technology, and the flow of ideas changed the role of a number of cities from regional and national centers to world centers. We pursued this analysis in several chapters, describing two different dimensions along which global cities might be conceptualized, which resulted in a ranking of leading cities each dimension produced. In this chapter, we will combine the two dimensions to produce a single overall hierarchy and typology, that will enable us nominally to define the leading global cities in more detail and provide a more exacting picture of global cities than was previously possible.

The final objective in this chapter is to return to another set of questions raised earlier in this book in order to discuss how increased immigration and the growth of agencies that monitor the world's economy have modified the nature of citizenship and national sovereignty. We will address the possibility that the political role of global cities will expand in the future, and that they will take over the functions previously associated with nations, hence becoming modern city-states.

DESIGNATING GLOBAL CITIES

In earlier chapters we described the place of the leading cities in the world's economy (Chapter 4) and the world's cultural industries (Chapter 7). In both analyses, we offered a hierarchy based on cities' roles as headquarters of either conventional economic activities or the cultural industries. Combining the ranks makes it possible to offer some generalizations about a global urban system in which both dimensions are simultaneously involved (see Figure 8.1).

Figure 8.1 presents a composite rating and ranking based on scores on all the economic indicators (from Chapter 4) and all the cultural industries indicators (from Chapter 7). Given the total of seven indicators, with cities scored on

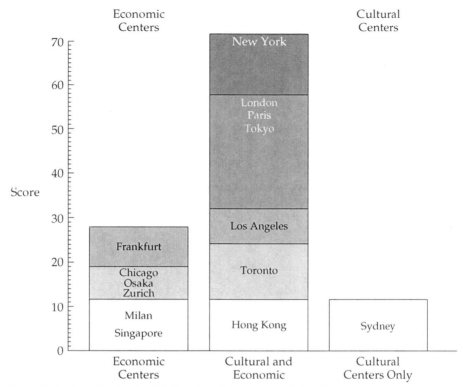

Figure 8.1   Leading Global Cultural and/or Economic Centers.

a 10-point scale on each, any city could receive a total score that ranged be-tween 0 (meaning it was never ranked on any indicator, the pattern that would characterize most of the cities in the world had they all been included here) and a perfect score of 70. Only New York obtained that maximum possible tally.

The thousands of cities with scores of 0 have not been included in any of our past summaries and they are not presented here due to space limitations. Figure 8.1 also excludes those cities whose combined score was less than 10, though we shall discuss some of them later in this section. Cities were consid-ered centers of either economic activity or the cultural industries only, and placed in the two corner columns of Table 8.1, when their score was due solely to activities in one of the two realms. The middle column, which is where all of the leading global cities are located, contains only places that served as the headquarters of a large number of both economic enterprises and cultural industries.

Beginning at the top of Figure 8.1, recall that New York was slightly ahead of London, Paris, and Tokyo in economic activity and somewhat more ahead of the others where cultural industries' location was concerned. Especially when cities' scores on the economic dimension were examined separately, we con-

Figure 8.2 Below the apex of global cities are cities like Frankfurt and Chicago, which are leading economic centers. (Pictured is Frankfurt's commercial center, in 2001.)

cluded that, based on the small differences between New York and the three cities immediately behind it, New York could be considered in a class by itself or all four cities could be placed into the top group. The small difference was consistent with either arrangement. When both dimensions are combined, however, as in Figure 8.1, New York's small edge in each is magnified. The difference between New York and the other leading cities now seems too large to support any interpretation other than that, on these indicators, New York stands alone at the global city apex.

London, Paris, and Tokyo strongly resemble each other, both in economic and cultural profiles as well as total scores. Based on these overriding similarities, they are grouped together behind New York and followed by a large empty space in the column until Los Angeles appears. Therefore, if London, Paris, and Tokyo are to be considered the second tier of global cities, it is important to add that everyone else lags substantially far behind them.

Trailing Los Angeles are nine other cities, and only two (Toronto and Hong Kong) are both cultural and economic centers. The other seven are either economic or cultural centers, hence they cannot be readily placed along the central (i.e., combined) column. This leaves us with two possible overall interpretations. Alternative one is to focus primarily on cities in the middle column, that is, the cities that contain significant amounts of both economic and cultural activities. Los Angeles might be considered in tier three with Toronto and Hong Kong placed into a fourth tier on the global cities hierarchy. The five remaining cities might then be considered specialized economic centers (Frankfurt, followed by Chicago, Osaka, and Zurich, then Milan and Singapore) or specialized cultural centers (Sydney), though in the latter case it is difficult to justify the category when only a single city is involved.

Sydney, as the one city to be placed among the leading global cities based solely on housing centers of the cultural industries, appears to be an anomaly. That may be a temporary condition, however, if either of two scenarios occur. First, Sydney's economic stature may grow to match its cultural standing, placing the city somewhere between Los Angeles and Toronto in the overall hierarchy. Congruent with that possibility has been growth in the capitalization of Sydney's stock exchange. In 2000, it was only slightly behind Chicago's in size. In addition, Fox Studios in Sydney is likely to become a more significant producer of global entertainment, and we have noted a tendency for studios frequently to portray their home cities in films. That media-generated accent on Sydney's image could fuel various types of investments and corporate relocations, enhancing the city's global economic standing.

The second scenario is that the number of global cultural centers will increase so that Sydney will no longer be the sole city of that type. A substantial number of cities, such as Mumbai and Rio de Janeiro, were considered regional, rather than global, cultural centers in Chapter 7. That designation reflected the fact that the penetration of the cities, while extensive, was confined to a distinct geographical-cultural region, or, if they provided cultural media across the globe, it was directed almost exclusively to one distinct population. The reach of many of the cultural industries headquartered in these cities may expand in the future as multiculturalism leads to wider audiences for entertainment originally designed for only one ethnic or racial group. However, if such expansion is substantial, it will likely attract the interest of the cultural behemoths headquartered in the major (economic and cultural) global cities who will then want to add that type of programming to their repertoire. Over the long run, therefore, the best guess is that there will probably be few major cultural centers that are not also economic centers.

A related question concerns whether the lower-ranking specialized economic centers will extend their reach with respect to the cultural industries they house. Given the interplay between the cultural and economic dimensions—as illustrated earlier in the book by Chicago's use of its Art Institute to attract Boeing's headquarters—it might be reasonable to expect that these cities will attempt to extend their reach. At the very least, we can note a strong commitment in some of these specialized financial centers to attract or build more significant cultural enterprises. Frankfurt, in particular, has a municipal cultural committee that is committed to trying to expand the city as a cultural center by supporting its ballet, opera, and row of museums on the south shore of the Main river facing the rows of banks of the north slope of the river. Officially, Frankfurt has expressed an ambition to be a European cultural center, rivaling Paris, though its cultural accomplishments to date have not been very notable.[1]

CITIES AND NATION-STATES

Michael Keating, who has written extensively on global politics, recently observed that "the nation-state faces twin pressures from above and below."[2] Its sovereignty over the territorial units within is being squeezed from above by supranational organizations and agencies. At the same time, nations' prerogatives are being abridged from within by the economic and cultural concentrations headquartered in their global cities. In this section we turn first to pressures on nation-states from above, then consider the future political role of global cities and speculate on the possibility that they will evolve into city-states, taking over some or all of the functions historically associated with nations.

Supranational Organizations

One of the major factors that led to some diminution of the independence of nation-states was the extensiveness of immigration over the last third of the twentieth century. The large numbers of foreign-born people living in the economically most advanced nations has fragmented the cultural dimension of nations, constricting the shared traditions of residents. In addition, because citizenship has often been withheld from immigrants, there has been international concern over their living conditions and treatment. Agencies of the United Nations and private human rights groups, such as Amnesty International, have pressured nations with large immigrant populations to accord them privileges formerly limited to citizens, despite their status as noncitizens, and to treat them in accordance with international human rights standards. The self-determination of a nation's citizens and the ability of nations to govern autonomously within their jurisdictional areas have been reduced as a result.

A second group of pressures on nation-states emanates from supranational agencies that have been established to monitor the world's finances. Two of the most notable, as discussed in Chapter 5, are The World Bank (TWB) and the International Monetary Fund (IMF). These agencies make billions of dollars available that most nations in dire need of loans could not obtain elsewhere. The interest rate is nominal, but there are other costs to be paid. Specifically, the agencies usually insist on long-term oversight of domestic economic policies, pressuring nations to privatize, deregulate, and avoid enacting any regulations or tariffs that compromise free markets.

To illustrate, in 1997, Indonesia was adversely affected by the recession experienced across Asia. Like many other Asian nations that suddenly found many of their largest companies and banks nearly insolvent, Indonesia was temporarily bailed out with IMF loans. Millions of dollars in loans later, in early 2000, the value of Indonesia's currency began to fall; within six months, the rupiah was down more than 18 percent against the dollar and imported goods were becoming more expensive. The government feared that further loss of purchasing power would trigger political unrest, and moved to impose capital controls. Specifically, the government announced that it would set a fixed rate of exchange within the country, and that would be the only legal rate, irrespective of supply and demand for any currency. After the announcement, the director of the IMF immediately flew to Jakarta for a breakfast meeting with Indonesia's president. "We are here to help and support, not to lecture and impose," the IMF chief told reporters, "But of course we offer frank advice."[3] With Indonesia awaiting another $372 million loan from IMF, that advice was persuasive, and immediately after the breakfast the government announced that it was canceling plans for capital controls.

During the 1990s, to illustrate further, Turkey was one of the leading recipients of IMF and TWB loans. In return, Turkey agreed to try to control consumer inflation (it had reached as high as 60 percent) and to bring its economy into line with other industrial nations, an agency euphemism for privatization. In particular, IMF wanted the government to sell both its telephone monopoly and Turkish airlines to private buyers, and to reduce corruption in its public banking sector. Turkey typically complied with each set of demands only in part, but soon had to turn to the agencies for more funds. Each time the government was given funds and told to make changes; and each time there was partial compliance. IMF and TWB aided economic development in Turkey, but in the process made it into a debtor nation, forced to accept agency edicts as the price of obtaining additional funds made necessary, in part, to pay off the former loans. According to public opinion polls, most Turks are rooting for the IMF to succeed in forcing economic reforms, but they are not happy about the price they are paying. As one university student in Istanbul explained, "I really appreciate what the IMF is doing . . . but I . . . feel powerless, because any power I have as a citizen has now been transferred to some international technocrats."[4]

Cities and Embedded Statism

Globalization, we have noted, involves an extensive movement of products and information, capital, ideas, and people among a number of key cities. It is the numerous linkages and connections among these cities—the world's economic and cultural centers—that maintain globalization. Why then has research and writing focused so much on nation-states? One answer is that underpinning most people's mental representations of the world is the familiar multicolored wall map of the nation-states found in every classroom and reinforced by the geopolitics of the twentieth century built on the premise of sovereign nation-states.[5] The nation-state even provided the dominant unit for analysis in comparative research in the social sciences because such studies almost always relied on examinations of nation-states.[6]

In discussing the twenty-first century's principal challenges confronting a more globally oriented urban sociology, Sassen emphasized the problem of "embedded statism." Embedded statism leads to the assumption, often implicitly, that only the nation-state contains the social processes that are most important to study, and that it is *the* appropriate unit in which to study them. We should recognize, Sassen writes, that the mere fact that something occurs within a nation-state's territory does not necessarily make it a national process.

When the nation-state is "unbundled," Sassen notes, we recognize that the places where the global processes come together are the major cities.[7] The intersections among these cities, which constitute the global urban system, seem frequently to bypass any national connection. Thus, the world economy might be described as resting primarily on *direct* linkages among global cities.

Within nation-states, the significance of the economic activity that occurs within major metropolitan areas is illustrated in the United States by recent figures compiled for the U.S. Conference of Mayors. The data indicate that the value of goods and services produced in the ten metropolitan areas with the largest output in 2000 accounted for about a third of the nation's total. Furthermore, the top three metropolitan areas (New York, Los Angeles, and Chicago, in that order) would, if they were nations, rank among the top-twenty nations in the world based on the size of their economies.[8]

City-States?

One vision of the future that is not predicated on the continuation of nation-states as they have existed in the past posits the possible rebirth of "city-states." Robert D. Kaplan, author of several award-winning books on foreign affairs, argues that cities (and their hinterlands) have been part of human history for much longer than nation-states, and cities have proven to be an especially enduring basis of social organization. Conglomerations of metropolitan areas may move from being centers of trade and commerce, just as nation-states did, to being core political centers. They will enter into alliances with each other, Kaplan predicts, and fight wars against each other—not over territory, but over trade privileges and bandwidths in cyberspace. To be specific, by 2010 or so, Kaplan expects North America to resemble the Greek city-states in a loose confederation of urban regions. One such region he calls, "Portcouver," and it extends from Vancouver, British Columbia, to just south of Portland, Oregon. By then, the fact that Vancouver was once in Canada and Portland and Seattle were in the United States will have little significance. Kaplan also envisions an East Coast corridor running from Boston to Washington, D.C. Why not, when these East Coast cities already have closer trade ties to European cities than to other North American cities?

Europe, according to Kaplan, will comprise several metropolitan complexes, including Amsterdam-Zurich and Munich-Budapest. Again, the fact that these federated urban areas include cities that were once in different nations will seem important only in history courses. Kaplan also expects that the Arab world will be dominated by the metropolitan areas of Beirut, Damascus and Amman. National boundaries will collapse in South America, as Rio de Janeiro, São Paulo, Montevideo, and Buenos Aires form an urban agglomeration along the Atlantic Coast. In some parts of Africa and Asia, however, Kaplan fears that the transition from nation-states will be especially difficult and involve conflict.[9]

On the other hand, arguing against the elaboration and extension of metropolitan area jurisdictions is the governing history of the locations. Although metropolitan areas are now the economically most important subunits within nation-states, and contain a large percentage of the total population, it may be difficult to envision them becoming more significant political entities any time soon because metropolitan governance is so poorly developed. In most of the world's largest metropolitan areas, city-suburban integration is limited to a few functional areas, such as coordinated transportation. Like Los Angeles or Mexico City, most urban areas have simply continued to expand across more municipalities, creating urban sprawl and expressway congestion without resulting in unified metropolitan governments.[10] This pattern could, of course, change, but it remains a far leap to see metropolitan areas developing into political units with functions that are equivalent to nation-states.

Conclusion

It is apparent that some diminution in the sovereignty of nation-states has accompanied globalization. It is difficult to imagine the trend not continuing with the future growth of supranational organizations: world courts, regional unions of nations, organizations that manage the world economy, and a continuing emphasis on human rights apart from citizen rights. There is no real substitute for the nation-state on the horizon, though. The European Union currently is the only transnational organization that exhibits the potential to replace nation-states, but it covers only a small part of the world, and further, even it does not seem likely to completely replace its members' nation-states. And as we have seen, little political infrastructure is in place from below with which to create functioning metropolitan governments outside of nation-states.

It is crucial to note that there is a marked difference between observing that nation-states are losing sovereignty and predicting the end of that political form. Sassen argues that it is important to remember that nation-states, backed by an elaborate body of law, still negotiate the conditions under which corporations, markets, or supranational organizations can enter their territory. In addition, nation-states (along with private firms) continue to play important roles in servicing, implementing, and financing global processes.[11] To fail to appreciate this role leaves one thinking about globalization as a product, somehow, of self-sustaining economic forces when, in fact, it requires continuous support. Further, while there are global forces external to every nation-state that cannot easily be ignored, these forces do not typically impinge upon each nation-state in an identical manner. Differences among nation-states persist, therefore, because globalization pressures intersect with economic practices and state policies that are embedded within each nation-state.[12]

Finally, it is important to recognize that nation-states provide institutional contexts that are likely to continue, unabated, to shape patterns of organizational governance, labor relations, wage structures, and other features of labor

markets. An interesting example is provided by the recruitment of foreign football players by clubs in the English football league. There is an international
market for players, with teams searching everywhere for talent. If the traditional constraints that nations placed on the movement of labor and capital
were gone—resulting in totally free markets—then the signing of foreign players would not be influenced by national boundaries. In fact, however, a study
of foreign recruitment over a fifty-year period suggests that clear national influences persist. The English teams show a marked preference for players from
similar cultures, who speak the same language and whose nations have historical ties to England (e.g., Scotland, Ireland, and Australia).[13] Thus, despite
deregulation and internationalization, labor markets continue to be embedded
in national contexts.

NOTES

1. Mark Landler, "Gray-Flannel City Wants to Dance to Its Own Hue," *New York Times*,
   26 September 2002, p. A4.
2. Michael Keating, "Governing Cities and Regions," in *Global City Regions*, ed. Allen J.
   Scott (Oxford: Oxford University Press, 2001), 371–90.
3. Mark Landler, "IMF Warns Indonesia Against Capital Controls," *New York Times*, 6
   June 2000, p. C4.
4. Thomas L. Friedman, "Turkey's Moment of Truth," *New York Times*, 5 June 2001,
   p. A23.
5. Ibid. See also Peter J. Taylor, D. R. Walker, and J. V. Beaverstock, "Introducing
   GaWC," United Nations University, Institute of Advanced Studies, Tokyo, August
   1999.
6. See the discussion of the epistemological shift that transnational analysis may require in William I. Robinson, "Beyond Nation-State Paradigms," *Sociological Forum*,
   13(1998):561–94.
7. Saskia Sassen, "New Frontiers Facing Urban Sociology at the Millennium," *British
   Journal of Sociology*, 51(2000):143–59.
8. The United States Conference of Mayors, *U.S. Metro Economies*, Washington, D.C.,
   July 2001.
9. These predictions were presented in Robert D. Kaplan, "Could This Be the New
   World?" *New York Times*, 27 December 1999, p. A23. The predictions are part of a
   rather pessimistic view of the future, involving social disorganization and conflict.
   For a fuller discussion of these views, see Robert D. Kaplan, *The Coming Anarchy*
   (New York: Vintage, 2001).
10. See the discussion in Peter M. Ward, "The Successful Management and Administra-
    tion of World Cities," in *World Cities in a World-System*, ed. Paul J. Knox and Peter J.
    Taylor (Cambridge, England: Cambridge University Press, 1995), 298–314.
11. Saskia Sassen, "Making the Global Economy Run," *International Social Science Jour-
    nal*, 161(1999):409–16.
12. A cogent summary of positions on this issue is presented by William Sites, "Primi-
    tive Globalization? State and Locale in Neoliberal Global Engagement," *Sociological
    Theory*, 18(2000):121–43. German ownership patterns provide an interesting exam-
    ple of nation-state persistence in Bruce Kogut and Gordon Walker, "The Small

World of Germany and the Durability of National Networks," *American Sociological Review*, 66(2001):317–35.

13. Patrick McGovern, "Globalization or Internationalization," *Sociology*, 36(2002):23–42. McGovern points out that English football is a critical case for globalized labor markets because (1) it is a global sport, (2) the quality of players is readily quantified and observed, and (3) labor is highly commodified as players can be readily sold or traded.

Index

CPSIA information can be obtained at www.ICGtesting.com
Printed in the USA
BVOW050551211011

274127BV00002B/1/P